Documents of the Marriage Liturgy

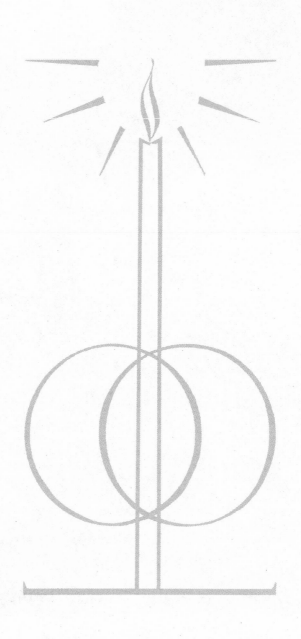

Mark Searle

Kenneth W. Stevenson

Documents of
the Marriage Liturgy

A PUEBLO BOOK

The Liturgical Press   Collegeville, Minnesota

A Pueblo Book published by The Liturgical Press

Design by Frank Kacmarcik

Library of Congress Cataloging-in-Publication Data

Searle, Mark, 1941–
    Documents of the marriage liturgy / Mark Searle, Kenneth W.
Stevenson.
        p.   cm.
    ''A Pueblo book.''
    Includes bibliographical references.
    ISBN 0-8146-6008-8
    1. Marriage service—Texts. I. Stevenson, Kenneth (Kenneth W.)
II. Title.
BV199.M3S43 1992
264'.0255—dc20   91-46162
                                                                         CIP

CONTENTS

FOREWORD

This collection of texts grew out of a set of translations I prepared for a course on the liturgy of marriage at the University of Notre Dame. When Kenneth Stevenson joined us as Visiting Professor in 1983, he was kind enough to suggest that the texts might be useful to a wider readership and offered to collaborate in preparing them for publication. He was to write an introductory essay situating the texts in the history of marriage and to prepare brief historical notes on each text. I was to provide notes on the theological interest of each text and a concluding essay on the potential contribution of the marriage liturgies to the development of a theology of Christian marriage. Together we were to expand and improve the selection of texts. And so, eventually, it has come to pass. Most of these texts are here translated for the first time. All have been laid out in such a way as to display as clearly as possible the structure of the rites, while the prayer texts have been recast into sense lines to enhance their readability. Further, ritual sections, rubrics, and prayers have been numbered for ease of referencing and cross-references provided where the same prayer recurs in different documents.

At a time when the need to clarify the vision of marriage in Christ and to re-think the pastoral issues associated with the marriage of Christians is felt more urgently than ever, the churches have to approach the task cognizant of their own traditions as well as of modern insights from the social sciences. Strangely, in most writings on marriage, from those of canonists, moralists, and theologians, to those of more popular authors, little attention is generally paid to the actual prayers and practices of believers in celebrating marriage over the centuries. It is to help remedy this neglect that this collection of texts, many of which are relatively inaccessible in their original form, is being made available. It is our hope that it might be of service not only to students of the liturgy, but to theologians and pastors, and to all who hold Christian marriage dear.

I am particularly indebted to Robert Peiffer and Martin Connell for their editorial assistance and especially for demonstrating to me the benefits of computerization.

Mark Searle
Notre Dame, August 1990

ACKNOWLEDGMENTS

The authors gratefully acknowledge permission granted to reproduce the following copyrighted materials:

the text of the Jewish marriage rite from *The Authorized Daily Prayer Book*, edited by J. M. Hertz. New York, Bloch, 1946;

the translation of the Byzantine rite from John Meyendorf's *Marriage: An Orthodox Perspective*. Crestwood, New York: St. Vladimir's Seminary Press, 1975;

Luther's marriage rite from vol. 33 of *Luther's Works*, edited by Ulrich Leupold and published by Fortress Press, Philadelphia, 1965;

the *Ecumenical Marriage Rite* is in the copyright of the Consultation on Common Texts, 1985, published by Fortress Press.

The following non-copyright texts are included in this volume:

the 1559 version of Cranmer's marriage rite, here reproduced from *The Prayer Book of Queen Elizabeth, 1559*, published in London by Griffith Farran, 1980, 122–128;

the marriage rite of John Knox is taken from *The Liturgy of John Knox Received by the Church of Scotland in 1564*, published by the Glasgow University Press in 1886;

for the Directory of Public Worship, we have reproduced the text given in I. Breward (ed.) *The Westminster Directory*, Bramcote, Grove Publications, 1980.

All other texts are translated by Mark Searle, copyright 1992.

BIBLIOGRAPHY

Texts and commentaries frequently cited are referred to as follows:

Farnedi, 1986: Giustino Farnedi (ed.), *Celebrazione cristiana del matrimonio. Simboli e testi.* [= Atti del II congresso internazionale di liturgia, Roma, 27-31 maggio, 1985] Roma: Studia Anselmiana 93, 1986.

Molin/Mutembe, 1974: Jean-Baptiste Molin and Protais Mutembe, *Le rituel du mariage en France du XIIe au XVIe siècle.* Paris: Editions Beauchesne, 1974.

Ritzer, 1970: Korbinian Ritzer, *Le mariage dans les Églises chrétiennes du Ier au XIe siècle,* Paris: Cerf, 1970, 57ff.; = French translation of *Formen, Riten, und religiöses Brauchtum der Eheschliessung in den christlichen Kirchen des ersten Jahrtausends* (Liturgiewissenschaftliche Quellen und Forschungen 38), Münster: Aschendorff, 1962 (reprinted 1982).

Stevenson, 1980: K. W. Stevenson, "The Origins of Nuptial Blessing." *Heythrop Journal* 21 (1980), 413f.

Stevenson, 1982: K. W. Stevenson, *Nuptial Blessing: A Study of Christian Marriage Rites* (Alcuin Collections 64), London: S.P.C.K., 1982.

Stevenson, 1987: K. W. Stevenson, *To Join Together: The Rite of Marriage.* Studies in the Reformed Rites of the Roman Catholic Church, vol. 5, New York: Pueblo, 1987.

In addition to the works cited above, the following articles may also prove useful for reference and study:

Kenneth Stevenson, "Benedictio nuptialis": Reflections on the blessing of bride and groom in some western mediaeval rites," *Ephemerides Liturgicae* 93 (1979) 457–478.

Kenneth Stevenson, "Van Gennep and Marriage—Strange Bedfellows? A Fresh Look at the Rites of Marriage," *Ephemerides Liturgicae* 100 (1986) 138–151.

Kenneth Stevenson, "Marriage Liturgy: Lessons from History," *Anglican Theological Review* 68 (1986) 225–240.

The above articles are reprinted in Kenneth Stevenson, *Worship: Wonderful and Sacred Mystery* (Washington: Pastoral Press, 1992).

INTRODUCTION—
AN OVERVIEW OF HISTORY

1 PROLOGUE

Marriage is both a social institution and a religious event, so
that it has a life that is somewhat different from baptism or Eucharist. In Soviet Russia, marriage was a valued bedrock of society, though the government would not openly encourage
citizens who were Christians to celebrate their marriage in
church; but many did, and they would maintain that, for them,
marriage was not complete without a celebration of it by the
Church.

In both baptism and Eucharist, there are certain common features that run through all the various Christian liturgies. The
presentation of the candidate, the renunciation and profession
of faith, and the baptism itself, together with various accom-
panying ceremonies which differ from one liturgical family to
another; and in the case of the Eucharist, the bare minimum of
celebrating God's Word, and then presenting bread and wine
for blessing, before consuming them in the presence of God,
has been richly embroidered, whether by Copts or Lutherans,
Presbyterians or Nestorians. The same is true of marriage. It is,
above all, *rite*, a combination of word in context, symbolic action, and the worshipping life of the Christian community.
Deep down, there are two basic movements which have been
interpreted variously through the ages, but they are inter-
twined. Human resolve, on the one hand, expresses the commitment of the man and the woman to marry each other before
God. Divine blessing, on the other hand, embodies the fact that
the couple seek God's presence and strength. One could almost
say that the interplay and centrality of these features will deter-
mine the clarity, even the success, of any given marriage rite.

From a slightly different angle, the three "stages" that Van
Gennep identified when he studied initiation (and other) rites
in primitive societies are also identifiable in marriage. The first
stage, that of "separation," when the couple are earmarked for
future marriage, corresponds to betrothal. The second stage,
that of "liminality," when the couple undergo the experience of
being on the edge of the community, is the period of engagement, which is a time of adjustment, planning, and distur-
bance, for both them and the community. The third stage, that

1

of "incorporation," is the celebration itself, which only comes as the culmination of the other two, and therefore has far greater impact because it arises out of a whole host of human experiences that have been, in some sense, "ritualized."

Marriage rites through history show us a number of astonishing things. In the period of origins right through to the early Middle Ages (and, in the East, beyond), these three stages have some connection with liturgy, and some rites even make full provision for each part, so that there are not just liturgies of betrothal and marriage, but also certain provisions for the time of liminality and preparation. Marriage liturgies "phase" through experience.

However, since that time in the West (from the twelfth century), these three stages have been put closely together, so that everything happens on the same day, and such phasing as there is moves through the church building, e.g. starting at the church-door (rite of consent), moving to the altar (marriage-prayers and Eucharist), and ending at home (blessing of the bed-chamber). The tale since then is of further attenuation, and most modern rites give little impression of phasing at all. They revert to the simple model of expressing human resolve and divine blessing, but apart from entering and leaving the church building, there is little dramatic phasing whatever, except in the hearts and minds of the people most closely identified with what is going on.

Other issues raise their heads from time to time. What kind of symbolism is appropriate? The ring, originally a pagan device given at betrothal, becomes almost indispensible at the marriage of Christians. The crown, originally an Eastern (and biblical) symbol of fertility, divine presence, kingship, becomes the standard focal point in all the Eastern liturgies. The joining of hands, which speaks volumes about love and commitment, undergirds nearly all the various liturgies. The veiling of the bride, a symbol of modesty and dignity, becomes central to the Roman liturgy, which (in its earliest form) makes the nuptial blessing of the bride alone the central part of the marriage Eucharist. The reading of Scripture is so important for Luther that a special portion has to be read "over" the couple before the solemn prayer.

The place of the Eucharist, likewise, varies from one tradition to another; whereas it is tangential in much traditional Protestantism, it is central in Roman Catholicism. What is the role of the president of such a liturgy? Even within the Catholic tradition, this has varied considerably, from the old Spanish custom of the priest "handing over" the woman to the man, to the later (originally Norman) practice of the priest "joining" them together. History gives no uniform answer to any of these questions. That is what makes it so interesting, since it informs the Christian collective memory at a time when marriage needs all the support and undergirding that it can get.

2 ORIGINS—TEXTS 1-3

The Bible has a lot to say about marriage, whether in the stories about certain married couples (e.g. Isaac and Rebecca, Gen 24), or in allusions to certain marriage customs (e.g. special clothes for the bride, Isa 49:18). But while there are no set liturgical texts for marriage within the Bible, there are sufficient allusions to the three stages of betrothal, engagement and marriage (e.g. Joseph and Mary, Matt 1, Luke 1 and 2) for the assumption to be made that marriage was phased in some way or another.

The Jewish evidence of a directly liturgical kind comes from two main sources. First, there are the prayers and actions in *Tobit*, which gives us a domestic marriage, ritualized carefully. Secondly, the *Talmudic* practice divides betrothal from marriage, and provides set liturgies for both, with characteristic blessings to be recited by the rabbi, ending with the shattering of a wineglass, as a symbol that the temple has been destroyed. The *Talmudic* liturgy poses problems, not because it is difficult to understand (which manifestly it is not), but for the simple reason that we do not know for sure its date of origin. If it goes back to the first century (or even earlier), then there is a strong chance that it will have influenced early Christian practice. If, however, it was all put together in the third century (which is unlikely), then any Christian developments in the first century would have been affected by other ideas and practices. Above all, however, marriage according to the *Talmud* was a corporate celebration, by the local community, in which the *huppah* (canopy) held over the couple and the recitation of the Seven Blessings were the culmination.

How did early Christians marry? This question has been asked frequently, and the answers given have differed widely. While some have maintained that there was no set liturgy of any kind, others have suggested some sort of procedure which (in the Roman Empire) would have met the requirements of the State. These were tolerant of any religion, provided that the consent of the partners was made. Such evidence as we have for this early period suggests, however, that there were set liturgies, and that they centered around the families concerned, and that local ministers were involved. In the *Apocryphal Acts of Thomas* (a Syrian document, from the second or third centuries), a wedding is being celebrated, and the Apostle Thomas happens to enter upon the scene, and a blessing is prised from him. The text for this prayer is a long thanksgiving for the goodness of God in creation and preservation, which ends with prayer for the couple.

Such a two-fold movement of ideas, which begins with blessing and thanksgiving, and moves into supplication for the couple, is a basic structure which appears not only in later service-books, particularly at the nuptial blessing prayers, but also reflects the sequence of ideas within the Seven Blessings mentioned earlier in Talmudic practice. Could early Christian marriage rites have been influenced by Jewish procedures and forms? It is hard to give a definite answer either way, but tempting to suggest it as a distinct possibility. After all, so many of the early Christians were Jews, and research into Jewish origins of the liturgy has yielded so much fruit in other services, that a parallel development is likely.

The New Testament contains four main passages that recur in marriage rites through the ages. Paul commends both celibacy and marriage (1 Cor 7:1-10); and the man should love his wife, as Christ loves the Church (Eph 5:22-33). For the gospel, Jesus teaches that marriage is binding, and that what God has joined together must not be put asunder (Matt 19:1-6); and the first "sign" performed by him in the Fourth Gospel is when Jesus was present at a marriage in Cana (John 2:1-11). While other texts appear in various rites, these four are the most common, and whereas 1 Cor 7:1-10 and Matt 19:1-6 are commonest in the West, Eph 5:22-33 becomes the standard epistle in the East, and John 2:1-11 the basic theme for Eastern prayers.

3 THE ROMAN SACRAMENTARIES—TEXTS 4-6

The three Roman Sacramentaries provide us with the first proper texts for marriage Eucharist—and no more. While other evidence can tell us that the two commonest Western Bible-readings just mentioned were used as epistle and gospel for these occasions, there are still substantial gaps in the story.

Betrothal was still the common practice at the time, for in the sixth–eighth centuries, those who were going to get married expressed this commitment beforehand, in order that the families concerned could make the necessary arrangements, financial and other. But there are two imponderables. First, in the West (except in Spain, as we shall see below), there appears to have been no proper betrothal liturgy; or, if there was one, no text has come down to us. This suggests that betrothal was a semi-private, domestic affair, without direct, official, liturgical intervention by the Church. This is not to suggest that it was therefore unsatisfactory, only that it was markedly different from what we know to have been the custom of the old Spanish rite (from the sixth century), as well as all the Eastern rites.

Secondly, how many people actually went to church for their marriage? Again, evidence is sparse, but it suggests that by no means all did; it is even possible that the nuptial Eucharist was a minority interest, or that couples lived together prior to their marriage Eucharist. Some later texts of domestic marriage rites (e.g. the *Italian Formulary*) supply a partial answer, that besides the deluxe church weddings there was a (perhaps larger) group of people who were married at home, by the simple device of the priest coming to recite some simple prayers over them.

As for the Sacramentaries themselves, we should remember that the "Leonine" book is a local collection of mass-prayers, whereas the Gregorian and Gelasian have a more official status. Each one has a set of mass-prayers which includes a long prayer over the bride. It is not entirely clear in the "Leonine" at what stage this prayer is to be recited, but in both Gregorian and Gelasian, it comes before communion. To a certain extent, such a position is a surprising one, but it was the traditional place for any special blessing of old in the Roman tradition, which is why, for example, the blessing of the oil for the sick has occupied this position since at least the third century. (The form for blessing the oils on Maundy Thursday issued after the Second Vatican Council keeps this tradition, but also allows for all the oil-blessings to take place at the end of the Liturgy of the Word.) Blessing the *bride only* reflects the pagan Roman emphasis on the bride herself, since by marriage she became a fully legal person in her own right. It also provides us with an anomaly when we are faced with virtually every other Christian liturgy, where nuptial blessing is for both partners. In the East, there is no question of crowning only one of the partners—both bride and groom are crowned together. Both the "Leonine" and the Gregorian texts describe the service as of *veiling* the bride. Neither of them mentions any veiling in any of the prayers, and we may therefore assume that the bride came to church with her long veil, and that the prayer over her was intended to reflect general interpretations of the meaning of that veil. After all, the prayers mention a catalogue of Old Testament women, whose virtues are held up to be admirable and worthy of imitation.

The other mass-prayers are full of different kinds of imagery— legal, social, pastoral.

Preoccupation with the bride persisted right down to the time when the Roman Rite was revised in 1969. But it also generally persists in Western culture, and it raises problems when one tries to square the biblical tradition, with its teaching about mutuality and fidelity, with the modern emphasis on equality of the sexes. Marriage and culture are not always separable in the liturgy.

4 THE EAST—TEXTS 7 AND 8

Whereas the Roman Rite has no proper liturgy of betrothal, and blesses the bride at a nuptial Eucharist, all the Eastern rites have full betrothal liturgies, bless and crown both partners, but have a more tenuous link with the Eucharist. The crowning was taken over from Jewish and pagan Near Eastern customs, and each of the Eastern rites leads up to the crowning as the great climax of the liturgy in question. Crowns have to be removed, and while this used to take place some days after the marriage, nowadays it happens at the end of the service.

If you were able to attend a nuptial mass according to each of the various Western Medieval rites, and then went to each of the Eastern liturgies (Byzantine, Coptic, Armenian, and the three Syriac rites), you would immediately notice that while the Western services differed over many things, but shared the Latin language, the Eastern rites by contrast differed in languages used, but shared a common base. This base probably goes back to the fourth century, if not before that, because the evidence we have, while slim, nonetheless shows that betrothal, followed by engagement, led up to a public liturgy, presided over by a bishop or presbyter, in the course of which the couple were blessed and crowned.

These "deep structures," then, run right through the liturgical families of the Orient, and they are celebrated in various ways all over the Western world by the Christian communities that have emigrated there. The Byzantine rite, which gives us the earliest text of the East (the eighth century prayer book, *Barberini 336*), is a simple series of prayers at betrothal, followed by a service of marriage consisting of a more complex set of prayers, with crowning, and a blessing of a wine-cup which contains an allusion to Christ's presence at Cana. The betrothal rite is called the order of "pledges" (*arrhabon*) and the marriage rite is called the crowning (*stephanoma*). As we saw earlier with the two Roman Sacramentaries, what a service is actually called can reflect accurately how ordinary people understand it. For Byzantine-rite Christians, betrothal is about offering pledges, i.e. pledges for a future act of marriage; and marriage itself is about being crowned by the Christian community. Such a basic core becomes elaborated as time goes on and the texts become more explicit, e.g. about the betrothal taking place at the narthex, to symbolize its preliminary character. Some texts stipulate that the Eucharist should be celebrated, others do not. Interpretative ceremonial is added, like the "dance of Isaiah," when the priest leads the couple in a circle, to symbolize their unity in love, and God's love incarnate between them. We are in a different world from the Latin West.

The Coptic rite has undergone a richer evolution over the years, but it still has the same basic shape as the Byzantine. The betrothal rite has proper Bible readings, clothed round with thanksgiving and intercessory prayers. Toward the end, three symbolic actions provide a special focus for the marriage that is yet to be. First, the bride's robes are blessed. Then the bridegroom goes to the bride to give her a cross and the ring. Finally, the couple are enveloped in a large veil together, symbolizing their being "apart" from the community. The marriage liturgy itself begins with the consent of the partners, and after the readings, there is a special litany, with twelve petitions for the couple, which lead into three solemn prayers for them. (The symbolism of twelve and three is, surely, deliberate.) The couple are then anointed with chrism (a peculiarity of the Coptic rite), and the crowns are blessed and then placed over the heads of the couple. There used to be a Eucharist to follow and, whereas betrothal was once separated from marriage, the two rites are now celebrated on the morning and afternoon of the same day.

Symbolism is indeed the hallmark of the Eastern rites; in the case of the Copts, anointing with chrism suggests the baptismal liturgy, seeing marriage as a vocation within the Christian community, and within society as a whole.

The other Eastern rites are no less interesting, not least for their symbolism. Each has a special symbolic action at betrothal, as if there were a need to give it a special focus, in order to show its importance in the lives of the couple, their families, friends, and the wider community.

5 RELICS AND EXTRAS—TEXTS 9-13

The twelfth century marked the drastic change in the West that brought betrothal and marriage together into a single liturgy, solemnized publicly by the Church. But before that development, three further features affected our story.

First of all, local rites in France and England begin to put together the nuptial mass in the Gregorian Sacramentary with a short series of prayers over the couple that were originally entirely separate. The eleventh century *Benedictional of Robert* shows this clearly, for most of the prayers that come at the end of the mass also appear in the *Pontifical of Egbert*, which dates from the tenth century but reflects earlier practice. *Egbert*, however, does *not* contain a Mass, but it does have *two* sets of marriage prayers, one of which has a blessing of the ring, whereas the other does not.

The *Pontifical of Egbert* could well take us to an informal, missionary church, in which marriage was as often performed at home by a priest as celebrated in church with a Nuptial Mass. (In those days, Mass was *only* permitted to be said in church.) Moreover, the presence of a ring-blessing in one of the rites and its absence in the other suggests that some folk used the ring at marriage whereas others did not. (Whether those who did not have a ring blessed used one at betrothal is unknown.)

Secondly, in putting these two parts together (the Nuptial Mass and the old domestic rite), the question remains, was the old domestic rite performed at home or was it now conducted in church? Earlier manuscripts of this type leave the question open, whereas much later ones do stipulate that the prayers after Mass should be said at home. But the very fact that the two parts are linked shows that the Church is trying to "take over" marriage, and to make a link between the simple marriage-prayers that collective memory would associate in the home and the fulsome Nuptial Mass that would be representative of the church's public functions.

Thirdly, Benedictionals and Pontificals, being bishops' books, contain blessings for various occasions, including those blessings that were given at Mass to the faithful immediately before Communion. These texts, which provided the inspiration for the seasonal blessings in the 1970 Missal, are in a different literary genre altogether from anything we have so far seen. They normally come in three (or four) short paragraphs, each ending with an "Amen." Probably inspired by Spanish tradition (from the old Visigothic rite), they become a significant part of the Nuptial Mass, because they begin a tendency to add prayers after the nuptial blessing, even when the celebrant was himself not a bishop. Some would call this tendency "clutter"; others would describe it as a genuine and authentic development.

Both the *Benedictional of Robert* and the *Canterbury Benedictional* provide texts at this point. *Robert's* text comes from a ninth century collection, the *Lanalet Pontifical*. Unlike the nuptial blessings in the Sacramentaries, this prayer blesses both partners throughout. Starting with Adam and Eve, it moves through Tobias and Sarah, to Christ at Cana, and prayer for the couple's "health of mind and body." The *Canterbury* prayer, on the other hand, starts with Cana, and moves straight into prayer for the couple, in their life together in the future. We are well into an era of considerable work at composing liturgical texts.

The prayers after Mass in *Robert* presume a certain formality. The ring must be placed on the woman's hand, with the invocation of the Trinity, and Psalm 127 appears for the first time, as a suitable invocation of God's blessing and presence on the couple. But *all three* of the prayers over the couple with which the rite ends are inspired by the marriage of Tobias and Sarah in the book of Tobit. First of all comes the prayer of Raguel (father of the bride), word for word. Then come two prayers which allude to the presence of Raphael, the angel, and to the God of Abraham, Isaac, and Jacob. The three patriarchs were clearly important; after all, their respective wives, Sarah, Rebecca, and Rachel would all have been mentioned for their superlative virtues in the nuptial blessing at Mass.

Finally, the eleventh century *Italian Formulary* gives us a complementary slant to the story. This was probably celebrated at home, and it contains no blessing of the ring. Whereas the first two prayers bless both partners, the third blesses the man and the fourth blesses the woman. No attempt has been made to differentiate the marital roles in these last two prayers. And un-

like a Mass in church, this simple little rite would have been
over in a matter of minutes.

6 VISIGOTHIC CREATIVITY—TEXTS 14-17

The old Spanish rite, which was so different from the Roman,
and which survived into the eleventh century (when it was
replaced by the Roman), is no mere antiquarian's toy. To the
contrary, in the liturgy of marriage, it gives us the earliest evidence of a number of significant features, not least of which is
the custom of binding the partners together. Hispanics in North
America still perform this practice, though usually at the wedding reception. The Spaniards took it (and others) with them on
their imperial voyages. It is alive both in the Philippines and in
Mexico today.

Isidore of Seville is the giant of the seventh century Spanish
Church. He gave it a strong impetus towards better organiza-
tion, greater pastoral care, and (one suspects) an ever-developing
liturgy. In his *De ecclesiasticis officiis*, much of this comes
through, and in the section dealing with marriage, we get a
glimpse of his way of approaching an issue. The Church
blesses marriage through its priests, and it does so as a tradition that goes right back to God's blessing of Adam and Eve
(Gen 1:28). Then he mentions what are probably folk-customs,
that virgins are escorted by married women at their marriage,
and they are veiled. The fact that they are veiled, Isidore maintains, is to show that they are subject to their husbands, for
Rebecca was veiled at her marriage to Isaac. (It is a little hard to
follow Isidore's logic at this point!) Then he returns to the
marriage-rite. The couple are bound together by a cord, which
is to show that marriage is indissoluble, and also that they are
to remain continent. Finally, the man gives his fiancee (N.B. so-
called, and therefore at betrothal) a ring, as a sign of the marriage bond. And on the marriage-contract, the first reason given
for matrimony is the procreation of children. (Both his quota-
tion of Gen 1:28 and the mention of procreation of marriage on
the contract appear regularly in the writings of Augustine.)

It is not until much later (tenth and eleventh centuries) that
Isidore's liturgy was written down in a form that has come
down to us. The two main texts, *Liber Ordinum* and *Liber Antiphonarius*, probably reflect a stage a bit later than Isidore's evidence. But here we find not only a considerably richer liturgy
than the Roman, but also full provision for betrothal, prepara-

tion of the chamber, prayer at the Liturgy of the Hours, as well as a lengthy and fulsome nuptial Eucharist, which ends with a nuptial blessing, and the handing over of the woman to the man by the priest.

Apart from the quite distinct character of language used in this tradition, three features need to be noted for this old Castillian rite. First, the blessing of the chamber and the offering of the "arras" ("pledges," as in the Byzantine rite) are domestic rites that were celebrated as separate and proper entities in themselves. Secondly, the community appears to be involved in the interim and preparatory rites, and not just in the Nuptial Mass. Thirdly, the connection between baptism and marriage is implicit throughout; just as the Fathers preached the importance of persevering and holding on to baptism, so these venerable prayers speak of the importance of preserving and holding on to marriage.

Was this rich and complex scheme what "ordinary people" did? The answer is partly given by a short sequence of prayers, all of them from *Liber Ordinum*, which appears in the eighth century *Bobbio Missal*, a book that was probably used by missionary monks in parts of France. Its clear descent from the old Spanish tradition perhaps brings us near to the average, tiny village church, or peasant-hut.

The Spanish liturgy as a whole was suppressed from the eleventh century, but many of its peculiarities survived, albeit Romanized. The Sacramentary of Vich shows a Catalonian attempt at bringing old Spanish euchology into the Roman Rite. While the betrothal (with two rings, now) and chamber-blessing rites persist (the Roman Rite made no provision for these), the Nuptial Mass itself keeps the old Gregorian Sacramentary nuptial blessing, but the binding of the cord and the handing over of the woman to the man remain.

These survivals are not just the result of liturgists at work. They are also eloquent testimony to the conservatism of ordinary women and men when it comes to a rite of passage, where people hold on to their own customs because they need the familiar to enable them to cope with an important aspect of their lives.

7 THE ANGLO-NORMAN SYNTHESIS—TEXTS 18–20

England and Normandy were united after the Battle of Hastings, in 1066. One of the less obvious results was that the litur-

gical lives of communities on each side of the English Channel
became more closely linked. Although differences persisted, it is
from this area that we have evidence of the most significant in-
novation in all the marriage rites of the Western Middle Ages—
a form of consent by the couple, made in the *vernacular.* For us,
who live in a world of mass-produced vernacular liturgies of all
kinds, it is hard to understand the impact of such a novel idea.
For instead of consent being expressed explicitly or implicitly by
an informal rite of betrothal, or even by the giving of a ring,
from the twelfth century it becomes standard practice for all
those seeking the blessing of the Church on their union to have
to stand at the church door and say, in the mother-tongue, that
they want each other.

Various forces were at work to cause such a development.
Scholastic theologians made a sharp distinction between consent
at betrothal (*verba de futuro*) and consent at marriage (*verba de
praesenti*). Such a wedge was a convenient device, because it
enabled them to popularize the pagan Roman imperial legislation that required consent to be given at marriage, whatever religious rite happened to be used. The consequences of this
teaching are familiar, and become enshrined in the Roman
Catholic Church at the Council of Trent; although marriage
must be in church, and the priest must be present to preside,
the partners must give their consent, as the irreducible minimum for the marriage to be valid. For the couple, rather than
the canon lawyer, one may hazard a guess that, for all the nov-
elty of this consent, the nuptial blessing at the Eucharist would
have held just as great an impact, for this blessing was now frequently given extra prominence by such devices as the canopy/
pall and by having it sung to the same elaborate chant as the
preface. This might echo the 1969 *Ordo Celebrandi Matrimonium*
of the Roman Catholic Church, which requires *both* the consent
of the partners *and* the nuptial blessing to be given, whether
the Eucharist is celebrated or not.

The *Reims Pontifical* gives us evidence of the rite of consent
before Mass in a sort of embryo. The couple must be betrothed
before they enter church. No formulae are given, no directions
as to what the priest, or the man or the woman are to say. It
would appear that this is an interim practice, which looks as
much back to an older, informal rite of betrothal, as it looks forward to a newer, formal rite of consent.

The big change is first met in the twelfth century rite of *Bury
St. Edmunds* (1125-35), which was an important center, a

Benedictine abbey as well as a place of pilgrimage. What was done there would have been significant, and probably copied elsewhere. There are four stages, the first of which is the lengthy pre-Mass rite. After the blessing of the ring, the consent has to be given, and a Latin direction states what this should contain. This is followed by the giving of the dowry and other gifts, and the ring. After a few prayers, the priest leads the couple into church while Psalm 127 is recited. Before the altar, a lengthy series of short prayers and blessings are recited over them.

The second stage is the Mass, for which the Trinity votive prayers are used on Sundays. Thirdly, two extra blessings come at the end, including a (new) blessing of a wine-cup (like Byzantine practice). Finally, the chamber and the couple are blessed at home.

This new shape dominates all that follows. Architecturally, the new design has been brought to life, the breakthrough has taken place. All that remains is for further enrichment to be given. Thus, in Barbeau, in fourteenth century France, the first active *vow* appears in French, and probably around the same time, in Salisbury (England) the vow appears in English, "I (Kenneth) take thee (Sarah) to be my wedded wife. . . ." The Sarum Missal's text comes in various forms in England and the British Isles, but the rhyming blank-verse prose shows a remarkable cohesion, perhaps a common original; because of their linguistic character, they would be easily picked up from a priest and recited and "owned" by a couple.

What happened to betrothal? In some places, it persisted (as at *Barbeau*), perhaps as an option, but definitely affected by the other consent, given at marriage, because like it, it is now made up of question and answer, and is followed by an "active" vow to marry at a certain date in the future. The Scholastic theologians, with their incisive minds, imposed their interpretation of the rules on the liturgy itself.

While the shape was the same, in Anglo-Norman rites, and (increasingly) elsewhere, there was some uncertainty as to what the priest was there to do. This becomes apparent when one looks at what he *says* after the consent has been given, and the vows have been said. Eventually, in Rouen, the priest "joins the couple together." Southern French rites cause the priest to say that "I hand her over to you. . . ." In England, he says nothing at all, thus providing the foundations for Cranmer's work of Reform in the sixteenth century.

8 COUNTER-REFORMATION—TEXTS 21-23

The Decree *Tametsi* of the Council of Trent in 1563 gives the results of that Council's debate on marriage. Marriage is indissoluble, it *is* a sacrament (the Reformers had disputed this), and it *must* be celebrated in church, before a priest. While local rites were encouraged to continue in their (considerable) variety, two features must be clear. The partners must give their consent, and the priest must say a formula to ratify that the marriage is contracted; here the Rouen form, "I join you together in matrimony . . .," is provided as the preferred text, though other official ones are permitted. Trent also stressed the importance of sound teaching about marriage, and many of the books that were printed therefore contain specimen addresses for the priest to read at marriage-liturgies. The catechetical function of the Church could be improved greatly by the new technology of printing.

The *1570 Missal*, however, gives little that is new, for all that it contains is the Nuptial Mass, the idea being that it should be employed in conjunction with the local *Rituale*. Following the now-established practice of a Missal, everything is printed together, mass-prayers, lections, and chants. The prayers themselves are those appointed in the Gregorian Sacramentary. (No votive forms, such as the Trinity, appear at all.) At the end of the Mass, an extra blessing of the couple appears. This is probably because it was felt necessary to provide a blessing in cases where the nuptial blessing itself was not given (i.e. when the bride was a widow). But the 1570 Missal in all other respects shows itself to be austere when compared with the elaborate texts provided by, say, the *Barbeau* and *Sarum* books.

Local rituals usually took note of Trent, adjusting the contents of their books to clarify the public character of marriage, if this had not been done before. Many of the local missals, however, kept their own features, such as the canopy/pall held over the couple during the nuptial blessing. Once again, central bureaucracy cannot eradicate local conservatism, though it must be admitted that the purpose of the 1570 Missal was to provide a sober, Roman book.

When the *Rituale Romanum* eventually did appear, for the first time, in 1614, all it did for marriage was to provide the irreducible minimum that had been defined in 1563, and put it in liturgical form. While local rites flourished, the result of the 1614 book was that new territories tended to use the minimum version contained in it, rather than acculturate, or even adapt, which the Second Vatican Council (in theory at least) has recently encouraged. Among the later medieval customs not mentioned so far that *do* appear in the 1614 rite are sprinkling holy water on the ring and the couple. Priests also began to wrap their stoles around the couple's hands whilst reciting the special formula, "I join you together. . . ."

In France, especially, a rich liturgical life persisted, often taking note of the more prudential enactments of Trent, but sometimes ignoring them. In *Coutances*, an interesting shift takes place between 1616 and 1744 that demonstrates the impact of Trent in a delayed fashion, as well as local customs persisting. These latter even include prayer to rid an unfortunate couple of infertility! Betrothal also persists, and children born before the marriage are said to be 'legitimized' if placed under the canopy during the nuptial blessing. This latter practice was known as early as the twelfth century. Today's so-called "permissive society" seems to have antecedents, as well as several generations of church-life that did not sniff at cohabitation before marriage.

During the nineteenth century, the movement called "Ultramontanism" put an end to local liturgical customs in many places, and the liturgical books of Trent were observed strictly, with little adaptation. Pastoral issues began to be raised, such as what should be done when a Roman Catholic married a Christian not in communion with Rome. The official line was to discourage these unions from ever taking place. But a few books make careful provision for these marriages to be celebrated, such as the 1839 Paris *Rituale*. (It was soon to be swept aside by the tide of Ultramontanism.) But this issue was to raise itself when the Second Vatican Council came to look at marriage.

9 THE REFORMATION—TEXTS 24-27

The Reformers rejected much of the late medieval teaching and practice on marriage, including the Scholastic view that marriage is a sacrament. While the Orthodox have an open mind on how many sacraments there should be, Catholicism insisted on seven; the Reformers tended to go for two (baptism and Eucharist), but most of them held to the *importance* of ordination and marriage. Through the piety of Lutheranism, Calvinism, and Anglicanism there is a strong understanding of marriage as the foundation of the Christian community, made partly explicit by the fact that its clergy were allowed to marry. The consequences of having a married presbyterate go far beyond the permission itself. They affect the whole nature of the way sacraments and sacramental rites relate to each other.

Among the features rejected by the Reformers were the blessing of the ring, references to marriage as a sacrament in any of the texts, and the nuptial blessing of the bride immediately prior to Communion. On the other hand, among the aspects which the Reformers introduced into their rites were the need for catechesis, the reading of Scripture, a simplified shape to the rite, prayers in the vernacular, and solemn prayer for *both* the bride and the groom.

Luther's *Traubüchlein* (1529) was only intended to be a sample for pastors to use as they wished. In fact, it became the standard Lutheran rite, with some adaptation as it travelled round Germany, Scandinavia, and beyond. Its simplicity is partly explained by the fact that in many areas of medieval Germany, non-Eucharistic rites of marriage were common. Held in church, they resembled elongated versions of the *Italian Formulary*, though they often included the nuptial blessing. Luther's theology is nonetheless apparent in his 1529 rite. Consent must be given immediately, and it is followed by sacred reading, catechesis, and solemn prayer at the altar. Scripture must be linked to prayer by teaching.

John Knox's *Book of Common Order* (1564) produces the English-language version of Calvin's 1542 rite that became typical throughout much English-speaking Protestantism. It also contains many features of those Calvinist rites that appeared in Holland, and elsewhere. Austere by comparison with Luther (no ring), it is fulsome in the didactic character of the rite, so that the couple are *taught* about marriage, and Scripture is *read* to them. Whereas Luther liked to have consent at the churchdoor, and the rest of the service at the altar, though there is no Eucharist, the Calvinist rites do not use the building symbolically, and Calvin himself directed that marriage should not be celebrated on those Sundays when the Lord's Supper was held.

By comparison with Luther and Calvin and Knox, Cranmer's "solemnization of Matrimony" in the *Book of Common Prayer* is an elaborate affair, even when one attempts to forget his matchless prose. Nonetheless, under the post-medieval surface there lies what is in all essentials a Reformed rite. Marriage is important, but not a sacrament. The couple make consent, but the priest does not say anything like the Trent formula, "I join you together. . . ." Even though Cranmer uses numerous medieval sources, including the nuptial blessing, all the prayers are for *both* the man *and* the wife. In 1549, he still allows gold pieces to be given with the ring, but these (officially at least) disappear in 1552, in the Second Prayer Book. And there is even a direction that Holy Communion should follow, although by 1662 this has become only a recommendation that the couple should receive Communion as soon as is convenient.

Cranmer nearly lost his job for being married before the official split with Rome in 1534, so we may assume that for him, marriage was a significant liturgy. While he omitted from the *Sarum Manual* vow the more overtly sexual promises of the wife ("to be bonere and buxsom in bed and at bord"), he steered a middle course when it came to the matter of theology. For example, whereas the Sarum vow speaks of marriage as "if holy church it will ordain," he substitutes a more neutral term which accords with Reformed doctrine, "according to God's holy ordinance." One weakness Cranmer inherited—and continued—from the medieval Church: there is no *prayer* for the couple until *after* the consent has been given. This sort of consideration prompted more radical thought about structure when the recent revisions were under consideration.

10 EPILOGUE—MODERN RITES

Before the Second Vatican Council, various attempts were made in Roman Catholic and Protestant Churches to revise the marriage rites, as these had been inherited and adapted since the sixteenth and seventeenth centuries. Roman Catholics wanted to enrich their rite, and coexistence among Protestants who were no longer seen as heretics, but Christians in their own right, spurred on a debate about what type of rite was appropriate when a Roman Catholic married a Protestant. Equally, many Protestants felt the need for a less verbose liturgy, clearer in its shape, and they had reintroduced the wedding-ring without fear of the accusation that it was a popish spectacle. The position of the Eucharist also came in for scrutiny. Catholics questioned its appropriateness on every occasion, whereas Protestants began to see that there were occasions when it was indeed desirable, as an option.

Theologically, too, there has been considerable rapprochement. Both sides, after all, had stressed the need for the consent of the partners, in the sixteenth century. Roman Catholics began, in the second half of the twentieth century, to talk of marriage as a *covenant* rather than as a *contract*. Both biblical and patristic in origin, covenant seemed to provide a genuine way forward, as Catholics and Protestants began to see each other as companions, called by God to walk together in a proclamation of the Gospel in the midst of an increasingly alien society.

The results of all the scholarship, the tapping of the Christian collective memory, and a realization of the world in which we now live, are clear in the various rites that have been produced over the past twenty years. The 1969 *Ordo Celebrandi Matrimonium* sets the whole liturgical action of the marriage-rite within the shape of a Liturgy of the Word, whether or not the Eucharist is actually celebrated. The couple only make their consent having heard the Word of God read and preached. Moreover, the nuptial blessing must be given on all occasions if possible, and alternative prayers are provided, in order to give variety of theme, image, idea. The strongly corporatist view of contemporary liturgy is apparent, too, in that maximum participation is encouraged, so that family and friends, even the bride and bridegroom, can read the biblical texts.

On the other hand, like the other modern rites, the 1969 *Ordo* has no phasing whatever, not even in the building. The couple walk in for the service and walk out again afterwards. The nuptial blessings are ambiguous, because a difference of opinion over whether that blessing should remain exclusively bridal could not be properly resolved, and a compromise had to be reached. Also, the nuptial blessing remained (at least in the official Latin version) in its traditional position, before Communion. However, many people have observed how much better it works when given after the consent and ring-giving, earlier in the rite, where it is supposed to be when there is no Eucharist. Clearly, there is considerable room for further adaptation, and more symbolism needs to be worked at, whether in old ones being revived, or entirely new ones being brought to birth.

Among the other modern rites, two deserve particular mention. The 1979 *Book of Common Prayer* (American Episcopal) brings Cranmer's tradition into the orbit of twentieth century revision, so that its shape is very similar to the 1969 Roman Catholic *Ordo*, with the main liturgical action taking place after the homily. The nuptial blessing, however, comes after the intercessions, immediately following consent and ring-giving, whether or not the Eucharist is celebrated. (The Eucharist is a preferred option now.)

Two other features, however, should be highlighted. First, the congregation is asked for its support in upholding the couple in marriage, and the partners may be "presented" for matrimony, in a way comparable to candidates for baptism. Secondly, the *passive* consent ("Do you . . .? I will") is now separated from the *active* vow ("In the Name of God, I take you . . .") by the collect, readings, and homily. Such a device as this brings into sharper focus the resolve of the couple; their basic intention is expressed, then they hear something of what it all may involve, and only *then* do they make their vows to each other in the presence of the Church.

These embellishments are incorporated into the *Consultation on Common Texts* Rite (1985), which also includes an (optional) question to the families present, asking for their support. Like the 1979 *Book of Common Prayer*, it begins with an address which bears some of the marks of Cranmer in updated form. Ecumenical questions are dealt with sensitively, such as whether the Eucharist should be celebrated, and a 'co-presidency' is maintained throughout.

The story, of course, is endless. As people respond to the wonders of God in creation and redemption in the mystery of marriage, it is only to be expected that liturgical forms should vary, and should go on varying. While contemporary renewal of liturgy is so much an ecumenical exercise, it is very much to be hoped that the next stage will also be a cooperative venture, which surely will involve more attention to basic questions such as the "deep structures" of betrothal-celebration prior to marriage, as well as the search for more and better symbolism, a more imaginative use of different parts of the church building, and the provision of some domestic rites for use at the wedding feast and for the blessing of the new home of the married couple.

1. THE BOOK OF TOBIT[1]

The *Book of Tobit,* a work of edification dating from about 200
B.C.E., belongs among the *Apocrypha* of the Hebrew Bible. Its
place of origin is unknown (Palestine?), though the story is set
in Nineveh at the time of the Exile. The textual tradition is uncertain at several points, but the purpose of the work is clear:
to assert the importance of faith at a time when God has apparently abandoned his people. It reflects the beliefs, practices and
ideals of late Judaism, particularly ideals relating to uprightness
of life, Jewish separatism and the married state.

Clearly, marriage is a family affair. Here it takes place in the
bride's house, with her father presiding, although under normal
circumstances the sealing of the marriage would have taken
place in the bride's house, followed later by the reading of the
marriage contract, the wedding feast and the commencement of
cohabitation—all in the house of the groom. *Tobit* describes a
ceremony beginning with a blessing of God, during which the
bride's father joins her hand to that of her groom. A marriage
contract is drawn up and the wedding feast follows. Consum-
mation of the marriage, however, is postponed (for three days
and three nights) to accentuate the holiness of marriage (8:5, 8),
a provision which was to have considerable influence on medieval Christianity. The same must be said of the texts, especially
the prayer of Raguel (7:15) and of Raguel and Anna (8:17-19),
which found their way into many medieval Christian marriage
rites.

The ideal marriage is presented as an act of divine service.
God is glorified both in the celebration of marriage (the
benedictions) and in the motives for which it is undertaken
(procreation rather than passion), and will continue to be glorified by the offspring born of such a holy marriage.

TEXT

Biblia sacra iuxta Vulgatam Clementinam. Paris: Desclee, 1947.

BIBLIOGRAPHY

Charles, R. H. *The Apocrypha and Pseudepigrapha of the Old Testament,* I,
Oxford: University Press, 1913, 174ff.

[1] Passages found only in the Vulgate.

Ritzer, 1970:56–57.

Stevenson, 1982:5–6.

Stevenson, 1980:413–14.

7:15
And taking his daughter's right hand, he (Raguel) placed it in the right hand of Tobias, saying:

May the God of Abraham,
the God of Isaac,
and the God of Jacob
be with you;
may he join you together
and fulfill his blessing in you.

7:16
And taking the scroll, they drew up a writ of marriage.

7:17
And after this they all feasted, blessing God.

8:4
Then Tobias exhorted the virgin (Sarah) and said to her:

Sarah, arise:
let us pray to God today,
and tomorrow,
and the day after tomorrow,
because for these three nights
we are joined to God,
and when the third night is over
we shall be joined in our own wedlock.

8:5
For we are the children of saints,
and we must not be joined together
as those nations marry that know not God.

8:6
And so, rising up together, they both prayed earnestly that health might be restored to them.

8:7
And Tobias said:

Lord, God of our Fathers,
may the heavens, the earth,

the sea, and the fountains, and the rivers,
and all the creatures that are in them,
bless thee.

8:8
Thou madest Adam of the slime of the earth
and gavest him Eve for a helper.
And now, Lord,
thou knowest,
that not for earthly lust
do I take my sister to wife,
but only for the love of posterity,
in which thy name may be blessed for ever more.

8:10
Sarah also said:

Have mercy on us, O Lord,
have mercy on us,
and let us grow old together in health . . .

8:16
And when (the maid) returned, she announced the good news,
and they blessed God, Raguel, that is, and Anna his wife.

8:17
And they said:

We bless you, Lord,
God of Israel,
because it has not turned out as we feared;

8:18
for you have acted mercifully towards us
and have cut us off from the enemy who was pursuing us;

8:19
and you have shown pity to two only children.
Make them, Lord,
to bless you even more
and offer you a sacrifice to your praise
and for their own well-being,
that all the nations may know
that you alone are God in all the earth.

9:9
May the God of Israel bless you,
for you are the son of the best of men

of a man who is righteous and God-fearing
of a giver of alms;

9:10
and may your wife be blessed and your parents,

9:11
and may you see your children
and your children's children
to the third and fourth generation;
and may your seed be blessed by the God of Israel
who reigns for ever and ever.

9:12
And when all had said, "Amen"
they went in to the banquet;
but they conducted the banquet
in the fear of the Lord.

2. JEWISH MARRIAGE RITE

Contemporary Jewish wedding rites, though differing somewhat
in the form of the ceremony and in their use or non-use of the
opening versicles and psalm (medieval), are based on the texts
of the Talmud, which date from the third century C.E., but may
incorporate older practices. If this is so, early Christians of Jewish background may well have used similar rites, but no direct
link between Jewish and Christian marriage rites has yet been
established.

The Jewish rite of marriage is in two parts and these were
originally quite separate celebrations. Each begins with a blessing over a cup of wine, evidence of the originally domestic
character of the rites. The first part, the *Kiddushin* (=sanctifica-
tion), commonly called "Betrothal," constitutes the essential
marriage rite. After the groom pronounces the formula (III, d),
and the bride accepts the ring, they are as good as married, although in Talmudic times a year or more may have passed before the second part of the rite, *Nissu'in* (=marriage), was
celebrated. The *Nissu'in* (V–VIII) marks the beginning of cohabitation. In earlier times, the first part took place in the house of
the bride and was presided over by the bride's father, who pronounced the blessing over the cup of wine (mixed with water).
The second part was held in the groom's house and was
presided over by the groom's father. It culminated in the wedding feast and its table prayers (VII–VIII).

Especially to be noted is the view of marriage as a covenant
between husband and wife which is entered into and lived out
within the larger covenantal relationship of God and Israel. The
couple in some sense embody that larger relationship, so that
they represent the whole people and their hopes, joys and
prayers are those of Israel as a whole. In the words of Jacob
Neusner, "Lover and beloved . . . are transformed from literal
to mythical figures. The blessings speak of archetypal Israel,
represented here and now by the bride and groom." The inter-
twining of the destiny of the couple and the destiny of Israel is
suggested by the references to the Garden of Eden and to the
eschatological restoration of God's people, as well as by the
messianic allusion in I and possibly by the breaking of the
glass, which is commonly interpreted as a gesture of mourning
for the destruction of Jerusalem.

A *huppah* or canopy is commonly held over the couple during
the ceremony. The "Seven Benedictions" are a blessing of God,

rather than of the couple, and have a shape which is reproduced in the prayer texts of Latin, Greek and Syriac churches of Christian antiquity.

TEXT

J. Hertz, ed., *The Authorized Daily Prayer Book* (New York: Bloch, 1946) 1008ff. (text and commentary).

BIBLIOGRAPHY

Greenberg, B. "Marriage in the Jewish Tradition." *J Ecum St.* 22 (1985) 1, 3–20.

Hoffman, L. *The Canonization of the Synagogue Service.* Notre Dame: University of Notre Dame Press, 1979, 140–145.

Hruby, K. "Symboles et textes de la célébration du mariage judaique," in Farnedi, 1986:15–28.

Neusner, J. *The Way of Torah.* Belmont, CA.: Wadsworth, 1979, 36–38.

Ritzer, 1970:57–62.

Stevenson, 1982:7–9.

Stevenson, 1987:13–15.

THE MARRIAGE SERVICE

I

Blessed is he that cometh in the name of the Lord:
we bless you out of the house of the Lord. [Ps 118:26]

O come let us worship and bow down;
let us kneel before the Lord our maker. [Ps 95:6]

Serve the Lord with joy;
come before him with exulting.

Ps 100 is recited.

He who is mighty, blessed and great above all things,
may he bless the bridegroom and the bride.

II

PRAYER OR ADDRESS

III

1.

Blessed art thou, O Lord our God,
king of the universe,
who createst the fruit of the vine.

2.

Blessed art thou, O Lord our God,
king of the universe,
who hast hallowed us by thy commandments,
and hast given us command concerning forbidden marriages;
who hast disallowed unto us
those that are betrothed,
but hast sanctioned unto us
such as are wedded to us
by the rite of the nuptial canopy
and the sacred covenant of wedlock.
Blessed art thou, O Lord,
who hallowest thy people Israel
by the rite of the sacred canopy
and the sacred covenant of wedlock.

3.

*The bridegroom places the ring upon the forefinger of the right hand
of the bride, and says:*

4.

Behold, thou art consecrated unto me by this ring,
according to the law of Moses and of Israel.

IV

*The Hebrew Marriage Document is read by the celebrant, after which
the following Seven Benedictions are said:*

V

1.

Blessed art thou, O Lord our God,
king of the universe,
who createst the fruit of the vine.

2.

Blessed art thou, O Lord our God,
king of the universe,
who hast created all things to thy glory.

3.
Blessed art thou, O Lord our God,
king of the universe,
creator of man.

4.
Blessed art thou, O Lord our God,
king of the universe,
who hast made man in thine own image,
after thy likeness,
and hast prepared for him,
out of his very self,
a perpetual fabric.
Blessed art thou, O Lord,
creator of man.

5.
May she who was barren [Zion]
be exceedingly glad and exult,
when her children are gathered with her in joy.
Blessed art thou, O Lord,
who makest Zion joyful through her children.

6.
O make these loved companions greatly to rejoice,
even as of old thou didst gladden thy creature
in the garden of Eden.
Blessed art thou, O Lord,
who makest bridegroom and bride to rejoice.

7.
Blessed art thou, O Lord our God,
king of the universe,
who hast created joy and gladness,
bridegroom and bride,
mirth and exultation,
pleasure and delight,
love, brotherhood, peace and fellowship.
Soon may there be heard in the cities of Judah,
and in the streets of Jerusalem,
the voice of joy and gladness,
the voice of the bridegroom and the voice of the bride,
the jubilant voice of the bridegrooms from their canopies,
and of youths from their feasts of song.
Blessed art thou, O Lord,
who makest the bridegroom to rejoice with the bride.

VI

A glass is broken by the bridegroom, and the celebrant pronounces the benediction.

VII

GRACE AFTER THE WEDDING FEAST

He who says grace commences thus:

Banish, O Lord,
both grief and wrath,
and then the dumb shall exult in song.
Guide us in the paths of righteousness.
Regard the benediction of grace by the children of Jeshurun.[2]

With the sanction of those present
we will bless our God,
in whose abode is joy
and of whose bounty we have partaken.

R.   Blessed be our God in whose abode is joy
and of whose bounty we have partaken
and through whose goodness we live.

He who says grace repeats the last sentence and continues in the usual way.

VIII

At the conclusion of the grace, the Seven Benedictions [above] are said.

---

[2] This short Hebrew poem was written in the tenth century by the poet-scholar Donash ibn Labrat.

3. PAULINUS OF NOLA

Paulinus of Nola (c. 353–431) was bishop of Nola from 409 until his death. A friend of many people in high places and an assiduous correspondent, he wrote odes (*carmina*) for various occasions, including one for the marriage of a church lector, Julian, son of Bishop Memor of Capua, to Titia. It is unclear from the text whether Aemilius, the bishop who presides at the wedding, was actually Titia's father. This is the earliest description of a Christian marriage liturgy in the West.

The ode reflects or, perhaps more accurately, preaches a very sober vision both of the marriage rite practiced among Roman Christians in late antiquity and of their ideal of marriage. In any case, this is very definitely a clerical marriage and can hardly be said to reflect the outlook of the average Christian family. It takes place, for example, in church, a practice unlikely to have been universal at this time but required for the marriage of the (lower) clergy. Most Christians married according to local laws and customs; regulations requiring the "blessing of the Church" originated in the fifth century with clerical marriages and were only extended to all Christians, at least in the West, much later on.

The ritual elements of the rite, alluded to in passing (199–230), seem to be a mixture of classical Roman marriage rites (the joining of the hands, the nuptial veil) and specifically Christian forms (hymn-singing, prayers of blessing and consecration). Notably absent is any mention of exchange of rings or vows (which would have taken place earlier in the home) or of the celebration of the Eucharist.

Throughout, the emphasis is on the holiness of the baptized, heightened in this case by the fact that the man (and perhaps the woman) had a bishop for a father. There is a self-conscious distancing from the "secular display" of pagan marriages, an accent on simplicity, modesty and, above all, submission to the law of Christ. The ideal is promoted even to the point of suggesting to the couple that they live a virginal marriage (231ff.). While the tirades against accommodation to the spirit of a venal age may still be appropriate, it is above all the positive accent on marrying "in Christ" as a counter-cultural act and on the importance of a shared life of holiness which speak the loudest. Themes which will recur in the later history of Christian marriage texts include: the marriage of Adam and Eve as prototype of this celebration; an allusion to the marriage of the Patriarchs;

references to the transcendence of gender differences in baptism and to the unity of Christ and his Church symbolized in marriage. The young couple are identified as children of the Church, as brother and sister in Christ who already prepare for yet greater nuptials in the kingdom of God.

TEXT

Paulinus of Nola, *Carmen XXV*, 199–232 (*CSEL* 30, 244–245).

BIBLIOGRAPHY

The Poems of St Paulinus of Nola, trans. and annotated by P. G. Walsh, New York: Newman Press (*Ancient Christian Writers*, v. 40), 1976, 245–253 and 399–403. (The translation given below mostly follows this text.)

Ritzer, 1970:225, 227.

Stevenson, 1980:414–415.

Stevenson, 1982:28.

Studer, B. "Zur Hochzeitsfeier der Christen in den westlichen Kirchen," in Farnedi, 1986:51–85.

POEM 25[3]

1
Souls harmonious are being joined in chaste love,
a boy who is Christ's virgin and a girl who is God's.
Christ God, draw these paired doves towards Your reins,
and govern their necks beneath Your light yoke;
for Your yoke, O Christ, is light indeed
when taken up eagerly
and borne willingly for love.
This holy burden of the law of chastity
weighs upon the reluctant,
but for the devout
it is a pleasant imposition
for the subjugation of the flesh.

9
None of the wanton conduct of the mindless mob
must mar this marriage.
Juno, Cupid, Venus,

[3] The numbers refer to the lines of the Latin text.

all symbols of lust,
must stay well away.
The chaste, dear child of a bishop
is being joined in a holy alliance,
so let peace, modesty, and
holiness be in attendance.
For a marriage compacted in harmony
is a holy and honourable love,
and peace with God.
With His own lips, God consecrated marriage,
and with His own hand made human beings in pairs.
He made two to abide in one flesh
to make them share a love more indivisible yet.
While Adam slept,
he lost the rib which was taken from his side,
and gained a partner formed of his own bone.
He felt no loss in his side,
for his flesh grew to replace it;
but he recognized one like to himself.
And, beholding this other self,
sprung from him, flesh of his flesh,
he prophesied with a new voice, saying:

"This flesh is the flesh of my flesh.
I recognise the bone of my bones.
She is the rib from my side."

27
Since Adam and Eve are the original model
for the holy alliance now being sealed
between these children of Aaron,
let our joy be sober and our prayers discreet.
Let the name of Christ echo everywhere
from the lips of his devoted people.
Let there be no dancing crowds in decorated streets,
nor strewing of the ground with leaves,
nor of the threshold with foliage.
Let there be no riotous parades
through a city where Christ dwells.
I would have no displays of worldliness
besmirch the lives of devoted Christians.
Let no wind waft the scent of alien rites.
All that we do must be characterized
by the elegance of chastity.

Holy people know that their only perfume
is that of Christ's name,
which smells of the chaste fragrance of God.

39
Let there be no trays overflowing with useless gifts,
for character, not wealth, is the sign of true worth.
The holy wife of a bishop's son,
the spouse of a boy already consecrated,
must receive as dowry the light of life.
For her no garments tricked with gold or purple,
the splendor of God's grace will be her robe of gold.
Necklaces of motley jewels are not for her:
for she herself shall be a shining jewel
for the Lord her God.
No weight of wealth should burden a neck
committed to the yoke of Christ the Lord.
Rather, her adornment designed to please
must depend on an inward grooming,
and her mind must be decked
with the dowry that brings salvation.
She must not long to squander her income
on costly jewels or silken wraps;
instead, let her soul be adorned with chastity.
Then, far from being a liability to her husband,
she will be his most precious asset.
Someone who seeks a reputation by the way they dress
is only cheapened and devalued thereby.
Such misconceived pursuits sorely blind the mind
and the body decked in gaudiness coarsens the soul.
Shamelessness fails to realise the foulness
of garments which cheapen the wearer.

61
God forbid that one who has become a daughter
in the house of an apostolic family
should ever look like the daughter
of a temple where idols are worshipped.
Not for her to disguise her skin with rouge,
her eyes with mascara, or her hair with yellow tint.
The girl who spurns the pure beauty nature gave her
is guilty of the sin of pride,
for she finds fault with the way God made her.
Any woman making herself up with such different looks
will hardly be believed when she claims to be chaste.

69

Young people, you belong to Christ;
steer clear of enjoyments bringing damnation and death.
Believe the words of God:
such adornments lead to punishment
for those whose hearts crave them.
So warns Isaiah the prophet[4]
that women now clad in dresses of white silk or purple,
in long robes of bright purple, glinting with gold,
with folds flowing down to the ankles,
will be fastened with a rope tight-drawn;
tied up with ropes, they will wear sackcloth forever,
and will turn huge grindstones in their prison-mill.
And those who pile their heads high with hair
will be made bald for their shame.
But you, new bride of a saintly husband,
do not bedeck yourself with such adornments;
only an empty mind can delight in such things.
Do not walk about with scented clothes and hair,
hoping to catch the nostrils of the men you pass;
do not sit with your hair coiffured and braided,
piled high in interwoven locks.
Let not your beauty be another's undoing,
nor a snare to lead others astray.
You should not even seek to seduce your own husband
by thus adding inches to your height.

91

And you, saintly boy, devoted to the sacred books,
your love must be one that goes deeper than good looks.
Christ has made up to you by endowing your soul
with riches that endure.
Both of you He has enriched with holy wedding gifts:
hope, devotion, fidelity, peace, and chastity.
God's Word is your silver,
your gold the Holy Spirit;
the jewels you possess are the brightness of good works
glowing in your hearts.
If people of standing are ashamed of shabby clothes,
if proud hearts take pleasure in expensive things,
then the example of our saints

---

[4] Cf. Isaiah 4:18-23.

and the holy simplicity of our first ancestors
must dispel such shame.

103

Consider our parents in paradise of old,
for whom a single field comprised their whole world:
sheepskins were their only covering.
Are we now ashamed of woven garments spun from wool?
When the lovely Rebecca came as bride to blessed Isaac,
she was simply dressed and veiled herself with modesty.
She came, we read, not decked out in jewels,
but muffled in a cloak.
With this she modestly concealed her face,
fearing to confront her bridegroom's eyes.

113

Or would you prefer the dancing girl Herodias,
whose performance won the head of John the Baptist?
Avenging her mother's anger, frustrated lust,
the reward her lewdness won her was a human head:
the very head that had proclaimed to the nations
that the Lamb of God was at hand.
It was her lascivious dress gained this wicked reward
for that godless dancing-girl.
Truly, her father's daughter!
Having made up her mind, she got her way,
and made him, despite himself, commit this crime.
With the enticements of her attractive body,
by her gyrations and clever footwork
she won the applause of guests
no better than the wicked king who had invited them.
If sandals of glittering gold
had not adorned her slim ankles,
or allowed her to kick up her heels more wantonly;
if she had not draped herself in a garment with curling train,
or pulled her hair back to reveal the jewels on her gleaming
    brow,
would she have won the depraved hearts of her audience
    or been so successful in her awful mission?
Herod, too, loved to strut in royal robes;
he grew crazy, puffed up by his raiment;
blasphemously proud, he forgot the honour owed to God.
He perished, stinking, from a worm-infested wound.
His punishment was what he deserved:

he who, in his majestic robes,
had come to consider himself divine,
died covered with unsightly sores.
Perhaps such illusions befit the hearts of kings,
but what have we to do with Pharaoh?
The kingdom we seek has nothing in common
with the empty vanities of the world:
the light of the saints does not mingle with the darkness of the
    enemy.

141
A cleric must love a wife
who glories in Christ as her hair,
whose beauty lies in her heart's radiance.
A lector must learn from sacred history
that God made her as man's helpmate.
The woman, for her part,
should seek equality with her consecrated husband
by humbly welcoming Christ's presence in her spouse.
Thus she can grow into his holy body
and be interwoven with his frame,
so that her husband may be her head
as Christ is his.
In a marriage such as this
Eve's subservience came to an end,
and Sara became the free equal of her holy husband.
When Jesus' friends were married like this,
He attended as a groomsman,
and changed water into wine like nectar.

153
And Mary, mother of the Lord,
will be at such a wedding,
who gave birth to God without losing her virginity.
In Mary, this virgin consecrated to God,
God built himself a temple of delight
with a secret opening in the roof.
So silently He glided down
silent as the rain that falls as dew
from a cloud on high upon a fleece.
None was ever privy to this secret visitation
when God took human form from his virgin mother.
How wonderful the Lord's deception
for the sake of humankind!

Without intercourse, a woman's womb conceived new life.
This bride submitted to no mere human husband.
She was a mother and bore a child
without the woman's role in intercourse.
The marriage made her a spouse,
but physically she was never a wife.
Though untouched by any husband
she became the mother of the boy-child.

167

What a great mystery this was!
The Church was wedded to Christ,
and became at once both sister to the Lord and bride!
The bride with the status of spouse is a sister
because she is not subject . . .[5]
Through the fructifying seed of the eternal Word,
she continues her maternal role,
conceiving and giving birth to nations.
She is sister and spouse:
her intercourse is not of the body but of the soul,
her husband is not human but divine.
Her children number old and young alike,
and are of either sex.
Blessed are they, these children of our God,
sprung from no human seed, a heavenly race.
Hence the teaching of the Apostle Paul:
in Christ there is neither male or female,
but one only body and one faith;
for we who acknowledge Christ to be our Head
are all one body, and members of him.
Having stripped off Adam, we have put on Christ;
thus now we are approaching the form of angels.
For all reborn in baptism there is thus one task:
both sexes must incorporate the perfect man,
and Christ as all in all must be our common Head,
our King who delivers his members
to the Father in the Kingdom.
And once our bodies are raised immortal,
human frailty will no longer require
that men and women should marry or be given in marriage.

---

[5] A line is missing from the text at this point.

191

So remember me, and keep your marriage chaste.
Let the holy cross be the yoke that pairs you together.
As children of a mother who is both spouse and sister,
discipline your hearts
to be worthy of the holy names you bear.
As brother and sister together
hasten to meet Christ the Bridegroom,
so that you may become one flesh in his eternal body.
Let that same love contain you
by which the Church clings fast to Christ,
and by which Christ holds her close in his embrace.

199

May your father the bishop bless you,
and lead the singing of holy chants
along with the choir of singers.
Kindly Memor, lead your children to the Lord
and before the altar commend them
with a prayer and a blessing of the hand.

But what fragrance is this hanging in the air
and wafting to my nostrils?
Whence comes this strange light to fixate my eyes?
Who is this, so remote from human life,
who walks with tranquil step,
trailing Christ's abundant grace,
escorted by a train of heaven's children
as by the angelic host?
I know him: the fragrance of God clings to him
and the beauty of the heavens shines in his face.
This is Emilius:
a man so rich in the countless gifts of Christ,
a man in whom the light of heaven shines.

213

Memor, arise;
venerate him as a father,
embrace him as a brother;
Aemilius is both of these to you.
Memor is both junior and senior.
How remarkable the gift and work of God,
for here the younger is the father!
The one born later is the older,
because as bishop of his see

he wears in his heart the gray hairs
marking his seniority as successor of the apostles.
Memor, being son and brother to Aemilius,
delights in the presence of him
who is father to himself and his dear ones.
Justice and peace embrace each other
when Memor meets Aemilius of like mind.
As bishops they are one in their godly reputation;
as friends their loyalty binds them to each other.

225
Thereupon Memor, mindful of his duty,
hands over, as is customary,
his dear ones to the hands of Aemilius.
Aemilius, yoking their heads together in nuptial peace,
veils them with his right hand
sanctifying them with prayer.

Christ, hear your priests!
Christ, hear the prayers of those who call on you!
Grant the pious wishes of your anointed supplicants!

231
Christ,
train these newly-weds through your holy bishop.
Help these pure hearts through his chaste hands,
that they might agree on a compact of virginity,
or be themselves the source of consecrated virgins.
Of these prayers, the first is preferable:
that they keep their bodies innocent of the flesh.
But if they consummate their marriage physically,
may their chaste children become a priestly race.
May the whole house of Memor be a house of Aaron.
May this house of Memor be a house of anointed ones.
Preserve the memory of Paulinus and Therasia,
and Christ will preserve the memory of Memor forever.

4. VERONENSE OR LEONINE
SACRAMENTARY

This collection of Mass prayers was once attributed to Leo the
Great (+461), but is now regarded as a more informal collection
of texts, probably of Roman origin, compiled at Verona in the
early sixth century. The first three prayers correspond to the
Opening Collect, the Prayer over the Gifts, and the *Hanc igitur*
of the Roman Mass. The fourth prayer clearly looks forward to
the nuptial blessing that follows (five-six), but in its present position seems to serve as a Postcommunion prayer, which would
suggest that the solemn blessing took place at the end of the
Mass and not, as later tradition had it, at an earlier point in the
Mass. The fifth prayer is a prayer that the main prayer (six) be
heard—a doubling quite common in the Roman liturgy in such
rites as ordination, baptism and the consecration of altars.

It is important to note that the Verona Sacramentary has no
provision for the actual betrothal or wedding rites, but only for
the celebration of the Eucharist and a solemn blessing of the
bride. Presumably, the actual contracting of marriage took place
elsewhere (at home) in accordance with local custom.

Some echo of classical Roman marriage customs is found in
the *Hanc igitur* (three), which speaks of two maidservants of
God, one of whom (the Roman *pronuba*?) offers gifts at the Eucharist on behalf of the other (the bride). The *pronuba* was an
older, happily married woman (a woman with one husband!),
who in Roman custom prepared the bride and led her to her
wedding.

Another echo is found in the title of the text: "The Nuptial
Veiling Begins." The orange-yellow veil was the characteristic
headdress of the Roman bride and was traditionally worn when
she appeared at her wedding. This title would seem to suggest
that, in Christian practice, the celebrant of the Eucharist actually
gave the bride her veil, though the prayers make no mention of
it and the origins of the later custom of veiling either the bride
alone or both bride and groom are exceedingly obscure. In any
case, it is likely that this nuptial Mass took place sometime between the concluding of the marriage contract (a domestic affair
between the families concerned) and the beginning of cohabitation, thereby interrupting or displacing the infamous ceremonies
of *domumductio* where the bride was led to her future home to
the accompaniment of much noise and bawdy songs.

The exclusive focus on the bride is one of the most remarkable features of this and other nuptial blessings in the Roman tradition. The clear implication is that the woman is the weaker partner, a view for which a biblical "rationale" is given in 6a. This account of the creation story reflects a reading of Gen 2 which was common in late antiquity, viz. that God made man in his own image, whereas woman was made in the image of man: her weakness derives from the fact that she reflects the image of God only indirectly! The social value of (arranged) marriages for establishing bonds between families as well as for perpetuating the human race, alluded to in the same paragraph, is probably also a reflection of the inferior social status accorded to women. The second half of the prayer (6b) sketches the ideal of the married woman, an ideal also to be understood against the background of the woman's subordination to man (first her father, now her husband), but also as a reaction to the license and immorality of late antiquity. Thus the prayer reflects both cultural presuppositions and a counter-cultural exaltation of marriage as a form of the Christian life.

TEXT

L. C. Mohlberg, L. Eisenhöfer, P. Siffrin, *Sacramentarium Veronense*, (Rerum ecclesiasticarum documenta; series maior: Fontes; 1), Rome: Herder, 1965, 139ff. The translation of the nuptial blessing given here follows Ritzer, 1970:240. (Full texts in Ritzer, 421–424.)

BIBLIOGRAPHY

Ritzer, 1976:238–243.

Stevenson, 1982:35–37.

HERE BEGINS THE NUPTIAL VEILING

1.
Hear us, almighty and merciful God,
that what is done by our ministry
may be brought to completion by your blessing.
Through.

2.
Receive, we beseech you, O Lord,
the gift we offer for the holy law of marriage;

be the guardian of the enterprise
which you have created.
Through.

3.
Be pleased, therefore, O Lord,
to accept the offering of your maidservant, N.,
which we offer you for your maidservant, N.
We humbly pray your majesty on her behalf,
that, as you have granted her
to come to the appropriate age for marriage,
so now that she is joined by your gift,
in the companionship of marriage[6]
you might fulfill her with the joy of the children she desires
and graciously bring her with her husband
to their hoped-for fullness of years.
Through.

4.
We beseech you, almighty God,
to accompany with your favor
what your providence has ordained
and to keep in lasting peace
those whom you will join in lawful union.[7]
Through.

5.
Listen favorably, O Lord, to our prayers
and graciously grant your help
to the institutions you have established
for the propagation of the human race,
so that what is joined by your authority
might be preserved by your help.
Through.

6a, i
Father, creator of the world,
you gave life to every living creature
and commissioned [human beings] to multiply.
With your own hands, you gave Adam a companion:
bones grown from his bones,
to signify identity of form
yet wondrous diversity.

---

[6] *consortio maritali.*
[7] *societas.*

Thus your command to share the marriage bed,
to increase and multiply in marriage,
has linked the whole world together
and established ties among the whole human race.
This you saw, O Lord, to be pleasing, even necessary:
that she who would be much weaker than man—
she being made in his image,
but he being made in yours—
once joined to the stronger sex,
they who were previously two become one;
while from that oneness of love both sexes derive.

6a, ii

Thus it was that generation was to follow generation,
those who came first
being succeeded by those who come after;
so that humankind,
though destined for death,
and despite life's brevity,
goes on without end.

6a, iii

To this end, then, Father,
bless the youth of your handmaid who is to marry.
Joined in a good and blessed union,
may she observe the mandates of the eternal law.
May she remember that she is called
not so much to the lawful pleasures of marriage
as to the safeguarding of her promise of fidelity.

6b, i

May she marry in Christ
as one faithful and chaste.

6b, ii

May she prove loving to her husband, like Rachel;
wise, like Rebecca;
long-lived and faithful, like Sarah.

6b, iii

May the author of lies never subvert her behavior;
may she adhere steadfastly to the bond of fidelity
and to the commandments.

6b, iv

May discipline lend strength to her frailty
as she devoutly serves the living God.

6b, v
Loyal to one bed,
may she flee all unlawful relations.

6b, vi
May she be serious and modest,
her honor above reproach,
instructed in the wisdom of heaven.

6b, vii
May she be fruitful with children,
a person of integrity and innocence.

6b, viii
And may she come at last
to enjoy the repose of the blessed
and to the heavenly kingdom.
Through.

5. A GREGORIAN SACRAMENTARY: THE "HADRIANUM"

The earliest version of the Gregorian type of sacramentary dates from the eighth century, but it is supposed to represent in all essentials the liturgy of Gregory the Great, two centuries earlier. Unlike the Verona book, the Mass Prayers here are clearly laid out, with the nuptial blessing and its introductory prayer coming before the Kiss of Peace and before Communion.

Though this sacramentary uses several of the Verona texts, it provides an original preface and a re-worked nuptial blessing. Nonetheless, the two books represent much the same understanding of marriage: the same view of the weakness of woman, which makes the bride the obvious and exclusive focus of the Church's prayer; the same emphasis on marriage as a divinely-instituted state into which people enter; the accent on the moral virtues expected of a Christian wife; marriage as a companionship, nonetheless, ideally lived in peace and harmony.

New to this text is the reference to Ephesians 5 (n. 6) and to the belief that even original sin and the need for a new, post-diluvian covenant had not obliterated the God-given holiness of the married state. In fact, the new opening sections of the nuptial blessing (nn. 6–7a) recall both the past dimension of marriage, rooted in the dawn of creation, and its future dimension, the marriage of Christ and his Church. The couple entering marriage, therefore, inherit the blessings of the original covenant which, surviving the fall and the flood, perdure through history, but they also assume the role of witnesses to the culmination of that history in the marriage of the Lamb (Rev 21). Thus the bridal pair assume a larger, archetypal identity, in which both past and future meet.

While the prayers continue to attend to the bride rather than to the groom, some shift in marriage customs seems to be registered in the *Hanc igitur* (n. 4), where the *pronuba* has disappeared and the offering is made by "your servants" (the families of the couple?). Some versions of the text also introduce plural forms into the nuptial blessing in an obvious attempt to broaden its application to include both partners. Moreover, while procreation still features as the chief reason for marriage, it is remarkable how, in comparison with the Verona Sacramentary, references to the social importance of marriage as a way of bonding families and ensuring the family line have given way to assertions about the importance of marriage for the Church in providing new candidates for baptism (n. 3).

The end of the blessing is re-worked to incorporate a prayer for long life and for the vision of "her children's children to the third and fourth generation"—a prayer which will frequently recur in later Western rites, and derives from the Vulgate text of the Book of Tobit (Tob 9:11).

TEXT

H. Lietzmann, ed., *Das Sacramentarium Gregorianum nach dem Aachener Urexemplar*, Münster: 1921, 110–112. Translation following Ritzer, 1970:427–429.

BIBLIOGRAPHY

Stevenson, 1982:40–43.

PRAYER FOR THE VEILING OF BRIDES

1.
Hear us . . .[8]

OVER THE GIFTS

2.
Receive, we beseech you, O Lord,
the gift we offer for the holy law of marriage;
be the guardian of the enterprise which you have given.
Through.[9]

PREFACE

3.
It is truly right and just,
fitting and for our salvation.
For you have joined people in marriage
with the sweet yoke of concord
and the unbreakable bond of peace,
so that the chaste fruitfulness of holy marriages
may serve to increase the adoptive children of God.
Your providence, O Lord, and your grace

[8]Ver, 1.
[9] Cf. Ver, 2.

serve to guide both things in wonderful ways:
what generation brings forth to enrich the world,
regeneration leads to the increase of the Church.
And therefore,
with angels and archangels,
with thrones and dominations,
and with the whole heavenly host,
we sing the hymn of your glory,
saying without ceasing:
Holy, holy, holy.

HANC IGITUR

4.
Be pleased, therefore, O Lord,
to accept the offering of your servants,
which they offer for your maidservant, N.,
whom you have deigned to bring to the age of maturity[10]
and to the day of marriage.
On her behalf
we pour out our prayers to your majesty,
that you would mercifully grant her
to be united with her husband . . . .

5.
Before the pax domini *[the priest] says this prayer:*

Listen favorably. . . .[11]

BLESSING

6.
O God,
you made all things out of nothing by your power.
When you had laid the foundations of the universe,
you created man in the image of God,
and made woman as man's inseparable helper,
bringing the woman's body into being
out of the man's flesh,
teaching us thereby
that what it had pleased to create
out of an original unity
must never be put asunder.

[10] *statum mensurae.*
[11] Ver, 5.

O God,
you have consecrated the bond of marriage
with such an excellent mystery
as to prefigure in the covenant[12] of marriage
the sacrament of Christ and his Church.

7.
O God,
through you a woman is joined to her husband
and society is chiefly ordered by that blessing
which was neither lost by original sin
nor washed away in the flood.

8a
Look with kindness upon your maidservant,
who is to be joined in marriage,
and who now seeks the help of your protection.

8b
May her yoke be one of love and peace.

8c
May she marry in Christ,
faithful and chaste.[13]

8d
May she remain an imitator of holy women:

8e
amiable to her husband, like Rachel;
wise, like Rebecca;
long-lived and faithful, like Sarah.

9a
May the author of lies never subvert her behavior;
may she remain steadfast in fidelity
and in keeping the commandments.

9b
Loyal to one marriage bed,
may she flee all unlawful relations.

9c
Let her shore up her weakness
with the strength of discipline.

---

[12] *foedus.*
[13] Greg, 8c–10b is mostly taken from Ver, 6b i–viii.

9d
May she be sober and modest,
her honor above reproach,
learned in heavenly wisdom.

10a
May she be fruitful with children,
a person of integrity
and beyond suspicion.

10b
And may she come at last
to enjoy the repose of the blessed
and to the heavenly kingdom.

10c
May she see her children's children
to the third and fourth generation,
and come to a desired old age.
Through.

10d
The peace of the Lord be with you always.

TO CONCLUDE

11.
We beseech you, almighty God,
to accompany with your love
what your providence has established,
so that those who are joined in lawful wedlock[14]
may be preserved by you in lasting peace.
Through.

[14] *societas.*

6. THE GELASIAN TRADITION

While clearly drawing on elements of both the Verona and Gregorian sacramentaries, the Gelasian marriage rite has some interesting differences. Once again, it should be noticed, we have a Nuptial Mass rather than a wedding rite, but the two seem to be getting closer since the Mass appears to be celebrated on the day of marriage (4). The offering of gifts at the Eucharist continues to be made, but the agent of the offering is no longer "your maidservant," the *pronuba* (Ver. 3), but "your maidservants" in the plural (bridesmaids, perhaps?). There is also provision for the Mass to be celebrated on the thirtieth day after the marriage, in which case the couple make the offering themselves (7).

It has sometimes been suggested that the practice of blessing people *before* Communion arose with the decline in the number of people receiving Communion, so that those not communicating would be blessed and permitted to leave before Communion was distributed. Certainly, the removal of the nuptial blessing to its now traditional place (in the Roman Rite) after the Canon and before Communion might be thought to indicate that the bride and groom were not expected to communicate, especially since the blessing itself makes no reference to Communion. However, the rubric (10a) states clearly that, after the kiss of peace, the priest is to give them the sacrament and then pronounce a blessing over them. This blessing, which precedes the postcommunion prayer and seems directly attached to the communion of the bridal pair is unique in the Roman sacramentaries in that it prays for both the bride and groom. As such, it may well be a Frankish addition, inserted by a scribe who felt uncomfortable with the exclusive focus of the Roman texts on the bride alone. Nonetheless, with its succinct references to Christ, to the origins of marriage at creation, and to the marriages of the patriarchs, it is entirely in keeping with the rest of the rite.

TEXT

Mohlberg-Eizenhoeffer-Siffrin, ed., *Liber sacramentorum romanae ecclesiae (Vat. Reg. 316).* (Rome, 1960.) 208–210.[1]

---

[1] This translation based on text in K. Ritzer, 1970:424ff.

BIBLIOGRAPHY

Ritzer, 1970:passim.

Stevenson, 1982:37–40; 1987:30–31.

Studer, B. "Zur Hochzeitsfeier der Christen in den westlichen Kirchen der ersten Jahrhunderte," in Farnedi, 1986:51–86.

HERE BEGINS THE MARRIAGE RITE

1.
Listen favorably . . .[2]

2.
We beseech you . . .[3]

OVER THE GIFTS

3.
Be present, O Lord, to our prayers.

4.
Accept with pleasure and kindness[4]
the gift of your maidservants, N. and N.,
which we offer for your maidservant, N.
You have deigned to bring her to the state of maturity
and the day of marriage.
May your grace bring to completion
what your providence has made possible.
Through.

PREFACE

5.
It is truly right and just . . .[5]
For you have joined [people] in marriage
with the sweet yoke of concord
and the unbreakable bond of peace,
so that the chaste fruitfulness of holy marriages
might serve to increase the adoptive children of God.
Your providence, O Lord, and your grace
serve to guide both things in wonderful ways:

---

[2] Ver, 5.
[3] Ver, 4.
[4] Cf. Greg, 4.
[5] Cf. Greg, 3.

what generation brings forth to enrich the world,
regeneration leads to the increase of the Church.

INFRA ACTIONEM[6]

6.
Be pleased, therefore, O Lord,
to accept the offering of your maidservants, N. and N.,
which they offer for your maidservant, N.
We humbly pray your majesty on her behalf . . .
Graciously bring her with her husband
to their hoped-for fullness of years.
Order our days in your peace . . .

INFRA ACTIONEM ON THE 30TH DAY
OR ON THE ANNIVERSARY OF MARRIAGE

7.
Be pleased, therefore, O Lord,
to accept the offering of your servants, N. and N.,
which they offer you on the thirtieth day
(or on the anniversary) of their marriage.
On their wedding day
you were pleased to unite them in the conjugal bond.
For this reason, then, they render their offerings[7] to you,
their God, living and true.
Humbly we pour out our prayers to you on their behalf,
asking that they might grow old together in peace
and see their children's children
unto a third and fourth generation
and bless you all the days of their life.
Through.

8a
You complete the whole canon and then you say the Lord's prayer and
bless her using these words:

HERE BEGINS THE PRAYER

8b
O God,
at the beginning of the growing world

---

[6] Literally, "within the act [of thanksgiving]," i.e., within the Canon of the
Mass. Cf. Greg, 5; Ver, 3.
[7] *vota.*

you blessed it with the multiplication of offspring.
Graciously hear our prayers
and pour out your blessing upon this your maidservant,
that they may be joined together in the union of marriage
by mutual affection, similar minds, and shared holiness.
Through.

9a
Father, creator of the world . . .[8]

9b
May she marry in Christ . . .[9]

10a
After this you say:

Pax vobiscum.

And then you communicate them.

Then after they have received Communion, you say this blessing over them as follows:

10b
Lord, holy Father,
almighty and eternal God,
with renewed prayer we humbly beseech you,
we for whom Christ himself intercedes with you.
Deign to bless the joining of your servants.
May they prove worthy of your blessings,
that they may be fruitful with children in succession.
Confirm their marriage,
as you did that of the first human being.
Avert from them every onslaught of the enemy,
that they who, by your providence,
have deserved to be married,
might imitate the holy patriarchs
even in their own marriage.
Through.

ALSO AFTER COMMUNION

11.
Hear us, Lord, holy Father,[10]
almighty and ever-living God,

[8] Ver, 6a, i.
[9] Ver, 6b, i.
[10] Cf. Ver, 1.

so that what is done by our ministry
may be brought to completion by your blessing.
Through.

7. BYZANTINE RITE

The marriage service of the Byzantine (Greek and Russian) Churches substantially dates in its present form from at least the eighth century (Barberini 336). Then, it was two distinct rites, but the two became merged, as can be seen from the following outline:

Betrothal:
Litany
Collect
Prayer of inclination
Declaration of
  Betrothal Crowning
Solemn blessing of couple

Marriage:
Litany
2 longer prayers
Shorter prayer

Word:
Eph 5:20-33
John 2:1-11
Litany
Prayer

Cup:
Litany
Lord's Prayer
Common cup
Dance
Removal of crowns

The presence of the clergy at Christian betrothals and marriages is attested as early as the third century in the East, but it was as honored guests that they attended and their role was restricted to giving a blessing at some point in the proceedings. By the seventh century, however, the practice was becoming universal and mandatory, and the scene of both rites shifted from house to church. With that, the ritual we have was born.

Betrothal, originally quite separate from marriage, or the beginning of cohabitation, could take different forms, some more binding than others. The form that has entered into the liturgy was the most solemn and binding of all, including as it did the gift of money or ring from the groom to his fiancée and her family. This was a solemn pledge (*arrhabon*) of marriage, and as the functional or economic aspects of the arrhabon declined, the symbolism of the engagement ring moved to the forefront (cfr. I.5).

The move from the narthex to the main body of the church (II.1) marks the transition from betrothal to marriage. (The declarations of freedom—II.2—are a modern Western interpolation.) The rite opens with a litany and then three lengthy prayers, of which the third and shortest is the oldest (II.4c). In all three, the remembering of the role of marriage at creation and throughout salvation history will be noted, together with the solidly realistic petitions for prosperity, peace and children which contrast strongly with the moralism of the Roman tradition.

The liturgical meaning of the crowning is clearly to associate the bride and groom with Christ and the martyrs as living witnesses to the victory of life over death. This is followed by a Liturgy of the Word (II.6-8) and a sharing of a common cup. The triple procession around the lectern is a rare example of liturgical dance (13) and the chant that accompanies it, celebrating the incarnation and Christ, "the apostles' boast, the martyrs' joy," is indicative of the theological depths of this liturgy of marriage. Finally, the crowns are removed, a ritual act which originally took place eight days after the wedding had been celebrated.

TEXT

Meyendorf, John, *Marriage: An Orthodox Perspective* (Crestwood, NY: St. Vladimir's Seminary Press, 1975) 126–144.

BIBLIOGRAPHY

Charalambadis, S. "Marriage in the Orthodox Church." *One-In-Christ* 15 (1979):204–223.

Dalmais, I.-H. "Le liturgie du mariage dans les églises orientales: Structure–histoire–signification." *La Maison Dieu* 50 (1957):58–69.

Gelsi, D. "Punti di reflessione sull'ufficio bizantino per la 'incoronazione' degli sposi," in Farnedi, 1986:283–306.

Stevenson 1987:75–79.

I

THE SERVICE OF BETROTHAL

The betrothal is celebrated in the narthex, or in the back part of the church.

Deacon: Bless, Master.

Priest:	Blessed is our God, always, now and ever and unto ages of ages.
Choir:	Amen.

1.

Deacon:	In peace let us pray to the Lord.
Choir:	Lord, have mercy. *Repeated after each petition.*

For the peace from above
and for the salvation of our souls,
let us pray to the Lord.
   For the peace of the whole world,
   for the welfare of the holy churches of God,
   and for the union of all,
   let us pray to the Lord.
For this holy house
and for those who enter with faith,
reverence, and the fear of God,
let us pray to the Lord.
   For our Metropolitan _____,
   for our Bishop _____,
   for the honorable priesthood,
   the diaconate in Christ,
   for all the clergy and the people,
   let us pray to the Lord.
For the servant of God _____,
and for the handmaiden of God _____,
who now plight each other their troth,
and for their salvation,
let us pray to the Lord.
   That they may be granted children
   for the continuance of the race,
   and all their petitions
   which are unto salvation,
   let us pray to the Lord.
That He will send down upon them
perfect and peaceful love, and assistance,
let us pray to the Lord.

That He will preserve them in oneness of mind,
and in steadfast faith,
let us pray to the Lord.
That He will preserve them
in a blameless way of life,
let us pray to the Lord.
That the Lord our God will grant to them
an honorable marriage and a bed undefiled,
let us pray to the Lord.
For our deliverance from all affliction,
wrath, danger, and necessity,
let us pray to the Lord.

Help us, save us, have mercy on us,
and keep us, O God, by thy grace.

Choir: Lord, have mercy.

Deacon: Commemorating our most holy, most pure, most
blessed and glorious Lady Theotokos and ever-
virgin Mary,
with all the saints,
let us commend ourselves
and each other,
and all our life
unto Christ our God.

Choir: To Thee, O Lord.

Priest: For unto Thee are due all glory, honor, and
worship:
to the Father, and to the Son,
and to the Holy Spirit,
now and ever and unto ages of ages.

Choir: Amen.

2.

Priest: O eternal God, who hast brought into unity
those who were sundered,
and hast ordained for them
an indissoluble bond of love,
who didst bless Isaac and Rebecca,
and didst make them heirs of Thy promise:
Bless also these Thy servants,
_____ and _____,
guiding them unto every good work.

> For Thou art a good God
> and lovest mankind,
> and unto Thee we ascribe glory:
> to the Father, and to the Son,
> and to the Holy Spirit,
> now and ever and unto ages of ages.

Choir: Amen.

Priest: Peace be unto all.

Choir: And to your spirit.

Deacon: Bow your heads unto the Lord.

Choir: To Thee, O Lord.

3.

Priest: O Lord our God,
> who hast espoused the Church
> as a pure virgin among the gentiles:
> Bless this betrothal,
> and unite and maintain these Thy servants
> in peace and oneness of mind.
> For unto Thee are due all glory, honor, and
>> worship:
> to the Father, and to the Son,
> and to the Holy Spirit,
> now and ever and unto ages of ages.

Choir: Amen.

4.

Then taking the rings, the priest blesses the bridal pair, making the sign of the cross with the ring of the bride over the bridegroom, and with that of the bridegroom over the bride, saying to the man:

> The servant of God, _____,
> is betrothed to the handmaiden of God, _____,
> in the name of the Father,
> and of the Son,
> and of the Holy Spirit.
> Amen.

And to the woman:

> The handmaiden of God, _____,
> is betrothed to the servant of God, _____,
> in the name of the Father,

and of the Son,
and of the Holy Spirit.
Amen.

*And when he has said this to each of them three times, he places the
rings on their right hands. Then the bridal pair exchanges the rings,
and the priest says the following prayer:*

5.

Deacon: Let us pray to the Lord.

Choir: Lord, have mercy.

Priest: O Lord our God,
who didst accompany the servant
of the patriarch Abraham into Mesopotamia,
when he was sent to espouse a wife
for his lord Isaac,
and who, by means of drawing water,
didst reveal to him
that he should betroth Rebecca:
Do Thou, the same Lord,
bless also the betrothal
of these Thy servants, _____ and _____,
and confirm the promise that they have made.
Establish them in the holy union which is from
  Thee.
For in the beginning
Thou didst make them male and female,
and by Thee the woman is joined unto the man as
  a helper
and for the procreation of the human race.
Therefore, O Lord our God,
who hast sent forth Thy truth upon Thine
  inheritance,
and Thy covenant unto Thy servants or fathers,
Thine elect from generation to generation:
Look upon Thy servant, _____,
and Thy handmaiden, _____,
and establish and make firm their betrothal,
in faith and in oneness of mind,
in truth and in love.
For Thou, O Lord,
hast declared that a pledge should be given
and confirmed in all things.

By a ring power was given to Joseph in Egypt;
by a ring Daniel was glorified in the land of
    Babylon;
by a ring the uprightness of Tamar was revealed;
by a ring our heavenly Father showed His bounty
    upon His Son,
for He said:
Bring the fatted calf and kill it,
and let us eat and make merry.
By Thine own right hand, O Lord,
Thou didst arm Moses in the Red Sea;
by Thy true word the heavens were established,
and the foundations of the earth were made firm;
and the right hands of Thy servants
also shall be blessed by Thy mighty word
and by Thine upraised arm.
Therefore, O Master,
bless now this putting-on of rings
with Thy heavenly blessing,
and let Thine angel go before them
all the days of their life.
For Thou art He that blesses
and sanctifies all things,
and unto Thee are due all glory, honor, and
    worship:
to the Father, and to the Son,
and to the Holy Spirit,
now and ever
and unto ages of ages.

Choir: Amen.

II

THE SERVICE OF CROWNING

The bridal couple, preceded by the priest, moves in procession to the center of the church.

1.

Priest and Choir:

Refrain: Glory to Thee, our God,
             glory to Thee!
             Blessed is every one who fears the Lord,
             who walks in his ways!

You shall eat the fruit of the labor of your hands;
you shall be happy,
and it shall be well with you.
Your wife will be like a fruitful vine
within your house;
your children will be like olive shoots
around your table.
Lo, thus shall the man be blessed
who fears the Lord.
The Lord bless you from Zion!
May you see the prosperity of Jerusalem
all the days of your life!
May you see your children's children!
Peace be upon Israel! (Ps 127)

An exhortation may follow.

2.

Then, according to Slavonic editions of the marriage service, the priest shall inquire of the bridegroom:

Do you, _____,
have a good, free and unconstrained will
and a firm intention
to take as your wife this woman, _____,
whom you see here before you?

Bridegroom: I have, reverend father.

Priest: Have you promised yourself to any other bride?

Bridegroom: I have not promised myself, reverend father.

And the priest, looking at the bride, shall inquire of her:

Do you, _____,
have a good, free and unconstrained will
and a firm intention
to take as your husband this man, _____,
whom you see here before you?

Bride: I have, reverend father.

Priest: Have you promised yourself to any other man?

Bride: I have not promised myself, reverend father.

3.

Deacon: Bless, master.

Priest: Blessed is the Kingdom of the Father,
        and of the Son,
        and of the Holy Spirit,
        now and ever
        and unto ages of ages.

Choir: Amen.

Deacon: In peace let us pray to the Lord.

Choir: Lord, have mercy.
        Repeated after each petition.

        For the peace from above and for the
        salvation of our souls,
        let us pray to the Lord.
            For the peace of the whole world,
            for the welfare of the holy churches of God,
            and for the union of all,
            let us pray to the Lord.
        For this holy house
        and for those who enter with faith,
        reverence, and the fear of God,
        let us pray to the Lord.
            For our Metropolitan _____,
            for our Bishop _____,
            for the honorable priesthood,
            the diaconate in Christ,
            for all the clergy and the people,
            let us pray to the Lord.
        For the servants of God, _____ and _____,
        who are now being united to each other
        in the community of marriage,
        and for their salvation,
        let us pray to the Lord.
            That He will bless this marriage,
            as He blessed the marriage in Cana of Galilee,
            let us pray to the Lord.
        That He will grant to them chastity,
        and of the fruit of the womb
        as is expedient for them,
        let us pray to the Lord.
            That He will make them glad
            with the sight of sons and daughters,
            let us pray to the Lord.

That He will grant to them
enjoyment of the blessing of children,
and a blameless life,
let us pray to the Lord.
   That He will grant to them and to us,
   all our petitions which are unto salvation,
   let us pray to the Lord.
That He will deliver them and us
from all affliction, wrath, danger, and necessity,
let us pray to the Lord.

Help us, save us, have mercy on us,
and keep us, O God, by Thy grace.

Choir: Lord, have mercy.

Deacon: Commemorating our most holy, most pure,
most blessed and glorious Lady Theotokos and
   ever-virgin Mary, with all the saints,
let us commend ourselves and each other,
and all our life unto Christ our God.

Choir: To Thee, O Lord.

Priest: For unto Thee are due all glory, honor, and
   worship:
to the Father, and to the Son,
and to the Holy Spirit,
now and ever and unto ages of ages.

Choir: Amen.

4.

Deacon: Let us pray to the Lord.

Choir: Lord, have mercy.

Then the priest recites aloud the following prayer:

4a

O God most pure,
fashioner of every creature,
who didst transform the rib of our forefather Adam
   into a wife,
because of Thy love towards mankind,
and didst bless them
and say to them:
Be fruitful and multiply,

and fill the earth and subdue it;
who didst make of the two one flesh:
Therefore a man leaves his father and mother
and cleaves to his wife,
and the two shall become one flesh,
and what God has joined together,
let no man put asunder:
Thou didst bless Thy servant Abraham,
and opening the womb of Sarah
didst make him to be the father of many nations.
Thou didst give Isaac to Rebecca,
and didst bless her in childbearing.
Thou didst join Jacob unto Rachel,
and from them didst bring forth
the twelve patriarchs.
Thou didst unite Joseph and Aseneth,
giving to them Ephraim and Manasseh
as the fruit of their procreation.
Thou didst accept Zechariah and Elizabeth,
and didst make their offspring to be the
    Forerunner.
From the root of Jesse according to the flesh,
Thou didst bud forth the ever-virgin one,
and wast incarnate of her,
and wast born of her
for the redemption of the human race.
Through Thine unutterable gift
and manifold goodness,
Thou didst come to Cana of Galilee,
and didst bless the marriage there,
to make manifest
that it is Thy will that there should be
lawful marriage and procreation.
Do Thou, the same all-holy Master,
accept the prayers of us Thy servants.
As Thou wast present there,
be Thou also present here,
with Thine invisible protection.
Bless this marriage,
and grant to these Thy servants,
    _____ and _____,
a peaceful life, length of days, chastity,
mutual love in the bond of peace,

long-lived offspring,
gratitude from their children,
a crown of glory that does not fade away.
Graciously grant
that they may see their children's children.
Preserve their bed unassailed,
and give them of the dew of heaven from on high,
and of the fatness of the earth.
Fill their houses with wheat, wine and oil
and with every good thing,
so that they may give in turn to those in need;
and grant also to those here present with them
all those petitions which are for their salvation.
For Thou art the God of mercies, and of bounties,
and of love towards mankind,
and unto Thee we ascribe glory:
to the Father, and to the Son,
and to the Holy Spirit,
now and ever and unto ages of ages.

Choir: Amen.

4b

Deacon: Let us pray to the Lord.

Choir: Lord, have mercy.

Then the priest recites aloud the following prayer:

Blessed art Thou, O Lord our God,
priest of mystical and undefiled marriage,
and ordainer of the law of the marriage of the
    body;
preserver of immortality,
and provider of the good things of life;
the same master who in the beginning
didst make man and establish him
as a king over creation,
and didst say: "It is not good
that man should be alone upon the earth.
Let us make a helper fit for him."
Taking one of his ribs,
Thou didst fashion woman;
and when Adam saw her he said:
"This is at last bone of my bones
and flesh of my flesh;

she shall be called Woman,
because she was taken out of Man.''
For this reason a man shall leave
his father and mother
and be joined to his wife,
and the two shall become one flesh;
what therefore God has joined together,
let no man put asunder:
Do Thou now also,
O Master, our Lord and our God,
send down Thy heavenly grace
upon these Thy servants, _____ and _____;
grant that this Thy handmaiden
may be subject to her husband in all things,
and that this Thy servant
may be the head of his wife,
so that they may live according to Thy will.
Bless them, O Lord our God,
as Thou didst bless Abraham and Sarah.
Bless them, O Lord our God,
as Thou didst bless Isaac and Rebecca.
Bless them, O Lord our God,
as Thou didst bless Jacob and all the patriarchs.
Bless them, O Lord our God,
as Thou didst bless Joseph and Aseneth.
Bless them, O Lord our God,
as Thou didst bless Moses and Zipporah.
Bless them, O Lord our God,
as Thou didst bless Joachim and Anna.
Bless them, O Lord our God,
as Thou didst bless Zechariah and Elizabeth.
Preserve them, O Lord our God,
as Thou didst preserve Noah in the ark.
Preserve them, O Lord our God,
as Thou didst preserve Jonah
in the belly of the whale.
Preserve them, O Lord our God,
as Thou didst preserve the three holy children
    from the fire,
sending down upon them dew from heaven;
and let that gladness come upon them
which the blessed Helen had
when she found the precious cross.

Remember them, O Lord our God,
as Thou didst remember Enoch, Shem, Elijah.
Remember them, O Lord our God,
as Thou didst remember Thy forty holy martyrs,
sending down upon them crowns from heaven.
Remember them, O Lord our God,
and the parents who have nurtured them,
for the prayers of parents
make firm the foundations of houses.
Remember, O Lord our God, Thy servants,
the groomsman and the bridesmaid of the bridal
   pair,
who have come together in this joy.
Remember, O Lord our God,
Thy servant, _____,
and Thy handmaiden, _____,
and bless them.
Grant them of the fruit of their bodies,
fair children
concord of soul and body.
Exalt them like the cedars of Lebanon,
like a luxuriant vine.
Give them offspring in number
like unto full ears of grain;
so that, having enough of all things,
they may abound in every work that is good
and acceptable unto Thee.
Let them see their children's children
like olive shoots around their table;
so that, finding favor in Thy sight,
they may shine like the stars of heaven,
in Thee our God.
For unto Thee are due all glory, honor, and
   worship:
to the Father, and to the Son,
and to the Holy Spirit,
now and ever and unto ages of ages.

Choir: Amen.

4c

Deacon: Let us pray to the Lord.

Choir: Lord, have mercy.

And again the priest prays aloud:

> O holy God,
> who didst form man from the dust,
> and didst fashion woman from his rib,
> and didst join her unto him as a helper,
> for it seemed good to Thy majesty that man
> should not be alone upon the earth:
> Do Thou, the same Lord,
> stretch out now also Thy hand
> from Thy holy dwelling-place,
> and unite this Thy servant, _____,
> and this Thy handmaiden, _____;
> for by Thee is the husband joined unto the wife.
> Unite them in one mind;
> wed them into one flesh,
> granting to them the fruit of the body
> and the procreation of fair children.
> For Thine is the majesty,
> and Thine is the Kingdom
> and the power
> and the glory:
> of the Father, and of the Son,
> and of the Holy Spirit,
> now and ever
> and unto ages of ages.

Choir: Amen.

5.

The priest takes the crowns, which recall those with which the ''martyrs,'' or witnesses of Christ, are crowned in heaven, and crowns first the bridegroom, saying:

> The servant of God, _____,
> is crowned unto the handmaiden of God,
>
> _____:
>
> in the name of the Father,
> and of the Son,
> and of the Holy Spirit.

So also he crowns the bride, saying:

> The handmaiden of God, _____,
> is crowned unto the servant of God, _____:
> in the name of the Father,

> and of the Son,
> and of the Holy Spirit.

Then he blesses them three times, saying each time:

> O Lord our God,
> crown them with glory and honor.

6.

Deacon: Let us attend.

Priest: Peace be unto all.

Reader: And to your spirit.

Deacon: Wisdom!

Reader:
The prokeimenon in the eighth tone (Ps 21):

> Thou hast set upon their heads
> crowns of precious stones;
> they asked life of Thee,
> and Thou gavest it them.

Verse: Yea, Thou wilt make them most blessed for ever;
Thou wilt make them glad
with the joy of Thy presence.

Deacon: Wisdom!

Reader: The reading is from the Epistle of the holy Paul to the Ephesians.

Deacon: Let us attend.

Reader: (Eph 5:20-33) Brethren: Give thanks always and for everything in the name of our Lord Jesus Christ to God the Father. Be subject to one another out of reverence for Christ. Wives, be subject to your husbands, as to the Lord. For the husband is the head of the wife as Christ is the head of the Church, His body, and is Himself its Savior. As the Church is subject to Christ, so let wives also be subject in everything to their husbands. Husbands, love your wives, as Christ loved the Church and gave Himself up for her, that He might sanctify her, having cleansed her by the washing of water with the word, that the Church might be presented before Him in splendor, without spot or wrinkle or any

such thing, that she might be holy and without
blemish. Even so husbands should love their wives
as their own bodies. He who loves his wife loves
himself. For no man ever hates his own flesh, but
nourishes and cherishes it, as Christ does the
Church, because we are members of His body.
"For this reason, a man shall leave his father and
mother and be joined to his wife, and the two
shall become one." This is a great mystery, and I
take it to mean Christ and the Church; however,
let each one of you love his wife as himself and let
the wife see that she respects her husband.

Priest:	Peace be unto you, reader.
Reader:	And to your spirit. Alleluia! Alleluia! Alleluia!
Verse:	(*Ps 12; tone 5*) Thou, O Lord, shalt protect us and preserve us from this generation forever.

7.

Priest:	Peace be unto all.
Choir:	And to your spirit.
Priest:	The reading from the Holy Gospel according to St. John.
Choir:	Glory to Thee, O Lord, glory to Thee.
Deacon:	Let us attend.
Priest:	(John 2:1-11) In those days there was a marriage at Cana in Galilee, and the mother of Jesus was there; Jesus also was invited to the marriage, with His disciples. When the wine failed, the mother of Jesus said to Him, "They have no wine." And Jesus said to her, "O woman, what have you to do with me? My hour has not yet come." His mother said to the servants, "Do whatever He tells you." Now six stone jars were standing there, for the Jewish rites of purification, each holding twenty or thirty gallons. Jesus said to them, "Fill the jars with water." And they filled them up to the brim. He said to them, "Now draw some out, and take it to the steward of the feast." So they took it.

When the steward of the feast tasted the water
now become wine, and did not know where it
came from (though the servants who had drawn
the water knew), the steward of the feast called the
bridegroom and said to him, "Every man serves
the good wine first, and when men have drunk
freely, then the poor wine; but you have kept the
good wine until now." This, the first of his signs,
Jesus did at Cana in Galilee, and manifested His
glory; and His disciples believed in Him.

Choir: Glory to Thee, O Lord, glory to Thee.

8.

Deacon: Let us all say
with all our soul and with all our mind,
let us say.

Choir: Lord, have mercy.

Deacon: O Lord almighty, the God of our Fathers,
we pray Thee, hearken and have mercy.

Choir: Lord, have mercy.

Deacon: Have mercy on us, O God,
according to Thy great goodness,
we pray Thee, hearken and have mercy.

Choir: Lord, have mercy. (3)

Deacon: Again we pray
for mercy, life, peace, health,
salvation, and visitation
for the servants of God, _____ and _____
(*and he mentions also whomever else he wishes*),
and for the pardon and remission
of their sins.

Choir: Lord, have mercy. (3)

Priest: For Thou art a merciful God,
and lovest mankind,
and unto Thee we ascribe glory:
to the Father,
and to the Son,
and to the Holy Spirit,

now and ever
and unto ages of ages.

Choir: Amen.

9.

Deacon: Let us pray to the Lord.

Choir: Lord, have mercy.

Priest: O Lord our God,
who in Thy saving dispensation
didst vouchsafe by Thy presence
in Cana of Galilee
to declare marriage honorable:
do Thou, the same Lord,
now also maintain in peace and concord
Thy servants, _____ and _____,
whom Thou hast been pleased to join together.
Cause their marriage to be honorable.
Preserve their bed blameless.
Mercifully grant that they may live together
in purity;
and enable them to reach a ripe old age,
walking in Thy commandments with a pure heart.
For Thou art our God,
the God of mercy and salvation,
and unto Thee we ascribe glory;
to the Father, and to the Son,
and to the Holy Spirit,
now and ever
and unto ages of ages.

Choir: Amen.

10.

Deacon: Help us, save us, have mercy on us,
and keep us, O God, by Thy grace.

Choir: Lord, have mercy.

Deacon: That the whole day may be perfect,
holy, peaceful, and sinless,
let us ask of the Lord.

Choir: Grant it, O Lord.
Repeated after each petition.

An angel of peace, a faithful guide,
a guardian of our souls and bodies,
let us ask of the Lord.
  Pardon and remission of our sins and
    transgressions,
  let us ask of the Lord.
All things
that are good and profitable for our souls,
and peace for the world,
let us ask of the Lord.
  That we may complete
  the remaining time of our life
  in peace and repentance,
  let us ask of the Lord.
A Christian ending to our life:
painless, blameless, and peaceful;
and a good defense
before the dread judgment seat of Christ,
let us ask of the Lord.

Choir: Grant it, O Lord.

Deacon: Having asked for the unity of the Faith, and the
            communion of the Holy Spirit,
            let us commend ourselves and each other,
            and all our life unto Christ our God.

Choir: To Thee, O Lord.

11.

Priest: And make us worthy, O Master,
            that with boldness and without condemnation
            we may dare to call on Thee,
            the heavenly God, as Father,
            and to say:

Choir: Our Father,
            who art in heaven,
            hallowed be Thy name.
            Thy kingdom come.
            Thy will be done,
            on earth as it is in heaven.
            Give us this day our daily bread;
            and forgive us our trespasses,
            as we forgive those who trespass against us;

and lead us not into temptation,
but deliver us from evil.

Priest: For Thine is the Kingdom,
and the power,
and the glory:
of the Father,
and of the Son,
and of the Holy Spirit,
now and ever
and unto ages of ages.

Choir: Amen.

Priest: Peace be unto all.

Choir: And to your spirit.

Deacon: Bow your heads unto the Lord.

Choir: To Thee, O Lord.

12.
Then the common cup is brought and the priest blesses it.

Deacon: Let us pray to the Lord.

Choir: Lord, have mercy.

Priest: O God,
who hast created all things by Thy might,
and hast made firm the world,
and adornest the crown
of all that Thou hast made:
Bless now, with Thy spiritual blessing,
this common cup,
which Thou dost give
to those who are now united
for the community of marriage.
For blessed is Thy name,
and glorified is Thy Kingdom,
of the Father, and of the Son,
and of the Holy Spirit,
now and ever
and unto ages of ages.

Choir: Amen.

13.

Then, taking the cup, the priest gives it to them three times: first to the
bridegroom and then to the bride. Then immediately the priest takes them,
the groomsmen behind them holding their crowns, and leads them in a circle
three times around the lectern. And the priest or the choir sings:

> Rejoice, O Isaiah!
> A virgin is with child;
> and shall bear a Son, Emmanuel.
> He is both God and man;
> and Orient is His name.
> Magnifying Him,
> we call the virgin blessed.
> O holy martyrs,
> who fought the good fight
> and have received your crowns:
> Entreat ye the Lord,
> that He will have mercy on our souls.
> Glory to Thee,
> O Christ God,
> the apostles' boast,
> the martyrs' joy,
> whose preaching
> was the consubstantial Trinity.

14.

Then, taking the crown of the bridegroom, the priest says:

> Be exalted like Abraham, O Bridegroom,
> and be blessed like Isaac,
> and multiply like Jacob,
> walking in peace,
> and keeping God's commandments
> in righteousness.

Then, taking the crown of the bride, he says:

> And you, O Bride:
> Be exalted like Sarah,
> and exult like Rebecca,
> and multiply like Rachel;
> and rejoice in your husband,
> fulfilling the conditions of the law,
> for this is well-pleasing to God.

Deacon: Let us pray to the Lord.

Choir: Lord, have mercy.

Priest: O God, our God,
who didst come to Cana of Galilee,
and didst bless there the marriage feast:
Bless also these Thy servants,
who through Thy good providence
now are united in wedlock.
Bless their goings out and their comings in.
Fill their life with good things.
Receive their crowns into Thy Kingdom,
preserving them spotless, blameless,
and without reproach,
unto ages of ages.

Choir: Amen.

Priest: Peace be unto all.

Choir: And to your spirit.

Deacon: Bow your heads unto the Lord.

Choir: To Thee, O Lord.

Priest: May the Father,
and the Son,
and the Holy Spirit,
the all-holy,
consubstantial,
and life-giving Trinity,
one Godhead and one Kingdom,
bless you;
and grant you length of days,
fair children,
progress in life and faith;
and fill you with all earthly good things,
and make you worthy to enjoy
the good things of the promise;
through the prayers of the holy Theotokos
and of all the saints.
Amen.

Deacon: Most holy Theotokos, save us!

Choir: More honorable than the Cherubim,
and more glorious beyond compare
than the Seraphim:

without defilement
you gave birth to God the Word:
true Theotokos, we magnify you.

Priest: Glory to Thee, O Christ our God and our hope,
glory to Thee.

Choir: Glory to the Father,
and to the Son,
and to the Holy Spirit,
now and ever
and unto ages of ages.
Amen.
Lord, have mercy. (3)
Father, bless.

Priest: May He who by His presence in Cana of Galilee
declared marriage to be honorable,
Christ our true God,
through the prayers of His most pure mother;
of the holy, glorious,
and all-laudable apostles;
of the holy, God-crowned kings
Constantine and Helen,
equal to the apostles;
of the holy great martyr Procopius;
and of all the saints:
have mercy on us and save us,
for He is good
and loves mankind.

Choir: Amen.

8. THE COPTIC RITE

The Coptic churches of Egypt and Ethiopia follow a rite which, like the Byzantine liturgy, is much older than the extant texts which date only from the late Middle Ages. Originally, as in all other churches, Coptic rites of betrothal and marriage were quite separate, but the distinction between them is still very clear since each has its own Liturgy of the Word. In actual fact, this full rite is seldom if ever used, usually being celebrated in an abbreviated form in which the vesting of the groom and the anointing of the bridal couple, and often other elements besides, are simply omitted.

The betrothal rite is celebrated with the bride and groom in different parts of the church (since the Copts retain the once common Christian practice of segregating the sexes in church). After the Word liturgy, three solemn prayers are offered for the couple (I.1.1-3) and the congregation assents to the prayers with intervening chants. The groom's garments are blessed and he is ritually vested (I.2.1-2). Bearing the ring, he is led to where his betrothed awaits and the betrothal is effected by the gift of the ring. The prayer (I.2.1) seems to suggest that the bride might also share the veil, and this apparently is done, though the text of the rite makes no explicit mention of it.

The bridal couple are led to the sanctuary, where the marriage rite begins with another Word liturgy. After the gospel, the church prays for the couple through the deacon's exquisite litany (II.2.2) which serves to situate the couple in the succession of generations which is salvation history. As in the betrothal rite, there follow three solemn prayers, concluding with the Prayer of Inclination, the congregation once again voicing its assent through the sung anthems interspersed between the prayers. Unique to the Coptic rite is the anointing of the bride and groom (II.4.1-4), but it is one more example of the assimilation by the Church's liturgy of elements integral to local marriage traditions. The anointing precedes the crowning, which is the key element of the Coptic liturgy as it is of all Eastern marriage rites. The symbolism is distinctly different from that of the Byzantine crowning, however, for the crowns here represent the blessings of God in this world and in the world to come. The meaning of the whole liturgy is summed up in the coronation chant: "The Father blesses, the Son crowns, the Spirit sanctifies and makes perfect." Through the ritual, the bride and groom themselves become symbols, not only assuming their place in salvation history after the great couples of the past, but actually assuming the role of the lovers in the Song of Songs, of the divine Word and the Virgin Mother, of Christ and the Church.

The liturgy concludes, after the final blessing and signing of the bride and groom, with the removal of the crowns, a rite which, as the rubric directs, should take place a week after the wedding but which is always done now at the conclusion of the rite. Whereas the Byzantine marriage rite still bears traces of the celebration of the Eucharist with which the marriage was at one time completed, no sign of it is left in the Coptic rite.

TEXT

A. Raes, *Le mariage dans les églises d'orient.* Editions de Chevetogne, 1958, 27ff.

BIBLIOGRAPHY

Burmester, O.H.E., *The Egyptian or Coptic Church. A Detailed Description of her Liturgical Services and the Rites and Ceremonies Observed in the Administration of her Sacraments.* Cairo: Publications de la societé d'archéologie copte, 1967.

Kopp, C., *Glaube und Sakramente der koptischen Kirche.* "Orientalia Christiana," Vol. 25, 1, Rome 1932, 192–204.

Morton, H.V., *Through the Lands of the Bible.* New York: Dodd, Mead and Co., 1938, 145–153.

Ritzer, 1970:159–162.

Stevenson, 1982:108–112; 1987:71-74.

J-Gh. Van Overstraeten, "Le rite de l'onction des époux dans la liturgie copte du mariage," *Parole d'Orient* 5 (1974), 49–63.

I

The bridegroom is received by the clergy at the doors of the church and led to his place in the men's section.
The bride, arriving afterwards, is greeted likewise and led to the women's section.
The rite opens with a liturgy of the word:

Prayer of Thanksgiving
Prayer of Incense
Reading: I Corinthians 1:1-10

Trisagion chant
Prayer of the Gospel
Psalm 84: Mercy and truth are met,
  justice and peace have embraced.
  Verse: Truth has come forth from the earth
  and justice looks down from heaven.
Gospel: John 1:1-17
Litany
Creed

RITE OF BETROTHAL

I.1.1

Priest: O God,
        you created man with your own hands
        and gave him woman
        to be his help and support.
        Be present now, O Lord,
        to stand between these young people.
        Betroth them for a life together,
        giving them this sign (the ring)
        as a symbol of their union.
        May they be united by the bond of love,
        for you have said,
        "My peace I give to you;
        it is I who give my peace to you."
        For you indeed are our peace,
        for all of us.
        We render you glory and honor,
        and to your only Son
        and the life-giving Spirit,
        now and always.

People: Christ,
        the Word of the Father,
        only Son of God,
        grant us your peace
        that fills us with all joy.
        Say to us, as you said to your holy apostles,
        "My peace I give to you;
        the peace I received from my Father
        I myself bequeath to you,
        now and forever."

Priest: Lord, lover of humankind,
            you have fulfilled the word of the prophet,
            "By the Lord a man shall be united with his wife."
            Make these betrothals celebrated here
            worthy of your blessing.
            Unite your servants
            that they may be without sin
            and may please your life-giving will.
            For it is you, our Lord,
            who created man out of the slime of the earth
            and gave him a helper made in his likeness,
            creating her by drawing her forth from him,
            to be his wife and companion,
            that they might lead a common life
            and bring forth sons and daughters into the world
            for the increase of the human race.
            Bless now, O Lord,
            the betrothal of your servants, N. and N.
            May they increase and multiply,
            thanks to your abundant mercies.
            Enable them to bring forth blessed fruit,
            to be devoted in their conduct,
            united in faith, knowledge, purity, and good works.
            Filled with the fear of your Name,
            let them be one both in flesh and in spirit.
            May they prove worthy of your blessing,
            through Christ our Lord.

I.1.2

Priest: Master and Lord, our God,[11]
            you accompanied Abraham's servant to Mesopotamia
                when,
            sent to find a wife for Isaac, Abraham's son,
            he pretended to be in need of water
            and so identified Rebecca
            as the one who was to be betrothed.
            Give your consent now,
            O Master and Lord and lover of humankind,
            to the betrothal of your servants, N. and N.
            Bless them.
            Safeguard the promise they have exchanged.

[11] Cf. Byzantine rite, I.5, p. 60.

Strengthen them with your own fullness of power.
Let their covenant be unshakeable.
Come to the aid of their youthfulness.
For it was you who made man and woman in the
  beginning.
It was you who gave the woman to her husband
to be his helper
and to perpetuate the human race.
As for all those gathered here to share our prayer,
our fathers and brothers,
sanctify them who are your servants.
Preserve them by the intercession of our Lady,
Mary, Mother of God,
and the prayers of the whole company of your saints.

People: Forget not your covenant with our fathers,
with Abraham, Isaac and Jacob,
Israel, your holy one.

THANKSGIVING FOR THE BETROTHAL

I.1.3

Priest: We give you thanks, Lord God,
Master of all things,
who exist from before the ages.
Master of the universe,
who adorned the heavens by your word,
who established the earth and all it holds,
who brought together things that were scattered
and who made two creatures (man and woman)
that they might become one.
We beseech you now, O Master,
to make your servants worthy of the mark and symbol
given by your word in the bond of betrothal.
May each have for the other an undivided love
on which their union will stand and be strong.
Build them up on the foundation of your holy Church,
that they may walk together in peace and harmony,
sealed by the word they have pledged to each other.
For you yourself are this bond of love
and the law which will guide their union.
May they be one in the union of their two persons,
according to your word.

> May they fulfill, O Lord,
> the commandment (of love) which your own Son,
> our Lord Jesus Christ, lived to perfection.
> With him and with the Holy Spirit,
> you are blessed now and for ever.

People: Bless the Lord,
all you peoples, tribes, and nations;
acclaim him, glorify him, and exalt him for ever.

The Lord's Prayer is recited and the dismissal and blessing are given.

BLESSING OF GARMENTS

I.2.1

The father of the groom presents the garments: a tunic of silk, a belt, and a white head-veil. These are blessed by the priest.

Priest: Master, Lord Jesus Christ our God,
who adorned the heavens with stars
and beautified the earth
with flowers of many kinds
and fruit-bearing trees,
and who gave pleasure to humankind
with your heavenly gifts
while giving us the earth to enjoy;
we pray you now,
you who are good and the lover of humankind,
bless these garments
which have been prepared.
Through your goodness and kindness,
let them be for your servants who wear them
garments of glory and salvation,
the raiment of joy and gladness.
Keep them pure in body, soul, and spirit.
May they pass their lives in peace and joy
and in the works of justice.
Grant them the enjoyment
of the goods of earth and heaven.
May they be rich in good works.
Fill their house and their barns
with all good things.
May they be found worthy
to do your will at all times,
for you are merciful,
abounding in faithfulness and compassion.

To you henceforth be the glory,
with your good Father
and with the Holy Spirit,
the giver of life,
of one being with you,
now and always and for ever.
Amen.

I.2.2
The groom is dressed in the silken tunic and the belt.

People: N. has been clothed in a spiritual robe,
he has been girded about
with a string of pearls.
The betrothed has been given
the garment of temperance
and on his head, a crown of joy.
As David the Psalmist sang:
"You have crowned him with honor and glory;
you have run to him
to bless him with goodness;
you have set upon his head
a crown of precious stones.
He asked you for life, O Lord,
and you have given him life for ever."
Amen.

I.2.3
Dressed in the tunic, and with a ring placed on the ring-finger of his
hand by the priest, the groom is led by the priest to the women's part
of the church, which they enter.
At the word of the priest, the man removes the ring from his own
hand and places it upon the finger of the woman.
With that the two are considered betrothed and the people sing the
hymn, "True Spouse, Mother of God."

II

THE MARRIAGE

II.1
The priest begins by questioning the two parties to assure their free
consent to the marriage.

II.2.1
Then the rite begins with the Liturgy of the Word:

Prayer of Thanksgiving
Prayer of Incense
Reading 1: Ephesians 5:22–6:3
Reading 2: I Peter 3:5-7
Reading 3: Acts 16:13-15
Psalm 19:5: As a bridegroom
   he comes forth from his wedding chamber;
   he rejoices like a giant to run his course.
Psalm 127:3: May your bride be like a fruitful vine
      beside your house,
   your children like young olive plants
      around your table.
Gospel: Matthew 19:1-6

II.2.2

People: Those whom the Holy Spirit has attuned like a zither
         bless God at all times.
         Night and day they raise their voices untiringly
         in psalms, hymns, and spiritual canticles.

Deacon: Lord God in heaven,
         Master of all things,
         God of our fathers,
         we beseech you, Lord,
         hear us and have pity on us.

People: Lord, have mercy.

Deacon: You who made the heavens, the earth,
         the sea and all they contain,
         and who have adorned them in your wisdom:
         we beseech you, Lord,
         hear us and have pity on us.
            You who made man
            in your own image and likeness
            and set him in a paradise of delights . . .
         You who drew forth woman from Adam's side
         and gave her to him
         as a helper fit for him . . .
            You who blessed Abraham and Sarah,
            giving her to him as his wife
            and granting him the rank of patriarch . . .
         You who protected Isaac,
         wedded him to Rebecca
         and saved him from his enemies . . .

You who blessed Jacob,
wedded him to Rachel as his wife
and made them heirs of the promise . . .
You who exalted Joseph,
wedded him to Aseneth as his wife
and through him gave life
to the whole country of Egypt . . .

> You who in these last times
> were born of a woman
> and shone forth upon
> the whole human race . . .

You who attended the wedding
at Cana in Galilee
and blessed it,
bless this marriage . . .

> You who by the power of your divinity
> changed water into real wine,
> let your blessing come to rest
> upon your servants, purifying them,
> O lover of humankind . . .

You who blessed the wedding
celebrated at Cana in Galilee
and by the power of your divinity
changed water into real wine,
bless and protect
the marriage of your servants, N. and N.,
keeping them in peace, unity, and love . . .

> Lord, merciful and beneficent,
> rich in pity and compassion,
> make us worthy to glorify your goodness,
> O lover of humankind.

People: Lord, have mercy.
Christ, Word of the Father,
only Son of God,
give us your peace which overflows with joy.

II.2.3
There follows another litany for peace, for the Church, and for the congregation.

II.2.4
The Creed is then recited.

II.3.1

Priest: God,
whose being and existence
know neither beginning nor end,
whose wisdom is infinite,
whose power unbounded;
you created man from the slime of the earth
and gave him a wife, drawn from his side.
You joined her to him as a help fit for him,
since your goodness and lordship determined
that it was not good for man to be alone.
We beseech you, O Lord,
to unite your servants, N. and N.,
that they might become one flesh.
Let them observe the law of joy
and remain faithful to the teachings.
Gladden them with the fruit of life, born of them.
May they enjoy good children
and calm and peaceful days.
Ready them for all good things,
through Jesus Christ our Lord.

Choir: Say to us, as you said to your apostles,
"My peace I give unto you."
The door at the East is the Virgin Mary,
the chaste wedding chamber
of the chaste bridegroom.

II.3.2

Priest: Lord our God,
Maker of all that is,
you created man from the slime of the earth
and gave him a helper
made from the rib you took from him.
You united them in the intimacy of marriage,
to live together
and to increase the human race.
You said to them:
"Increase and multiply,
replenish the earth and subdue it."
You who are good and the lover of humankind,
bless the union of your servants, N. and N.

Bless them who are joined
in accordance with your will.
May they multiply like our first fathers,
Abraham, Isaac, and Jacob, whom you blessed.
Bless them like Abraham and Sarah.
Exalt them like Isaac and Rebecca.
May they multiply as you multiplied Jacob and his seed.
Glorify them as you glorified Joseph in Egypt,
and make them chaste as he.
Make them numerous, as you did Elkana and Anna,
whom you blessed with the joy of a child,
the faithful Samuel, the prophet.
Make them worthy
of the visitation of your holy archangel,
as happened to Zachary and Elizabeth,
to whom you gave the grace of bearing him
who is the greatest born of woman,
John the Baptist,
forerunner of your only Son.
You also blessed Joachim and Anna,
Lord our Master,
for from them was born the spiritual ark,
Mary, Mother of God.
In her your only Son became flesh.
He came into this world.
He blessed the wedding at Cana in Galilee.
Bless your servants, N. and N., who are to be married.
Grant them wealth, wisdom, and health.
May they be one in body and spirit
in all devotion and holiness.
May they be worthy of your blessing
and glorify your holy Name,
with your only Son
and the Holy Spirit,
now and at all times.

Choir: "My peace, which I received from my Father,
I leave to you henceforth and forever."
All the kings of the earth walk in your light
and the peoples in the brightness of your splendor,
O Mary, Mother of God.
In the Song of Songs, Solomon calls her
"My sister, my companion, my own true city, Jerusalem."

II.3.3

Priest: Lord our God,
            great and everlasting,
            you made life spring up where there was none
            and by your word you gave existence to all that is.
            With your immaculate hands,
            you made man in your own image and likeness.
            From this one person you
            brought forth another.
            You said:
            "It is not good for man to be alone,"
            and you caused a deep sleep to overcome Adam
            who fell asleep.
            And you took one of his ribs
            and closed up the hole with flesh.
            Therefore shall a man leave father and mother
            and cleave to his wife,
            that they may be two in one flesh.
            What God has united, let no one put asunder.
            You blessed Abraham with Sarah,
            Isaac with Rebecca,
            Jacob with Leah and Rachel,
            and you have purified all
            who have shared in your blessing.
            Now, Lord our Master,
            cast your eyes upon your servant, N.,
            and N., his companion.
            Confirm their union.
            Keep their bed chaste.
            Protect them and their house
            with your strong right arm.
            Free them from all jealousy and deceit;
            keep them in concord and peace
            and grant them the joy of presenting to you,
            our living God,
            the living fruit they bring forth.
            Bless them
            as you blessed Abraham with Sarah,
            Isaac with Rebecca,
            and Jacob with Leah and Rachel,
            the builders of the house of Israel.
            And finally bless
            in the name of our Lord Jesus Christ,

these men and women gathered here with them.
Through him who is our Lord,
our God and our Savior,
Jesus Christ.

Choir: Forget not the covenant you made
with our fathers,
Abraham, Isaac and Jacob,
Israel, your holy one.
The angel of this day
soaring to the highest heaven.
Remember us before the Lord
for the forgiveness of our sins.
She (Mary) is more brilliant than the sun.
You are the Orient
to whom the righteous will look
with joy and gladness.

II.3.4

Priest:
With bowed head:

Incline your ear to us, O Lord, and hear us,
sinful and unworthy as we are.
Confirm the union of your servant, N.,
and N., his companion.
Free them from all evil.
May they live many days
in sweetness, holiness,
patience and submission.
Save them from all blame and bad example.
Enlighten the eyes of their understanding
and of their heart,
that they may ever act
in accordance with your will;
for you are merciful and rich in compassion
towards all who call upon you.
We render you glory, honor and adoration,
now and for ever.

Choir: May God bless you.
We bless his holy Name,
his praise always on our lips.
Blessed be the Father,
the Son

and the Holy Spirit,
perfect Trinity,
whom we adore and glorify.

PRAYER OVER THE OIL

II.4.1

Priest: Master and Lord,
God and ruler of all that is,
Father of our Lord,
God and Savior, Jesus Christ.
You anointed priests, kings and prophets
with fresh olive oil.
We pray and beseech you, Lord,
lover of humankind,
you who are good,
to pour out your blessing upon this oil.
Let it be an oil of sanctification for your servants.
Amen.
A weapon of truth.
Amen.
And of justice.
Amen.
An ointment of purity and incorruptibility.
Amen.
Unclouded light and unblemished beauty.
Amen.
For happiness and true consolation.
Amen.
For strength and health
and for overcoming the power of the Enemy.
Amen.
For their renewal and restoration
in body, soul and spirit.
Amen.
For prosperity and for the doing of good works.
Amen.
For the glory and honor of your holy Name,
of your only Son and of the life-giving Holy Spirit,
one with you in being,
now and forever.
Amen.

II.4.2

Choir:
While the bridegroom is anointed, the choir sings:

> May this oil destroy the demons.
> It is protection against evil spirits.
> It is the oil of holy spirits.
> It is protection
> against the assaults of impure spirits.
> Through Jesus Christ, the king of glory.
> Blessed be the Father,
> the Son and the Holy Spirit,
> perfect Trinity,
> whom we adore and glorify.

II.4.3

While the bride is anointed, the choir sings:

> With oil you have anointed my head
> and your cup inebriates me as the best (wine).
> Your mercy accompanies me all the days of my life.
> All peoples shall call them blessed
> and will say, "Amen, so shall it be."
> The Lord will send his angel.
> He took me from behind my father's sheep
> and anointed me with the oil of his anointing.
> My brothers are good and they are big.
> They shall call me blessed and say:
> "So be it, so be it, amen."
> For he is blessed. . .

II.4.4

Priest:
Following the anointing:

> Lord, God of powers,
> rich in mercy,
> whose goodness knows no bounds,
> accept our prayers.
> Protect your servants, N. and N.
> Watch over their union,
> keep their marriage bed chaste,
> surround them and us with your holy angels.
> Rain down upon us from your heavenly dwelling
> your abundant mercies.

For your goodness' sake,
wipe away our numerous transgressions
and grant us to enjoy the repose of your saints
in your heavenly kingdom,
through your only Son,
Jesus Christ our Lord.

II.5.1

The crowns are then presented and the following prayer is said over them:

Holy God,
you have crowned your saints
with imperishable crowns
and you have joined heaven to earth.
Bless, then, these crowns
which we are to place on the heads of your servants.
That they may be for them a crown
of glory and honor. Amen.
A crown of salvation and blessing. Amen.
A crown of joy and peace. Amen.
A crown of rejoicing and gladness. Amen.
A crown of virtue and righteousness. Amen.
A crown of wisdom and understanding. Amen.
A crown of strength and firmness. Amen.
Grant to your servants
who will wear these crowns
an angel of peace and the bond of love.
Strengthen them against all shameful thoughts
and indecent desires.
Save them from the wiles of the Evil One
and from all diabolical temptation.
Let your mercy be upon them.
Hear the cry of their prayer.
Put your fear into their hearts.
Lead them throughout a long life unto a ripe old age
and grant them joy in beholding
their sons and daughters.
Guide their children, too,
that they may prosper
in your one, holy, catholic, and apostolic Church,
and strengthen them in the orthodox faith.
Conduct them upon the path of truth,
according to the will of your good Father

and of the Holy Spirit,
now and at all times.

*The priest sets the crowns upon their heads as the following verse is
sung.*

Choir: Crown them with honor and glory.
The Father blesses,
the Son crowns,
the Holy Spirit sanctifies and makes perfect.
Worthy, worthy, worthy
are the groom and his companion.

II.5.2

Priest:
Meanwhile, setting the crowns on their heads, the priest prays:

Lord, crown your servants
with a crown of invincible grace,
a crown of mighty and powerful glory,
a crown of orthodox and undying faith,
and bless all their undertakings.
For you are the giver of all good gifts,
O Christ our God.
To you are due all honor and glory,
and to your good Father
and to the life-giving Holy Spirit,
one with you in being,
now and at all times.

II.5.3

Then the following responsory is recited:

The Lord has crowned this bridegroom of
Christ with imperishable crowns.
Shine forth, shine forth, O groom,
together with your true spouse,
who dwells in the habitation prepared for her.
Receive the joy and the gift of God.
It is Christ our God who gives them to you.
Go forward with joy to your nuptial chamber,
a chamber bedecked with decorations of every kind.

II.5.4

The Lord's Prayer is then said and the dismissal follows.

II.5.5

Then the priest traces the sign of the cross on the bridegroom's head.

> May he who blessed our father Adam
> and Noah and Abraham
> and Moses, in the land of Midian,
> bless you, O groom, you and your companion.
> May he who blessed
> his beloved Isaac and Abel,
> the first of the just,
> and Solomon with his father David,
> bless you, O groom, you and your companion.
> May he who blessed our father Jacob,
> called Israel, and Esau
> and Job, the just one,
> bless you sevenfold, O groom,
> you and your companion.

Then the priest makes the sign of the cross over the bride.

> May he who blessed Adam and Eve,
> our first parents,
> and Abraham and Sarah,
> and Isaac and Rebecca,
> bless this union.
> May he who blessed Jacob, called Israel,
> with Leah and Rachel,
> and Anna, the mother of Samuel,
> bless this union.
> May he who blessed Joseph and Aseneth,
> Zachary and Elizabeth,
> Mary the Mother-Bride
> and all blessed women,
> bless this union.

Choir:

The priest then addresses various admonitions to the bride and groom in Arabic, to which the choir responds by singing:

> The cherubim adore him,
> the seraphim worship him as they proclaim:
> "Holy, holy, holy are you, Lord, among thousands
> and honored among the thousands of thousands.
> You are a sweet perfume, O my Savior,
> because you have come to us and saved us.
> Have mercy on us.

My peace, the peace I received from my Father,
I myself leave to you,
now and for ever.
King of peace, grant us peace.
Confirm your peace in us.
Forgive us our sins.
Hear, my daughter, listen and see.
Forget your people and your father's house,
for the king desires your beauty,
he who is Lord.
Hear, O bride, listen and understand,
for the bridegroom desires your goodness,
he who is your husband
and who must be obeyed.
King of peace, grant us your peace.
Confirm your peace in us.
Forgive us our sins.
Lo, now is the time of blessing,
now is the time of exquisite perfume,
to sing to our Savior who is good
and the lover of humankind.

The Lord's Prayer is recited, the priest gives the blessing, and the choir sings this canon:

Hail, shining bride, mother of the light!
Hail, you who conceived the Word in your womb!
Hail, you who are revered above the cherubim!
Hail, you who gave us the savior of our souls!
Glory to the Father
and to the Son
and to the Holy Spirit,
now and always
and for ages of ages.
Sing a new song unto the Lord,
songs and hymns in honor
of our brother, the groom,
and of his companion.
Let us proclaim with joyful voice:
joy and gladness to the groom
and to his companion
from the Lord!
Let us say with David the Psalmist:

Jesus Christ will bring you to see
the prosperity of Jerusalem,
the city of the Lord.
Worthy, worthy, worthy are they,
the groom and his companion.

III

THE REMOVAL OF THE CROWNS

1.

*On the seventh day after the marriage, the crown is removed from the
heads of the groom and his bride.*

The rite begins with a Liturgy of the Word:

2.

Prayer of Thanksgiving
Prayer of Incense
Reading: Timothy 4:9-15
Trisagion
Prayer of the Gospel
Psalm 127: May your wife be like a fruitful vine
   beside your house.
   Verse: Your children like young olive plants
   around your table.
Gospel: John 1:14-17
Litany
Creed

3.

Priest: God of our fathers,
Father of our Lord, God and Savior, Jesus Christ,
you are our Master, O Lord, lover of humankind.
By your powerful hand and your raised right arm,
you have exalted your servants, N. and N.
We pray you, our Lord,
to protect both them and their marriage.
They have bowed their heads before you
in reverence and faith.
Confirm your peace in them,
the desire to do your will,
and all compassion.
May your blessing and mercy
rest ever upon their house.

Keep them both in your care,
so that he might walk in your good pleasure
and that she might live as becomes a woman.
Guide them in the ways of piety,
so that, in this as in all things,
your great and holy Name
might be glorified, exalted and blessed,
and that the Father,
the Son and the Holy Spirit
might be honored, blessed
and glorified in all things,
now and at all times.

Then the Lord's Prayer is said. The priest gives the dismissal and blessing, and removes the crowns from their heads.

9. BOBBIO MISSAL

The Bobbio Missal, an eighth century book from Northern Italy, is among the few surviving relics of the Gallican or non-Roman liturgy of Gaul. Though the manuscript is from the eighth century, it is based on an original probably dating from the sixth century. As the title indicates (*Blessing of the marriage chamber over the couple*), this is not a liturgy for getting married, but a blessing for the inception of marriage, and it takes place in the home of the newlyweds. The practice of blessing the wedding chamber and the bed was common throughout the Middle Ages and lasted until the French Revolution and even later in some places. In Bobbio there is no indication of how the marriage actually took place or of whether there was a Nuptial Mass.

The first text (550) is a lengthy call to prayer, and it speaks of marriage as a religious vocation, to be lived out in companionship, as well as a source of offspring. The prayer that follows (551) does not correspond closely in its contents to the invitation that preceded it. Nonetheless, the spirit is the same and the image of a companionate marriage, entered upon in obedience to God's command, is dominant, even to the omission of any reference to children. The references to Old Testament models of wifely virtue is reminiscent of the Roman nuptial blessing, but the prayer is for both partners and the style is considerably more homely.

The second prayer (552) is for second marriages. Remarriage after the death of a partner was frowned on in Rome and Italy, where the nuptial blessing was reserved for first marriages. This was not the case apparently in the churches of Gaul, at least until Roman influence came to make itself felt. Nonetheless, the emphasis is on legitimating the second union by reference to the need for children: perhaps the "single-minded desire for children" is deemed to compensate for the divided love of marrying two partners. Biblical precedent is cited in the example of Ruth and the concession made by Paul in 1 Cor 7:39. Presumably Leah and Rachel are mentioned because they were the first and second wives of Isaac (Gen 29) and because they competed in bearing him children (Gen 30)!

TEXT

The Bobbio Missal: A Gallican Mass Book. Edited by E. A. Lowe and J. Wickham Legg. Henry Bradshaw Society, vol. 53. London, 1917.

BIBLIOGRAPHY

Ritzer, 1970:275, 299.

Stevenson 1982:56–57.

BLESSING OF THE MARRIAGE CHAMBER
FOR THOSE MARRYING[12]

550
Dearly beloved,
let us call upon God,
who has deigned to pour out
the gift of his blessing
to multiply the offspring of the human race;
that he may himself guard his servants, N. and N.,
whom he has chosen for union in marriage;
and that he would give them peace,
oneness of mind and manners
and the ties of mutual love.
May they, by his favor,
have the children they desire
and may these children, being his gift,
also be endowed with his blessing,
so that these his servants, N. and N.,
might serve him in all things
in humility of heart.
Through.

ANOTHER PRAYER

551
We pray you, Lord, holy Father,
almighty and eternal God,
for your servants, N. and N.,
whom you have ordered
to come to the grace of marriage.
They desire your blessing,
albeit through our voice and prayer.
Grant them, Lord,
to live faithfully in the companionship of love.
May they be endowed with the charity of Sarah,
the wisdom of Rebecca,

[12] Paragraph numbers are those of the Lowe/Legg edition.

the love of Rachel,
and the grace and charity of Susanna.
May it descend upon these your servants, N. and N.,
as the gentle rain falls upon the face of the earth.
May they feel the action of your hand,
and your Holy Spirit,
and attain to everlasting joy.

PRAYER OVER THOSE WHO MARRY
FOR THE SECOND TIME

552
O God,
you mercifully offer many remedies for human frailty
and assure the increase of the human race,
so that nature is not deprived of the seed
by which the generating pair is increased in its offspring.
So it was that in early times
you blessed Ruth, the Moabite,
and in the latter days
you permitted second marriage through your apostle.
Grant, then, Lord, to your servants
the single-minded desire for children;
that the Lord may make this woman, N.,
who enters into your house,
to be like Rachel and Leah
who built up the house of Israel,
that she might be an example of virtue
in the church of God.
Through.

10. PONTIFICAL OF EGBERT

This tenth-century English pontifical probably reflects the influence of reform-minded centers on the Continent rather than any direct link to the eighth-century Egbert of York. Once again, there is no indication of any Nuptial Mass: the rite seems entirely domestic and appears to take place as the couple assume their married life.

The first two texts, under the title "Prayer for Marriage," are, in fact, a) a form of the Aaronic blessing, b) a brief collect. Only the collect has an explicit reference to marriage. It is not easy to see how or where these texts might have functioned. The others are clearer, being blessings given at the home of the bride and groom: a blessing of the bridal chamber, of the wedding ring, and of the bed. The blessing of the nuptial chamber is the first text we have seen to cite the Book of Tobit, but these references were widespread in Celtic and Gallican marriage prayers, with their tradition of blessing the marriage in the home. The blessing of the ring is very unimaginative, but its interest lies in its being the blessing of a *wedding* ring, as opposed to a betrothal ring. Why it is placed here between the blessing of the marriage chamber and the blessing of the bed is not at all clear, though Ritzer believes that the whole sequence took place in the marriage chamber and represents the ancient Gallican-Celtic marriage rite (except for the use of the ring: a specifically British contribution). The blessing of the bed begins with a collect which looks as though it could serve for blessing a house. Then follow two blessings directed to the man but extending to include his wife and his parents and future children. Noteworthy in all these prayers is the emphasis on married life as a life of holiness and not just as something to be tolerated for the sake of procreation.

The collection concludes with three other prayers for the blessing of the couple occurring later in the Pontifical, but they seem to constitute a different set. The influence of the Book of Tobit is very clear. The collect (II.5b i) is a reworking of the text of I.1b, while the final blessing is another version of the Aaronic blessing from that given in I.1a.

TEXT

Two Anglo-Saxon Pontificals. Edited by H. M. J. Banting. The Henry Bradshaw Society, vol. 104. London, 1989.

BIBLIOGRAPHY

Ritzer, 1970:312–318.
Stevenson, 1982:63–64; 1987:36–37.

I

PRAYER FOR MARRIAGE

1a
May the Lord bless you (*vos*)
and may Christ keep you,
and may the Lord show his face to you
and give you peace;
and may Christ fill you with every spiritual blessing
for the forgiveness of sins and for eternal life,
for ever and ever. Amen.

ANOTHER

1b
Look down from heaven, O Lord,
upon this marriage
and lavish your holy and noble blessing upon them.

ANOTHER

1c
May the Father bless you (*vos*)
and the Son
and the Holy Spirit,
who are three in number,
one in name.

BLESSING OF THE WEDDING CHAMBER

2a
Bless, Lord,
this bridal chamber
and all who dwell herein
that they might live in your love
and grow old
and be multiplied unto length of days.
Through our Lord.

ANOTHER

2b

Bless, Lord,
these young people
as you blessed Tobias and Sarah,
the daughter of Raguel.
Grant them your blessing, Lord,
that they might live in your love
and grow old
and be multiplied unto length of days.
Through.

BLESSING OF THE RING

3.

Eternal God,
creator and sustainer of the human race,
giver of spiritual grace;
send your Holy Spirit, the paraclete,
upon this ring.
Through.

BLESSING OF THE BED

4a

Lord, bless this bed
and all who dwell in it,
that there may be found in them
holiness, chastity, meekness,
fulfillment of the law and obedience to God,
Father, Son, and Holy Spirit.
Through.

4b

May God the Father bless you (*te*),
the Son heal you,
the Holy Spirit enlighten you
and preserve your body,
save your soul,
shine in your heart,
guide your senses,
and lead you to heavenly life.
Through.

4c

May the blessing of the Lord be upon your wife
and upon your parents;
may you see your children
and your children's children
to the third and fourth generation;
and may your seed be blessed by the God of Israel,
who reigns for ever and ever. Amen.

II

FOR THE BLESSING OF BRIDES

5a

God of Abraham,
God of Isaac,
God of Jacob,
bless these young people
and sow the seed of eternal life in their minds
that whatsoever they learn to their advantage
they might also desire to perform.
Through Jesus Christ,
the restorer of humankind,
who lives with you and your Holy Spirit.

ANOTHER

5b i

Look down from heaven, Lord,
upon this marriage.
Pour out your blessing
through Raphael, your angel of peace,
that health and honor might be theirs.
Through.

5b ii

May the Lord bless you (*vos*);
may God keep you
and have mercy upon you;
may the Lord turn his face to you
and grant you peace.
Through.

11. BENEDICTIONAL OF ROBERT OF JUMIEGES

Though it is commonly ascribed to Robert of Jumièges (Archbishop of Canterbury, 1051-1052), it is in fact more likely that this book of blessings was that of another Robert, who was Archbishop of Rouen at the beginning of the eleventh century.[1] In either case, it was edited in England, used in Normandy and preserved in Rouen. It is important because it represents the first example of the combining of the Roman practice of the Nuptial Mass and the Anglo-Norman practice of domestic wedding prayers. Even so, it appears that there are two parts to the rite: the Mass (and the blessings during Mass) held in church and the prayers (12a-g) for use in the home.

The Mass is that of the Gregorian Sacramentary, but the nuptial blessing is duplicated with a solemn blessing in Gallican style, i.e. in a sequence of blessings. This added text is also found in the Lanalet Pontifical (tenth c.) and later made its way into many French and English rituals. It is a fine prayer which begins by recalling "our first parents," then the memory of Tobias and Sarah, then the wedding feast at Cana, praying for the couple's sanctification and happiness in this life and life in the world to come. Despite the authority of the Roman text, it is not hard to understand why those who adopted the Roman liturgy would be reluctant to abandon their own blessings which were so much more inclusive.

The texts that follow the Mass begin with two prayers for blessing the ring, separated by a couple of verses of Ps 68, and then a rite of actually giving the ring appears for the first time. This is followed by Ps 127[128], which was to become the classic wedding psalm. Here it may serve to accompany a procession to the bridal chamber, for the last three prayers seem to

---

[1] Despite the fact that Rouen was a center of reform (see introduction to Bury St. Edmunds, below), this Robert, who was Archbishop of Rouen from 989 to 1037 and also Count of Evreux, seems unlikely to have been a proponent of tighter discipline. He was the son of Richard, Duke of Normandy, by the Countess Gunnor. According to the story told in the *Historia Normannorum*, when his father wanted Robert appointed as Archbishop of Rouen, he was told it was canonically impossible, since the duke and the child's mother had never been formally married. The duke thereupon married the countess, legitimizing all their children by bringing them, too, under the nuptial veil. As archbishop, Robert had three children of his own by his consort, Herleva, according to the chronicler Odoricus Vitalis. See *Gallia Christiana*, Paris, 1874.

belong there. The first is from *Tobit,* the second and third being variations on the blessings used for the nuptial chamber in *Egbert.*

TEXT

H. A. Wilson, ed., *The Benedictional of Archbishop Robert.* Henry Bradshaw Society, vol. 24. London, 1903, 149–51.

BIBLIOGRAPHY

Ritzer, 1970:311ff.

Stevenson, 1982:66–67.

MASS FOR THE BLESSING OF A BRIDE

1.
Hear us . . .[2]

2.
A Reading from the Epistle of the Blessed [Aposle Paul] to the Corinthians.
I Corinthians 7:1-10

ACCORDING TO JOHN

3.
John 2:1-11

OVER THE GIFTS

4.
Receive, we beseech you . . .[3]

PREFACE

5.
It is truly right and just . . .[4]

6.
Be pleased, therefore . . .[5]

---

[2] Greg, 1.
[3] Greg, 2.
[4] Greg, 3.
[5] *Hanc igitur:* variable prayer in the Roman Canon. Cf. Greg, 4.

7.
We beseech you . . .[6]

BLESSING

8.
O God,
you have made all things out of nothing . . .[7]

ANOTHER BLESSING

9.
May almighty God,
who by his own power
created our first parents, Adam and Eve,
sanctified them with his blessing
and joined them in a holy union,
sanctify and bless your hearts and bodies
and conjoin you in a union of true love.
Amen.
May he who sent the archangel Raphael
to prepare the marriage of Tobias and Sarah
send his holy angel from his heavenly throne
to comfort you in his holy service,
show you the path of righteousness
and protect you for ever from all evil.
Amen.
May he who willed that his only begotten Son,
our Lord Jesus Christ,
redeemer of the world,
should be born of a virgin,
and who consecrated marriage
by his presence and his miracle,
when he turned water into wine,
may he be present at your nuptials also
and deign to bless you and make you holy.
Amen.
And may he grant you quiet times,
health of mind and body,
joy in the birth of holy children,
and, when the labors of this present life are done,
may he grant you to come faithfully

---

[6] Greg, 11.
[7] Greg, 6–10.

into the company of his holy angels.
Amen.
(And may his peace be with you always.
Amen.)

POSTCOMMUNION

10.
We beseech you, almighty God, *as above.*[8]

11.
Listen favorably, Lord, to our prayers:[9]
since you ordained the propagation of the human race
graciously assist us;
so that what is joined by your authority
may be preserved by your help.
Through.

[HERE] BEGIN THE BLESSINGS
OVER THE YOUNG PEOPLE[10]

12a
Bless, O Lord,
this ring which we bless in your Name.
May she who wears it be kept in your peace,
live and grow old in your love
and be multiplied unto length of days.

Command, Lord, your power *until* silver.[11]
Glory be.

12b
Eternal God,[12]
creator and sustainer of the human race,
giver of spiritual grace,
send your Holy Spirit, the paraclete,
upon this ring.
Through.

---

[8] See n. 7, above (=Greg, 11).

[9] Greg, 5.

[10] *Incipiunt benedictiones super adholescentes.*

[11] Ps 68:28-30. For full text of these verses, see Bury St. Edmunds 6, below. The use of this corrupt text is strange. Molin and Mutembe call it "bizarre," but suggest it might have entered the marriage liturgy as a blessing or exorcism associated with the giving of money, in virtue of its mention of "those who have been tested by silver" (*op. cit.*, 139).

[12] Egbert, 3.

12c
He puts the ring on her hand.

In the name of the Father,
and of the Son,
and of the Holy Spirit.
Amen.

12d
Psalm.

Blessed are those who fear the Lord,
to the end (Ps 127).

12e
May the God of Abraham,[13]
the God of Isaac,
and the God of Jacob
himself join you together
and fulfill his blessing in you.
Through.

12f
Look down, O Lord,
from your holy heaven upon this marriage.[14]
Just as you sent your holy angel, Raphael,
to Tobias and Sarah, the daughter of Raguel,
so Lord deign to send your blessing
upon these young people,
that they might remain in your will,
persevere in your will,
live in your love,
increase and grow old,
and be multiplied unto length of days.
Through.

12g
God of Abraham,[15]
God of Isaac,
God of Jacob,
bless these young people
and sow the seed of eternal life in their minds,

---

[13] Tob 7:15.
[14] Egbert, 1b, 2b.
[15] Egbert, 5a.

so that whatever they may learn
that would be of help to them,
they will hasten to put it into practice.
Through Jesus Christ,
redeemer of humankind,
your only begotten Son,
who lives and reigns with you and the Holy Spirit,
now and always,
for eternal ages of ages.
Amen.

12. THE CANTERBURY BENEDICTIONAL

A benedictional is a book that contains only the blessings given by a bishop, so it has no Mass texts in it. The text given here, like the last one also from the eleventh century, is a series of short blessings for use over the bride and groom. It shows how, even when the Roman Nuptial Mass and its solemn blessing of the bride were adopted, the local approach to marriage was kept alive in the form of solemn blessings, perhaps given at the end of Mass, perhaps elsewhere. Two unusual features of this blessing are the reference to Cana and the mention of the bridal pair being "crowned by God" here and in eternity. Though the Cana miracle is mentioned in the *Benedictional of Robert* (9), it is more commonly met in the East, as is the crowning motif.

TEXT

R. M. Wooley, ed., *The Canterbury Benedictional*. Henry Bradshaw Society, vol. 51. London, 1917, 126.

BIBLIOGRAPHY

Stevenson, 1982:64–65.

BLESSING OF BRIDE AND GROOM

1.
May God,
who not only attended a marriage
but chose to make there a beginning of his miracles,
bless this his servant and maidservant
who are to be united in the marriage bed,
and the people here present.
Amen.

2.
May their life be marked by harmony,
continual charity,
modest chastity,
the attitude of humility,
moral discipline
and the highest beauty of all religiosity.
Amen.

3.
May the angel of God be with them
as an unfailing guard;
may the power of the devil
be utterly expelled from them;
may their days be multiplied in peace
and enriched with children;
thus may they be blessed,
that here and in eternity
they may be crowned by God.
Amen.

4.
The which may he deign to grant.

13. AN ITALIAN FORMULARY FOR THE BLESSING OF A MARRIAGE WITHOUT MASS

This short series of prayers for marriage is found in an eleventh century missal from Northern Italy and is a reminder that not everyone was married in church during a Nuptial Mass. It closely resembles the sort of prayers found in the pontifical of Egbert and in Archbishop Robert's book of blessings. The series is entitled, "Prayer over men and women when they are wed." It opens with a choice of collects. The first is rather generic, the second highly unusual. In Christian typology, Pharaoh is often a figure of Satan, so the prayer seems to envisage married life as something of a spiritual ordeal, praying that the couple may emerge unscathed to find favor at the last judgment. The third text, "A blessing over one man," looks suspiciously like an all-purpose blessing, but its accent on divine protection matches the mood of the previous collect. The last text is entitled "A blessing of the ring when a woman marries" but is also a generic prayer for the blessing of God's protection. Again, here is a series of blessings for marriage that, apart from a brief allusion to "increase and multiply," put little emphasis on procreation, focusing instead on the spiritual life of the couple.

TEXT

Ritzer, 1970:430–431.

BIBLIOGRAPHY

Stevenson, 1987:37–38.

A PRAYER OVER MEN AND WOMEN WHEN THEY ARE WED[16]

1.
Lord, almighty God,
deign to send your blessing
upon this your servant, N.,
and this your maidservant, N.,
so that they might live in your love

---

[16] *Oratio super masculos et feminas in conjugationem.*

and increase and multiply unto length of days.[17]
Through.

ANOTHER

2.
Lord Jesus Christ,
bless your servant, N.,
and your maidservant, N.,
through the prayer of Moses
whom you delivered in the Red Sea
from the face of Pharaoh,
that they might find favor before your face
and be saved on the day of judgment.
Through.

BLESSING OVER ONE MAN[18]

3.
May God the Father bless you.
May Christ his Son come to your aid,
guard and preserve your body in his service,
enlighten your mind,
guard your senses,
perfect your soul by his grace,
and keep you from all evil.
May his holy right arm protect you.
May he who always helps his saints
be pleased to help you.

BLESSING OF A RING WHEN A WOMAN MARRIES[19]

4.
Lord, creator and sustainer of the human race,
giver of everlasting salvation,
grant your blessing to your maidservant, N.,
that equipped with the strength of heavenly protection,
she may progress to eternal salvation.
Through.

---

[17] See Egbert, 2b and Robert, 12f.
[18] *Benedictio super hunum hominem.*
[19] *Ben(edictio) anuli quando mulier ad nuptia(s) accedit.*

14. ISIDORE OF SEVILLE:
DE ECCLESIASTICIS OFFICIIS,
II, 20.5ff.

With Isidore, who was the reforming archbishop of Seville
(Spain) from about 600 to 636, we come to the liturgies of the
Iberian peninsula, which are known as the Visigothic rites.
After being colonized by Rome in the century or so before the
Christian era, Spain enjoyed the best part of four centuries of
Roman civilization. Early in the fifth century, the first waves of
barbarians began to arrive en route to Africa, but the Arian
Visigoths arrived to stay and settled in alongside the Catholic
Christians. In 589, the Goths converted to Catholicism and a
period of national consolidation began, with Isidore as the
major ecclesiastical figure. The marriage rite which he describes
in his *Liber Ordinum*, quoted here, is a mixture of Roman and
Visigothic traditions and offers another example of how tena-
ciously people cling to their own customs in matters as close to
their lives as marriage.

Paragraphs 5–6 and 8 reflect Roman custom: the presence of
the once-married woman as companion to the bride, the nuptial
veil, the emphasis on the modest submission of the woman to
her husband, and the giving of the ring (to the bride). The
practice of symbolically binding the couple together with a
colored cord and of observing the "nights of Tobias"—the three
nights of abstinence—are more likely Visigothic. The curious
etymologies are characteristic of Isidore, while his explanation
of the colors of the cord and of the placing of the ring on the
fourth finger demonstrate his familiarity with popular modes of
thought.

Not the least important part of his testimony is his opening
remark on the "fact" that people who wed have their marriage
blessed by the priest. Certainly, it had not always been that
way and would not happen everywhere in the Church for centuries to come; but whether Isidore is referring to an established
practice in Seville or trying to encourage such a practice is hard
to say. The use of Gen 1:27-28 as a paradigm for the ecclesiastical blessing would become common, though few would express
the idea as succinctly as Isidore: "What happened at that time
in paradise is imitated now in the church."

TEXT

De ecclesiasticis officiis II, 20:5-8, 10. In Migne, *Patrologia latina* 83, 810c–812b; in Ritzer, 1970:432–433.

BIBLIOGRAPHY

Stevenson, 1982:54.

5 [20]

The fact that, when people marry, their marriage is blessed by a priest is something established by God at the very beginning of the human race. For it is written: "God made man; in the image of God he made him, male and female he made them, and he blessed them, saying, 'Increase and multiply'." What happened at that time in paradise is imitated now in the church. And when virgins marry lawfully, they are attended by women married only once,[21] and this is for the sake of monogamy: it is meant to be an omen, but a good omen.

6.

And when such women are married, they are veiled as a reminder to them that they are thereby subject to their husbands, and humble. That is why the veil is commonly called the *mavors* or "Mars," for it is a sign of the husband's dignity and his power.

For the husband is the head of his wife.[22] It is therefore right that women should be veiled when they marry, so that they might be mindful of womanly modesty, for there is that to follow regarding which they must be modest. So it was that, when Rebecca was led to her husband, she did not greet him or kiss him when she saw him, but immediately—knowing what was to come—veiled her head with a scarf.[23]

The verb *obnubere* means "to cover." Hence married women are called *nuptae* because they veil their faces, just as clouds[24] cover the sky.

7.

Moreover, those who are married are joined, after the blessing of the levite, by a single cord, and they should in no way dis-

---

[20] Paragraph numbers correspond to the Latin text.
[21] *univirae pronubae.*
[22] 1 Cor 11:3.
[23] Gen 24:65.
[24] *nubae.*

rupt the compact of marital unity. The cord they wear is woven of white and purple colors: the white standing for purity of life, the purple for the blood of [bearing] children. Thus this sign gives a warning that the rule of continence is to be kept by both partners for a while and that the marital debt is not hereafter to be withheld. This is what the Apostle enjoined on married people: "Keep continent for a while, that you may give yourselves to prayer"[25]—this is signified by the white in the cord—and then he adds "and then return to one another," which is signified by the purple color.

8.

The fact that the man gives his fiancée a ring means that it is a sign of mutual faithfulness or, rather, that their hearts are bound by a single pledge. Hence it is placed on the fourth finger, for in that finger, it is said, there is a vein which carries the blood to the heart. In ancient times, a woman could not be given in marriage more than once, lest her love be divided among more than one husband. Among the Israelites, moreover, it was forbidden to give a girl to a husband before she had reached menstruation.

10.

The dowry-contracts indicate that a woman is taken to wife for the sake of procreating children . . .[26]

---

[25] 1 Cor 7:5.
[26] For an example of a (much later) dowry contract, see Appendix I.

15. THE LIBER ORDINUM

The *Liber Ordinum* is a collection of old Spanish or Visigothic rites which was specially put together for presentation to Pope Alexander II in 1056 in order to prevent the romanization of the (now reconquered) parts of Spain which had preserved for centuries their own native liturgical usages under several centuries of Arab rule and were now threatened with losing them.

There are two marriage rites in this collection which resemble each other closely. Manuscript 'B' is reproduced here, since it contains a fuller provision for the various rites of matrimony. The Visigothic marriage rites work (like the Eastern liturgies) by celebrating marriage in several distinct phases, by providing a rich euchology, and by use of dramatic symbolism. Though the collection of texts dates from the eleventh century, its contents are much older and may represent practices going back to the early fifth century.

The collection given here provides for a celebration of marriage in four phases (I-IV) and appends two sets of prayers for use at a second marriage. Each of the four rituals is quite simply structured and the prayers are well developed without being verbose.

The first rite is that for the blessing of the wedding chamber (I) which, together with the blessing of arrhas (III), may be the oldest part of the whole ritual. The blessing of the chamber takes place early on Saturday morning, thus before the Nuptial Mass and blessing which are celebrated on Sunday. It begins with sprinkling the house with salt (exorcism?). The priest then arrives and, after a Scripture verse, recites a collect. All say the Lord's Prayer and the rite concludes with a typically Visigothic prayer of blessing, punctuated by the people's "Amen."

There then seems to be a form of Vespers (II), or Evening Prayer, attested elsewhere in Spain for weddings and other sacraments, but the received text is incomplete.

Next follows a Blessing of the Arrhas, or marriage-gift. Originally this would have been a form of bride price paid to the woman's family when the marriage was contracted (i.e. at betrothal). The ceremony of the giving of the arrhas constituted a binding betrothal rite, celebrated some time—often years—before the actual marriage. By the eleventh century, however, the old Germanic bride price had long since been confused with the Roman custom of making provision for the bride's future in the form of a settlement against the eventuality of her being widowed, a settlement which could often be quite extensive. In this rite, however, the arrha is simply a gift from the groom to the bride and appears to be identified, in any case, with the two rings. This suggests that the exchange of rings—which first appears here—has come to replace the bridal gift by the eleventh century. More significantly, it seems as though the solemn betrothal with the arrhas has now been absorbed into the celebration of the marriage itself, since it is placed between Vespers and the Nuptial Mass.

The fourth stage is the Mass, where the rubrics are confusing: first it is said that the nuptial blessing occurs at the end of Mass, before the dismissal; then the rubrics at the end of the blessing provide for the couple to receive Communion, and for a brief series of concluding rites. It was the Roman custom to give the nuptial blessing before Communion, and it looks as though these texts have been cobbled together out of traditional pieces to accommodate Roman practice. After an opening invitation to prayer, the main Visigothic marriage blessing follows. The blessing for the veiling of the bride which comes next in the text is certainly out of place: it is a different style of prayer and it is a prayer for the veiling of the bride, despite the fact that, at this point, both bride and groom are under the same veil! It is also followed by the saying of the Lord's Prayer, which is odd since it would have just been sung in the Mass. The last prayer (the second of the two mentioned in the rubric) completes the solemn blessing.

Despite the crude editing, the beauty and vigor of these rites is apparent. They are marked by a concern for both partners and for their wider circle and for children yet unborn. There is a solid spirituality of married life, though it is marked by some apprehension about the dangers of unbridled libido: they are always to live together in this world in such a way as to be worthy to inherit the next. Children are a blessing desired and prayed for, but procreative purpose does not dominate the text.

TEXT

M. Férotin, ed., *Le Liber Ordinum en usage dans l'église wisigothique et mozarabe d'Espagne du cinquième au onzième siècle.* Mon. eccles. lit. 6. Paris, 1904, 433–443.

BIBLIOGRAPHY

Pinell i Pons, J. "La liturgia nupcial en el antiguo rito hispanico," in Farnedi, 1986:87–105.

Ritzer, 1970:298–305.

Stevenson, 1982:48–53; 1987:45–49.

I

ORDER FOR BLESSING THE WEDDING CHAMBER

1.
First, at the third hour on the Sabbath, according to custom, salt is to be sprinkled in the dwelling or bridal chamber. Then, when the priest arrives to bless the marriage chamber, he recites this verse, saying:

2.
Look upon your servants
and upon your works, O Lord,
and direct their children
with blessings (Ps 89:16-17).

Then this prayer:

PRAYER

3.
O Lord,
those things which are blessed
by invocation of your name
are sustained by the fulness of your blessing.
Bless this room, set aside for honest marriage,
that no onslaught of evil might touch it.
May the chastity of marriage alone reign here
and may your compassion
attend its worthy celebration.

Our Father.

BLESSING

4a
May the all-powerful Lord
pour forth his plenteous blessings
upon this marriage chamber[27]
and bless with everlasting holiness
those who meet here together.
Amen.

---

[27] *receptaculo nuptiali.*

4b

May all evil spirits be turned back from this place
and may the angels take up their awaited station here.
Amen.

4c

Here by God's grace may marriage so be celebrated[28]
that the virtue of the married couple is never debased.
Amen.

4d

May the words and actions of those who enter here
to celebrate their marriage be so proper
that they are never swept away by desire
to the shipwreck of passion.
Amen.

4e

Thus may modest decency protect the newlyweds
and everlasting peace sustain those
who are joined in the joys of matrimony.
Amen.

II

ORDER FOR THOSE MARRYING[29]

VESPERS[30]

1.

. . . May they offer you the dedication of their marriage vow.
May they love one another
and love you not the less.
Living in peace and serving you faithfully,
may they never cease to beseech you with us, saying:

Our Father.

BLESSING

2.

May Christ the Lord receive the faithful vows
of his servants, N. and N.,
and forgive you all your sins.
Amen.

---

[28] *connubii celebritas habeatur.*

[29] *Ordo nubentium.*

[30] There is a folio missing from the manuscript, so only the end of the evening prayer is given.

May an unbreakable bond of love
be his gift to those who now enter
upon the grace of marriage,
that they might pass through this world in peace.
May they who are about to enter
into chaste wedlock
be kept unharmed in heart and body
before God at all times.

III

ORDER OF THE ARRHAS[31]

1.
If anyone wishes to give arrhas, he should approach the priest. A dish is presented, on it he lays a clean cloth and two rings.

PRAYER

2.
Lord, all-powerful God,
you commanded Abraham
to give Isaac to Rebecca
through the exchange of arrhas,
as an image of holy matrimony,
so that by the offering of rings
the number of children might be increased.
We pray you to sanctify with your power
this offering of arrhas
which your servant, N.,
makes to his beloved bride, N.
Graciously bless both them and their gifts
so that, protected by your blessing
and joined in the bond of love,
they may rejoice to be counted
among your faithful for ever.

BLESSING

3a
May the Lord fill you
with sweet reverence for his name
and fructify you with the seed of holiness.
Amen.

---

[31] For the arrhas, or pledges, see introduction to this text.

3b
May your life together
be like the fragrance of the lilies,
that your minds might rise easily
to heaven at all times.
May you remain true,
with God's help,
to the exchange of arrhas you have made
that they might be signs of united hearts
and that you might be the parents of virtuous children.

IV

ORDER FOR THE BLESSING OF NEWLY-WEDS[32]

1.
When people come to be married, Mass is celebrated according to cus-
tom and then, before the deacon dismisses the congregation, those to be
married approach the priest at the gates of the sanctuary.
   The parents of the girl, or other relatives if she has no parents,
come forward and hand the girl over to the priest. The priest veils the
couple with a pall or sheet, placing on top of it a cord of white and
purple.
   Then he recites this preface with the two prayers which follow it.

PREFACE

2.
Dearly beloved,
let us call upon almighty God . . .[33]
May they, by his favor,
have the children they desire
and may these children,
being his gift,
also be endowed with his blessing,
so that these his servants, N. and N.,
may serve in humility of heart
him whom they acknowledge to be their creator.
Amen.

[32] *Ordo benedicendi eos qui noviter nubunt.*
[33] This invitation to prayer is identical with that in Bobbio 550, apart from the ending.

PRAYER

3a

O God,
when the world itself was new-born,
you shaped woman out of the bone of man,
for the purpose of continuing the human race,
thereby revealing the unity of genuine love;
for, in making the two out of one,
you have shown that the two are one.
Thus you established the basis of the first marriage,
namely, that the man should take to wife
what was part of his own body,
knowing it to be made out of part of himself.

3b

Look graciously down from your heavenly throne
and be pleased to hear the prayers we offer
for your servants
whom we have joined in marriage
by blessing their union.
Bless them with your merciful kindness
and by the kindness of your mercy sustain them.
Amen.

3c

Grant them, Lord,
to be of one mind in the fear of your Name
and to show their love in the goodness
of their mutual behavior.
Amen.

3d

May they love one another
and never be estranged from you.
Amen.

3e

May they render to one another
the debt of marriage
in such a way as never to cause offense to you.
Amen.

3f
May they never turn aside after another,
but please you by remaining faithful
to one another.
Amen.

3g
Grant them, Lord,
an abundance of this world's goods
and a large family of children.
Amen.

3h
Let the sweetness of your blessing
so surround them
that whatever children may be born of their union
may find favor with their fellows
and be blessed by you.
Amen.

3j
Grant them, Lord,
to enjoy length of days in this life
and to desire the unending life that is to come.
Amen.

3k
Let them so negotiate all temporal business
that they will continue faithfully
to long for eternal things.
Amen.

3l
Grant them so to love all passing goods
that they may not lose those goods
that last forever.
Amen.

3m
Loving each other truly
and serving you faithfully,
let them see their children's children
and, after a long life in this present world,
let them come to the heavenly kingdom.
Amen.

BLESSING OF THE GIRL ALONE[34]

4.
O God,
by the teaching of the Holy Spirit,
you commanded that Rebecca should be veiled
when she first saw Isaac
and by angels you ordered
that women should veil their heads.
Vouchsafe to bless this your servant, N.,
who intends to marry.
May her chastity be her covering.
As she receives the veil of modesty
may the grace of modesty be hers.
Let her cleave to one man.
Let her marry one man in Christ.
Let her be aware that she marries
not in fornication but in truth.

Let her look to her father Abraham;
let her look to Sarah, her mother and model,
the mother of all holy children who marry.
And let her work out her salvation
in the bearing of faithful children.

Our Father.

BLESSING

5.
May the Lord bless you by the word of our mouth
and may he join your hearts
in the everlasting bond of sincere love.
May you flourish with an abundance of this world's goods;
may you be fittingly blessed with children;
may you always rejoice in your friends.
May the Lord grant you the goods that last,
to your parents a happy old age,
and to all everlasting happiness.
Amen.

6.
*Having finished these prayers, the priest hands the girl over to the
man, admonishing them that, out of respect for the Holy Communion,*

---

[34] *Benedictio solius puelle.*

they should keep themselves from pollution that night.[35] *And so they receive Communion.*

7a
Afterwards the deacon gives the dismissal, saying:

In the name of our Lord Jesus Christ,
the Mass is over.
Let us go in peace.

7b
And as they begin to process and to leave the church, the following antiphon is sung:

You who to the grace of marriage.[36]

7c
Then he says:

BLESSING

May the three-fold majesty
and single Godhead bless you.
Amen.
The Father, the Son, and the Holy Spirit.
May you be found on the day of judgement
just as you were when you left the font.

V

Preface for one person marrying for the first time, but marrying someone who is marrying for the second time.

1.
Dearly beloved,
let us join with all the faithful

---

[35] *. . . ut pro sancta communione a pollutione in ea nocte se custodiant.* The exhortation to continence on the first night(s) of marriage is very old, being inspired by Tobit 8:4 (*q.v.*) and first attested in the fifth century *Statuta ecclesiae antiqua:* "When [the bride and groom] have been blessed [by the priest], let them remain in virginity that night, out of respect for the blessing." A century later, Caesarius of Arles was accustomed to give the nuptial blessing in the basilica three days before the wedding, again so that continence would be observed out of respect for the blessing. See H. G. J. Beck, *The Pastoral Care of Souls in South East France During the Sixth Century* (Rome, 1950) 232–233. Here in eleventh century Spain, the motivation has changed, but the practice is still encouraged.

[36] The text refers to the folio that is missing. Cf. II.1 above. But the chant is also to be found in the Visigothic *Liber Antiphonarius*, II.2 (below).

in beseeching ever more devoutly
the God to whom all good things belong
and from whom all good things flow
to those who express their worthy desires in prayer.
Let us ask him to strengthen
those whom he has permitted to marry
with the grace of his blessing,
whereby they will succeed
both in obtaining without sin what they desire
and enjoying with God's blessing what they obtain.
Amen.

ANOTHER BLESSING

2a
O God,
source of all blessing
and goal of prayer for one who offers blessing;
the initial reproduction of the human race
you commanded with the words of your mouth,
decreeing:
"Increase and multiply and fill the earth."
Hear our prayers and mercifully grant
what we your petitioners request.
Grant to this your maidservant, N.,
whom we have just joined in the bond of matrimony,
genuine resources of gracious sweetness
and true love for the husband she is marrying.
Amen.

2b
Let her so cleave to him
as never to waver from your commandments.
Amen.

2c
Let her be so fruitful in the womb
that she may always be thinking
in the spirit of those things that are holy.
Amen.

2d
May she be so blessed with children by your grace
that, after a long and happy life,
she may deserve to arrive in the heavenly kingdom.
Amen.

BLESSING

3a
May the Lord of heavenly glory
and the king of all ages bless you.
Amen.

3b
May he give you
the sweetness of his sweetness
and happiness in this present life.
Amen.

3c
May he give you the joy of children
and, after a long life,
admit you to the dwelling-place of heaven.

VI

ANOTHER ORDER FOR SECOND MARRIAGES

1a
O God,
you help us in many ways,
with remedies for human weakness,
with the blessing of fertility
and with the multiplication of children.
So that nature should not be cheated of its seed
and that a line should be increased for posterity,
you blessed Ruth the Moabite
in the early days.
Amen.

1b
In the latter days
you permitted second marriages
through the teaching of your Apostle.
Grant them a shared desire for children
and remove from them all carnal lust and desire.
Amen.

1c
May their concern be, as Ruth's,
to have children out of love,
not to have pleasure out of lust.
Amen.

1d
May they be modest in their affections
rather than driven by their passions.
Amen.

1e
May the blessing that followed Ruth
accompany them also.
Amen.

1f
May the Lord make this woman,
who is entering your house,
to be like Rachel and Leah
who built the house of Israel.
Amen.

1g
May she be an exemplar of virtue
and be renowned in the Church of the living God.
Amen.

BLESSING OF THE SAME

2a
Holy Lord, everlasting Father, all-powerful God,
we beseech you on behalf of your servants,
N. and N.,
whom you have called to a second marriage
and who seek, by means of our unworthy prayers,
to obtain your blessing.

2b
Grant them, Lord,
faithful companionship in love
and an abundance of your blessings,
and grant to your maidservant, N.,
that she may put on the charity of Sarah.
Amen.

2c
The wisdom of Rebecca,
the love of Rachel,
the grace and chastity of Suzanna.
Amen.

2d
Bless your servant, N.,
as you blessed Abraham, Isaac, and Jacob.
Amen.

2e
May your blessing
and the gift of your grace
come down upon your servants, N. and N.,
as the rain and the dew come down upon the earth.
Amen.

2f
Let your blessing so flow
upon their hearts and bodies
that they might feel the touch of your hand
and, by the Holy Spirit,
be made sharers in everlasting happiness.

Our Father.

BLESSING

3a
Lord,
bless these your servants, N. and N.,
who have been joined
in the holy covenant of matrimony
by a second nuptial veiling
in accordance with the Apostle's command.
May it have all the merit of a first marriage.
Amen.

3b
May godly fear keep them continent,
and may they be fruitful in conceiving children.
Amen.

3c
May they be worthy of the merits
of the patriarchal couples.
May peace, meekness,
and the gentleness of holiness be theirs.
Amen.

3d
That rendered one in spirit
and one in body
by the grace of good works,
they may find joy
in the marriage they have chosen.
Amen.

16. VISIGOTHIC LIBER ANTIPHONARIUS

The old Spanish rites celebrated not only the Eucharist but also the Liturgy of the Hours for many special occasions, including marriage, as we see here. This Visigothic collection of chant-texts dates from the tenth century but, like the *Liber Ordinum*, its contents go back much further. Unfortunately, it is now virtually impossible to reconstruct, on the basis of the indications given in this text, what the nuptial Liturgy of the Hours might have been like in practice.

The tendency to look to the Old Testament for inspiration in understanding and celebrating marriage, characteristic of all Churches, is particularly marked in Spain. In these texts there is not a single reference to Christ, or to any New Testament text. Genesis, the patriarchal narratives, the psalms (especially Ps 127) and the Book of Tobit provide all the materials for this celebration. Blessings prayed for are, characteristically, those of fertility and long life, which will be seen as evidence of God's favor.

TEXT

J. Vives, A. Fabrega, L. Brou, eds., *Antifonario visigotico mozarabe de la Catedral de Léon*. Monumenta Hispaniae sacra, 5/1. Madrid-Barcelona, 1959, 454–455.

BIBLIOGRAPHY

J. Pinell, "El oficio hispanico-visigothico," *Hispania sacra* 10 (1957), 385–427.

Ritzer, 1970:298–300.

OFFICE FOR MARRIAGE[1]

I

VESPERS

Vr. Offer your evening sacrifice.[2]

---

[1] *Officium de nubentum* [sic!] Some of the abbreviations are obscure: "Ant." means "antiphon"; "Vr." indicates a verse to be sung; "Resp." may mean a response to a reading.

[2] Originally Ps 141, with a lamp-lighting ritual.

Sono.[3]   Lord, God of our Fathers,
may heaven and earth bless you,
the seas and all that is in them,
for you made Adam from the slime of the earth
and gave him Eve as helper,
that he might bless your name unto ages of ages.
Alleluia!

We bless you, Lord, God of Israel,
who have shown mercy to your two servants.
Make them bless you more and more,
and offer you a sacrifice of praise,
that all the nations may know
that you alone are Lord,
glorious over all the earth.

Ant.[4]   May the Lord, the God of Israel,
bless you,
that you may see your children
and your children's children
unto the third and fourth generation.
Praise (God)!

All.[4a]   May the Lord, the God of Israel,
bless you with an everlasting blessing,
that your seed may be blessed unto ages of ages.
Alleluia!

Vr.   Seek the Lord.

II

MATINS[5]

Ant.   The Lord has blessed the house of Israel,
he has blessed all those who fear the Lord,
the little as well as the great.

Vr.   The Lord has made known.

Ant.   You whom the Lord has brought
to the joy of marriage,

---

[3] A hymn. The text, like the rest of the Vespers texts, is based on Tobit.

[4] This antiphon was a refrain sung by the people as a cantor sang Ps 98(99):5 or 9ff.

[4a] An antiphon sung before and after psalm verses to which the people added an Alleluia. "Seek the Lord." See Psalm 68(69) or 104(105).

[5] Morning Prayer.

may he grant you length of life and lasting joy,
that you may rejoice
in your children and grandchildren,
after the example of Abraham and Sarah,
Isaac and Rebecca,
whom the Lord loved
and whom he enabled to conceive.

Vr.   Sing in the beginning.

All.   May the Lord extend a blessing over you
and over your children.
Alleluia!
You are blessed by the Lord,
the maker of heaven and earth.
Alleluia, alleluia!

Vr.   The Lord was mindful.

Resp.   May the blessing of the Lord be upon you.
Alleluia!
We bless you in the name of the Lord.
Alleluia!

Vr.   May the Lord extend a blessing over you
and over your children.
Alleluia!
You are blessed by the Lord,
the maker of heaven and earth.
In the name.

MASS[6]

Ps.   You shall eat the labors of your hands;
you are blessed
and all shall go well with you [Ps 127].

Vr.   Your wife shall be like a fruitful vine
on the wall of your house;
your children like young olive plants
around your table;
thus is blessed the man who fears the Lord.
And all shall go well with you.

Laudes.[7] I shall bless you says (the Lord).

   [6] *Ad missam.* Since this is an antiphonary, no prayers are provided. Ps 127 was sung after the first reading.
   [7] *Laudes.* Alleluia and versicle sung after the Gospel.

Sacrifi.[7a] He will form.
          In those days.

All.[7b]   May the Lord your God give you increase;
          may he add thousands to your number
          and bless you.
          Alleluia, alleluia!

[7a] *Sacrificium:* Visigothic term for the offertory chant. Two options are provided: Gen 2:2 or Gen 24:1.

[7b] *Alleluiaticum:* a chant usually sung at Vespers, but used here as an exit chant.

17. SACRAMENTARY OF VICH

The eleventh century sacramentary of Vich, in Catalonia, represents a synthesis of old Spanish and imported Roman features. The traditional Visigothic uses are retained: the blessing of the arrhas (pledges, chiefly rings since the sixth century), and the blessing of the wedding chamber. This rite has much in common with the *Liber Ordinum*, but the blessing of the arrhas here seems still to be distinct from the celebration of the marriage. That begins with the blessing of the marriage chamber, followed by the celebration of the Nuptial Mass. For this the texts of antiphons, prayers and readings are indicated and the admixture of Roman and Visigothic traditions is clear to see. The nuptial blessing appears in the Roman position, before Communion, but it is immediately preceded by the veiling of both bride and groom (done slightly differently from the *Liber Ordinum*). There is, in fact, a double blessing: the Roman blessing of the bride is followed by the Visigothic blessing of the couple. Striking in these prayers, and especially in the nuptial blessing (1422), is the this-worldly focus of the petitions which contrasts rather strongly with the asceticism of the Roman prayers and the mysticism of the Eastern euchology. Imagery from the New Testament (Cana, Eph 5) is entirely missing.

Note the role of the priest as intermediary: the hand of the bride and the hand of the groom are given by their respective fathers to the priest, who then joins them together. No longer simply a blesser of marriages (as he had been since at least the fourth century), the priest seems actually to be conducting the ceremony.

TEXT

A. Olivar, ed., *El sacramentario de Vich*. Monumenta Hispaniae sacra. Series liturgica, IV. Barcelona, 1953, 208ff.

BIBLIOGRAPHY

Ritzer, 1970:257–259, and *passim*.
Stevenson, 1982:54ff.; 1987:45–46.

CCXCIV. THE BLESSING OF ARRHAS[8]

1403
Lord, all-powerful God,
you commanded Abraham . . .[9]

ANOTHER

1404
May the blessing
which God poured out on Jacob through Isaac
descend upon you in all its fullness.
May the blessing
which Jacob invoked upon his beloved children
be increased by God
when he gives it to you.
May the blessing
which Moses pronounced over the children of Israel
attend, by the favor of Christ,
upon your hearts;
and just as the redeemer of all,
our Lord Jesus Christ,
gave the fullness of his blessing
to the disciples,
so may he also cause that same blessing
to abound in your minds and bodies.
Through our Lord.

ANOTHER

1405
Bless, O Lord, this arrha,
which your servant, N.,
has this day placed
in the hand of your maidservant, N.,
just as you blessed Abraham with Sarah,
Isaac with Rebecca,
and Jacob with Rachel.
Grant to them the grace of your salvation,
abundance of goods
and constancy in deeds.

---

[8] Paragraph numbers are those of the Olivar edition.
[9] *Liber Ordinum*, III, 2.

May they flourish
like the rose planted in Jericho.
May they fear and adore Jesus Christ,
who lives . . .

CCXCV. SERVICE FOR THE WEDDING CHAMBER[10]

First, at the third hour . . .[11]

1406
Look upon your servants . . .[12]

BLESSING OF THE WEDDING CHAMBER

1407
O Lord,
those things which are blessed . . .[13]

CCXCVI. MASS

1408
May the Lord, the God of Israel,
be with you;
may he himself wed you;
for he has shown pity to two single people.
Lord, make them bless you more and more.

Ps. Blessed are those [Ps 127].

1409
Hear us . . .[14]

1410
Do you not know that your members are members of Christ?[15]

RESPONSORIAL[16]

1411
Blessed are those who fear the Lord
and walk in his ways.

---

[10] *Ordo thalami.*
[11] *Liber Ordinum,* I, 1.
[12] *Liber Ordinum,* I, 2.
[13] *Liber Ordinum,* I, 3.
[14] Greg, 1.
[15] Reading from 1 Cor 6.
[16] Responsorial psalm [Ps 127].

Vr. You shall eat of the labors of your hands,
you are blessed and all will go well with you.

ALLELUIA

1412
May the Lord send you help from his holy place,
and out of Sion may he make you safe.

1413
At that time, Jesus spoke in parables, saying:

   "The kingdom of heaven is like a king who prepared a wedding for his son."[17]

OFFERTORY[18]

1414
May the Lord bless you;
may you see your children's children.
May he send you help from his holy place
and out of Sion may he make you safe.

PRAYER OVER THE GIFTS

1415
Receive, we beseech you . . .[19]

PREFACE

1416
It is truly right and just . . .[20]

CONCLUDING PRAYER

1417
Be pleased . . .[21]

BEFORE THE *PAX DOMINI* IS SAID[22]

Then those who are to be married come forward and approach the priest at the sanctuary gate. The father of the bride steps forward, or

---

[17] Gospel: Matt 22:2ff.
[18] Offertory antiphon.
[19] Ver, 2.
[20] Greg, 3.
[21] Ver, 3.
[22] Cf. *Liber Ordinum*, IV, 1.

another of her relatives, and taking the hand of the bride gives it to the priest. The groom's parents do the same. The priest joins them together and makes the bride stand to the left side of her groom. Then he veils them, covering the man's shoulders and the woman's head, and places the marriage cord over their shoulders, and he says:

"In the name of the Father,
and of the Son,
and of the Holy Spirit."

After which the priest pronounces over them the following blessing:

PRAYER[23]

1418
Dearly beloved,
let us call upon almighty God . . .
by whom they certainly know themselves
to have been redeemed
and richly endowed.

ANOTHER

1419
Be present . . .[24]

ANOTHER PRAYER

1420
O God, the source of all blessing . . .[25]
that, after a long life,
she may rejoice with them
in the company of the saints.

The Lord be with you.
And also with you.
Lift up your hearts.
We have lifted them up to the Lord.
Let us give thanks to the Lord our God.
It is right.

---

[23] *Oratio:* in fact a call to prayer. Cf. *Bobbio* 550.
[24] Gel, 3.
[25] *Liber Ordinum*, V, 2a-d except for the final clause, and without the Amens.

PREFACE

1421
It is truly right and just,
fitting and for our salvation.
For you have made all things out of nothing . . .[26]

ANOTHER PRAYER[27]

1422
O God,
when the world itself was new-born,
you shaped woman out of the bone of the man
for the purpose of continuing the human race,
thereby revealing the unity of genuine love;
for in making the two out of one
you have shown that the two are one.
Thus you established the basis
of the first marriage, namely,
that the man should take to wife
what was part of his own body,
knowing it to have been made out of part of himself.

Look graciously down from your heavenly throne
and be pleased to hear the prayers we offer
for your servants, N. and N.,
whom we have joined
in marriage by blessing their union.

Bless them with your merciful kindness
and by the kindness of your mercy sustain them.

Grant them, Lord,
to be of one mind in the fear of your Name
and to show their love in the goodness
of their mutual behavior.

May they love one another
and never be estranged from you.

May they render to one another
the debt of marriage
in such a way as never to cause offense to you.

---

[26] Greg, 6-10.
[27] See *Liber Ordinum*, IV, 3.

May they never turn aside after another,
but please you by remaining faithful
to one another.

Grant them, Lord,
an abundance of this world's goods
and a large family of children.

Let the sweetness of your blessing so surround them
that whatever children may be born of their union
may be pleasing to their fellow human beings
and be blessed by you.

Grant them to enjoy length of days in this life
and to desire the unending life that is to come.

Let them so negotiate all temporal business
that they will continue faithfully
to long for eternal things.

Grant them so to love all passing goods
that they may not lose those goods that last forever.

Loving each other truly
and serving you faithfully,
let them see their children's children
and, after a long life in this present world,
let them come to the heavenly kingdom.
Through.

ANOTHER

1423
May the Lord bless you . . .[28]
. . . and to all these goods
may he add everlasting joys.

May he who is named both one and three,
may he be glorified for ages of ages.
Amen.

ANOTHER

1424
God of Abraham . . .[29]

---

[28] *Liber Ordinum,* IV, 5.
[29] Egbert, 5a.

1425
In the name of the Father
and of the Son
and of the Holy Spirit.
May the God of Abraham,
the God of Isaac
and the God of Jacob
be with you
and fulfill his blessing in you.[30]

Afterwards he shall warn them to keep themselves from pollution until the third night, for the sake of Holy Communion, and then he shall communicate them.

Afterwards, he concludes, saying:

1426
In the name of our Lord Jesus Christ,
walk in peace.

1427
Thus shall be blessed everyone who fears the Lord;
you shall see your children's children,
peace upon Israel. [Ps 127:4-6]

POSTCOMMUNION

1428
We beseech you . . .[31]

PRAYER OVER SPOUSES[32]

1429
Lord,
bless these your servants, N. and N.,
who have been joined
in the holy covenant of matrimony
by a second nuptial veiling,
in accordance with the Apostle's command.
May it have all the merit of a first marriage.
May godly fear keep them continent
and may they be fruitful in conceiving children.

[30] See Robert, 12e.
[31] Greg, 11.
[32] *Oratio super nuptos.* See *Liber Ordinum*, VI, 3.

May they be worthy
of the merits of the patriarchal couples.
May peace, meekness and gentleness be theirs,
that rendered one in spirit and one in body
and marked by the grace of good works,
they may obtain the hoped-for fruit of marriage.
Through.

18. AN ENGLISH MISSAL:
BURY ST. EDMUNDS

In the eleventh and twelfth centuries a strong tide of reform washed over the European churches, largely prompted by the need to free Church life from secular control and to develop the social and legal structures which could assure some measure of social order. Part of this reform consisted of a determined assault on clandestine marriages which had long created problems not only for Christian monogamy, but for such important social and political issues as the legitimacy of offspring, inheritances and property rights.

The reform of marriage seems to have been launched in the area of Rouen where, in 1072, a provincial synod decreed that:

> marriages should not be contracted secretly, nor after dinner (*post prandium*). But the bride and groom should fast and be blessed by a priest, also fasting, in a monastery. And before they are joined in wedlock, diligent inquiry is to be made concerning their families (*progenies*). If there is any consanguinity within seven degrees they should be sent away, as also if either of them is divorced. Any priest acting contrary to this regulation is to be deposed.[33]

The reform, then, was aimed at regulating marriage more exactly, contracting it more publicly, and celebrating it more decorously. In the next couple of centuries it would find its way into the codification of canon law and into the thinking of the school theologians, in both instances laying a heavy accent on the need for a freely-given and publicly-witnessed exchange of consent.

So, for example, Peter Lombard (+1164), the great compiler and synthesizer of theological opinions, summarized contemporary thinking as follows:

> It is the bond which is established by the words of consent— when they say, "I take you for my husband . . . I take you for my wife"—which makes the marriage.
>
> The efficient cause of marriage is consent: not any kind of consent, but consent expressed verbally; and not referring to the future, but to the present. For if their consent refers to the future, saying "I shall take you for my husband . . . I shall take you for my wife," such consent does not effect marriage. Similarly, if

[33] Mansi, XX, 38.

they give their consent mentally, but do not express it verbally, such consent does not effect marriage. On the other hand, if they give verbal expression to something they do not mean in their hearts, still the force of those words of consent—"I take you for my husband" and "I take you for my wife"—is such as to constitute a marriage. (*Sentences*, Lib. IV, dist. xxvii, 3)

The marriage rite in the Bury St. Edmunds missal, preserved at Laon in France, is one of the earliest examples of the rearrangement of the rites of marriage in the wake of such developments. The betrothal rite, with explicit questions concerning consent to the marriage, is now held in a public place: outside the main door of the church. It is presided over by the priest who then leads the couple into the church, blesses them before the high altar, says the Mass and pronounces the nuptial blessing over them. Despite Rouen's desire to separate the formal ceremonies of marriage from the more popular customs, the Bury St. Edmunds missal still provides for a blessing of a cup (table prayer? Communion-substitute?) after Mass and a blessing of the couple in (or on) their matrimonial bed.

A number of elements from this rite survive in modern English-speaking marriage rites, especially the ceremony and formula for the giving of the ring and the practice of the nuptial kiss.

TEXT

Molin/Mutembe, 1974:289–291.

BIBLIOGRAPHY

Molin/Mutembe, 1974:*passim*.

Stevenson, 1982:68–71; 1987:39–43.

[HERE] BEGINS THE SERVICE FOR MARRYING A WOMAN[34]

I

Blessing the ring at the door of the church[35]

---

[34] *Incipit ordo ad desponsandam mulierem.*
[35] *Benedictio anuli ante hostium templi.*

1.
Bless, O Lord, this ring . . .[36]

2.
Creator and sustainer of the human race,
source of spiritual grace,
giver of eternal salvation,
vouchsafe to send your blessing upon this ring
which we bless in your most holy Name
that those who are thereby betrothed
may be armed with heavenly strength
and protected by your care
and experience the help of your blessing
unto eternal life.
Amen.

3.
*After this blessing has been pronounced, the man is asked by the priest
whether he wishes to take this woman, N., to be his lawful wife. The
same question is posed to the woman.*

4.
*When both have given their consent, the settlement and other gifts, as
agreed upon between them, are brought forward and given to the
woman. Then he who is to give the woman away steps forward and,
taking her by the right hand, gives her to the man as his lawful wife.
If she is a girl, her hand is covered; if she is a widow, her hand is
uncovered.*

5.
*Then the priest and the bridegroom place the ring on the right thumb
of the bride, saying:*

In the name of the Father,

then on her index finger, saying:

and of the Son,

then on her middle finger, saying:

and of the Holy Spirit.
Amen.

*And there let it remain.
Then the bridegroom says:*

[36] Robert, 12a.

With this ring I thee wed,
this gold and silver I thee give,
with my body I thee worship,
and with this dowry I thee endow.

Then the bride, having received the ring, the gold and silver, and the
dowry, falls to the feet of her husband.

6.

When she has returned to her feet, the priest says:

Command, O God, your power;
Confirm, O God, what you have wrought in us,
From your temple in Jerusalem.
Kings shall bear you gifts.
Put down the beasts of the reeds.
May the gathering of bulls among the cows of the people
Keep far away those who have been tested by silver.
[Ps 68:28-30][37]

7a

O God,
at the beginning of the growing world . . .[38]

7b

May the God of Abraham . . .[39]

8.

Having completed all these things, they enter the church carrying
lighted candles in their hands, following the priest to the altar. The
priest sings the psalm:

Blessed are they. [Ps 127]

II

1.

The Lord be with you.

Then the bride and groom stand before the altar,
bowing their heads to the priest. The priest then recites this prayer
over them, if they are minors:

---

[37] See Robert of Jumieges, note 11.
[38] Gel, 8b.
[39] Vich, 1425; Robert, 12e.

PRAYER

God of Abraham . . .[40]

ANOTHER PRAYER

2.
May the almighty and merciful God,
who created our first parents,
Adam and Eve, by his power
and sanctified them with his blessing
and joined them in a holy companionship,
himself sanctify your hearts
and join you together
in the companionship
and affection of genuine love.

ANOTHER PRAYER

3.
Look down, O Lord,
from your holy heaven . . .[41]

ANOTHER PRAYER

4.
May God the Father bless you,
may Jesus Christ keep you,
may the Holy Spirit shine upon you.
May the Lord show his face to you
and be merciful to you.
May he turn his face to you
and give you peace,
and fill you with every spiritual blessing
for the remission of all your sins,
that you may have eternal life
and live unto ages of ages.
Amen.

A prayer for those who have attained the age of majority:[42]

---

[40] Egbert, 5a.
[41] Robert, 12f.
[42] *Oratio super illos qui maioris aetatis sunt.*

PRAYER

5.

Look down, O Lord,
from your holy heaven upon this marriage[43]
and send Raphael,
your angel of peace,
that they might be healthy
and worthy and peaceable,
and pour out your blessing upon them.
Through our Lord.

ANOTHER PRAYER

6.

Vouchsafe, we beseech you, O Lord,
your blessing upon these people,
your servant and your handmaid,
that they may be obedient to you
and serve you together.
Through.

ANOTHER PRAYER

7.

Most merciful Father,
bless the marriage
of your servant and maidservant,
that, cleansed of all sin,
the love of your love might grow in their hearts,
which will please you on the dread judgement day.
Who live.

ANOTHER PRAYER

8.

May God the Father bless you,
may Jesus Christ keep you . . .[44]

III

1.

The Mass of the Holy Trinity if it is a Sunday.
Otherwise, the Mass Invocavit me.

---

[43] Cf. Robert, 12f; Egbert, 5b, i.
[44] Same as para. 4, above.

He has called upon me . . .
I shall fill him.
He who dwells [Ps 91].

2.
Before the pax domini *is said, the following prayers are recited over the bride and groom who are prostrate.*

Be present, O Lord . . .[45]

O God,
you made all things . . .[46]

May the God of Abraham,
the God of Isaac
and the God of Jacob
be with you in good times and in bad;
may he himself join you together
with the breadth of his favor;
may he fulfill his blessing in you,
that you may see the sons of your children;
and may your seed be blessed by the God of Israel,
who lives and reigns
for ages of ages.
Amen.

3.
After this, the pax domini *is said, the bridegroom is kissed, and then he kisses his bride.*

COMMUNION[47]

Lord, I shall be mindful.

IV

BLESSING OVER THE COUPLE AFTER MASS

1.
May you ever be blessed by the Lord of heaven,
who made all things out of nothing,
who lives and reigns in perfect Trinity,
for ages of ages.
Amen.

[45] Gel, 3.
[46] Greg, 6–10. The last section [10 b–c] is found here in the plural: ". . . may they come at last . . ."
[47] Communion verse.

BLESSING OVER THE CUP

2.
Bless, Lord.
this cup and this flagon,
as you blessed the six stone water-jars
at Cana in Galilee,
to make wine out of water;
bless and sanctify
this drink and this flagon with lasting blessing,
that whosoever drinks therefrom
may enjoy prosperity in the present age
and, in heaven,
the joys of the life to come.

BLESSING OF THE MARRIAGE CHAMBER

3.
Bless, Lord,
this marriage chamber[48]
and all who dwell herein,
that they may live in your love
and grow old
and be multiplied unto length of days.
Through.

Then the marriage chamber is to be incensed. Afterwards, he blesses
the couple as they sit or lie on their bed, saying:

Lord, bless these young people
as you blessed Tobias and Sarah,
daughter of Raguel,
that they may live in your Name
and grow old
and be multiplied unto length of days.
Through.

May he bless you,
Father, Son and Holy Spirit,
three in number
and one in name.
Through our Lord.

[48] Egbert, 2a.

19. RITUAL FROM
THE ABBEY OF BARBEAU

This marriage service is from the Cistercian abbey of Barbeau in
the diocese of Sens in central France, and dates from the late
fourteenth century. It is of interest for a number of reasons.
First, it presents a complete text of the marriage rite, prayers
and rubrics, from the initial betrothal to the final blessing of the
nuptial chamber. Second, it shows clearly how the betrothal
still remained a separate phase of the process of getting married: here the couple promise to wed "within forty days." On
the day of the actual wedding, the couple come to the door of
the church, where the banns are read for the last time, consent
to the marriage is established, vows are exchanged, the ring is
blessed, and the ring and coins given to the bride. After a formal entry into the church, the Mass with the solemn nuptial
blessing follows; after which there are the customary rites to be
performed at the newlyweds' house. Third, this is one of the
earliest texts to provide vernacular formulae for the questions
addressed to the couple and for the promises they make to each
other. Fourth, this rite clearly shows how the priest has now
emerged as the person who conducts both the betrothal and the
wedding, and how the families have receded into the background. All these developments are the result of the emphasis
placed by the canonists and the theologians on the necessity for
a public attestation of freedom to marry and of mutual consent.

Nonetheless, as the shape of modern Western marriage rites
begins to emerge here, older customs refuse to die. Apart from
the retention of the different phases of marrying, we find ves-
tiges of the old bride price in the gift of the silver coins, though
these are now given to the bride, not to her family. There is
also the blessing of bread and wine following the procession of
the newlyweds from the church to their home and, later that
night, the blessing of the bridal chamber. And there are elements which are still retained, but whose meaning has
changed: for example, the wedding ring, originally a symbol of
a woman's betrothal in the Romano-Gallic tradition, but now
clearly associated with the wedding itself.

The prayers themselves represent a now-familiar mixture of
Roman and Gallican traditions, but some new ones surface here
to remind us that uniformity between dioceses—or even within
the same diocese—was not something that anyone considered
important. For people who lived relatively settled existences

and traveled little, continuity in custom was more important than uniformity from place to place.

TEXT

Molin/Mutembe, 1974:305–308.

BIBLIOGRAPHY

Molin/Mutembe, 1974:*passim*.
Stevenson, 1982:75, 82; 1987:43, 121.

I

MARRIAGE SERVICE[49]

1.
After asking the names of the persons contracting (the engagement), the priest says to the man:[50]

N., will you take N.,
here present,
to be your wife and spouse,
if holy Church agrees?

If he answers "Yes," the priest shall ask the woman in the same words. If she answers "Yes," the priest shall take the right hand of each of them and say:

2.
N., say after me:
N., I pledge to you
that I will take you to be my wife and spouse
within forty days,
if holy Church agrees.

Then the priest shall say to the woman:

N., say after me:
N., I pledge to you
that I will take you to be
my husband and master, etc.

---

[49] *Officium matrimonii.*
[50] In this, as in other fourteenth century texts, the questions to be posed to the couple are actually given in the vernacular, the rest of the rite remaining of course in Latin.

3.

Then the priest should say:

May this be to the profit and salvation
of your bodies and your souls,
to the honor of God and of our Lady,
and of all the saints.
In the name of the Father.

4.

And he shall join their hands together.

II

1.

*When the marriage is to take place at the door of the church, after ask-
ing the names of the persons contracting (marriage), the priest says:*

We have published the banns between N. and N.
two/three times in the holy church.
They wish to be joined together in marriage.
Let us publish the banns a fourth time
and command, under pain of excommunication,
that if any man or woman
knows of any consanguinity or affinity
or any other impediment
standing in the way of this marriage,
let them say so before we proceed any further.

2.

*If the response of the people is that there is no such impediment be-
tween the persons, the priest shall say to the man:*

N., do you wish N. to be your wife and spouse,
since holy Church agrees?

If the answer is "Yes," he shall say the same to the woman.

3.

*If she answers "Yes," the priest shall take them both by the right
hand and say:*

N., say after me:
N., I take you to be my wife and my spouse
and I pledge to you the faith of my body,
that I will be faithful to you and loyal
with my body and my goods
and that I will keep you in sickness and in health

and in whatever condition
it will please the Lord to place you,
and that I shall not exchange you
for better or worse
until the end.

The woman shall say the same words after the priest.

BLESSING OF THE RING

4.
O God, send your strength;
O God, confirm what you have done among us.
From your holy temple which is in Jerusalem;
Let kings offer you gifts, etc. [Ps 68]
Glory be to the Father.
Kyrie eleison.
Christe eleison.
Kyrie eleison.
Our Father.

Let us pray:

5.
O Lord,
creator and sustainer of the human race,[51]
source of spiritual grace,
giver of eternal life,
vouchsafe to send your blessing upon this ring
which we bless in your most holy Name.
May both the man and woman
who are with it betrothed
be equipped with heavenly virtue
and shielded by your protection,
and may they receive the help
of your blessing unto eternal life.
Amen.

6.
*Then the priest asks for the rings and thirteen pieces of silver. He
gives away as much of the silver as he pleases and puts the remainder,
with the ring, in the palm of the woman's right hand, placing the
man's hand on top of it. Holding the hands in his own, the priest
says to the man:*

[51] Cf. Egbert, 3.

7.

N., say after me:
N., with this ring I wed you,
with this money I endow you,
and with my body I honor you.
To the honor of God,
and of our Lady St. Mary,
and of all holy men and women
and of Monseigneur N.,
here present.

Then the money is put in the bride's purse.

The priest tells the groom to take the rings in the first three digits of his right hand and, taking the bride's right hand, the priest makes the groom repeat after him, on the first finger,

In the name of the Father,

on the second finger,

and of the Son,

on the third finger,

and of the Holy Spirit. Amen.

And on this finger he pu . . .[52]

N., with this ring I wed you,
with my body I honor you,
and I endow you with the dowry
agreed upon by my friends and yours.

And there the ring remains.

7.

*Then the priest stretches his hand over the couple
and says the following prayers:*

The Lord be with you.
Let us pray.
Look down, O Lord . . .[53]

8.

Let us pray.
May the God of Abraham,[54]
the God of Isaac,

---

[52] Rest of the text is missing; the next section is a later insert, down to III.2.
[53] Robert, 12f.
[54] Vich, 1425; Robert, 12e.

the God of Jacob
be with you
and himself join you together,
and may the Lord fill you with his blessing.

9.
Then the priest takes the groom by his right hand and the bride by his left hand and leads them into the church.

And he shall sign them with the sign of the cross, saying: In the name of the Father.

III

1.
Then mass is celebrated.

2.
Before the pax domini *is said, the priest pronounces the following prayers over the couple, who are covered with a veil:*

Let us pray.

3.
Be present . . .[55]

PREFACE

4.
O God, you have made all things . . .[56]
May the peace of the Lord be with you always.
Lamb of God.

5.
Then the bridegroom approaches the priest and receives the pax *from the priest and gives it to the people.*

COMMUNION

6.
We bless the God of heaven
and confess him before all living beings;
for he has dealt with us according to his mercy.

7.
When the celebration of mass is over, the bride and groom leave.

---

[55] Greg, 5.
[56] Greg, 6.

IV

1.
They stand before the door of their house holding bread and wine and the priest pronounces the following blessing over the bread:

Bless, O Lord, this creature, bread,
just as you blessed
the five loaves in the wilderness;
may all who eat thereof
receive health of mind and body.
In the name of the Father.

Then the groom bites off a piece of bread.
The bride does the same.

BLESSING OVER THE WINE

2.
May the king of angels
bless the drink of his servants;
in the name of the Father.

Then the groom drinks.
The bride does the same.

3.
When this is done, the priest takes them by the hand and leads them into the house, saying:

In the name of the Father.

A BLESSING OF THE NUPTIAL CHAMBER IN THE EVENING

4.
Bless, O Lord, this marriage chamber . . .[57]

---

[57] Bury St. Edmunds, IV, 3.

20. THE SARUM MANUAL

The rite of the church of Sarum (Salisbury) was widely used in England and was influential beyond the British Isles. The text given here was printed in 1543 and can serve as an example of the way marriage rites looked on the eve of the Reformation. Like other fifteenth-century manuals from the British Isles, it reveals how the Anglo-Norman structures for public betrothal and public exchange of marital consent had now been elaborated into a rich vernacular ceremony of consent. The merging of betrothal and marriage has led to a double asseveration: a passive formula of consent ("Wilt thou have this woman to wife . . .?") and an active marriage vow ("I, N., take thee, N. . . ."), the latter in the blank-verse now familiar all over the English-speaking world.

The whole ritual takes place in the course of one day, being broken up into a series of stations, beginning at the door of the church. There the couple are met by the priest who proclaims the banns of matrimony for the last time (I.1–I.2). If no one objects, he then proceeds to elicit the free consent of the man and the woman (I.3). Then the marriage vows are exchanged (I.4), still outside the church, and the ring is blessed and given, with gold and silver coins, to the woman by her new husband (I.6a-h). There follows a procession into the church (II.1). It halts before the entrance to the choir, where a series of blessings are spoken over bride and groom (II.2a-g). This done, bride and groom are led to their places, on the right side of the space between the altar and the choir (II.3), where they hear the first part of the Mass (III.1). Throughout the canon of the Mass and the nuptial blessing—in its by now familiar place before Communion—the couple lie prostrate on the floor in front of the altar, with a veil held over them by four clerics (III.5b-6e). Finally, the Mass over, the couple repair to their new home for the wedding feast. A formula is provided for the blessing of bread and wine (IV.1) and, later, for the blessing of the bridal chamber and the bed (IV.2).

Unlike the Ritual or the Pontifical, which are strictly liturgical books, the Manual contains a great deal of commentary on the rites relating both to their execution and to their meaning. While the most important directives are reproduced here, some passages, indicated by square brackets, have been paraphrased. Furthermore, where Sarum indicates that the vernacular is to be used, but gives only a Latin text, the English text given in the

York Manual of the same period has been used where appropriate.

TEXT

A. Jefferies Collins, ed., *Manuale ad usum percelebris ecclesiae sarisburiensis.* Henry Bradshaw Society, v. 91. London, 1960, 44–59.

BIBLIOGRAPHY

Stevenson, 1982:79–81.

THE MARRIAGE SERVICE[58]

I

1.
To begin, the man and the woman are positioned in front of the door of the church, before God, the priest and the people, the man to the woman's right, the woman to the man's left.

It should be known that, although betrothal may be celebrated at any time—and the same holds good for marriage that is contracted privately by consent alone—nonetheless, the handing over of wives and the solemnization of marriage are prohibited at certain times; namely: from the Advent of the Lord to the octave of Epiphany, from Septuagesima to the octave of Easter, from Sunday before the Ascension of the Lord to the octave of Pentecost. On the octave day of Epiphany, however, marriage may lawfully be celebrated, for there is no prohibition then, although there is for the octave of Easter. Likewise, on the Sunday following the feast of Pentecost nuptials are lawful, since Pentecost does not have an octave day.

Then the priest calls the banns, speaking in the mother tongue as follows:[59]

2.
Lo, brethren, we are comen here
before God and his angels and all his halowes,
in the face and presence of our moder holy Chyrche,
for to couple and to knyt these two bodyes togyder,

---

[58] *Ordo ad faciendum sponsalia.* Literally, "Service of Betrothal," but by this time *sponsalia* had long since been used to mean marriage.

[59] The Sarum Manual gives the text in Latin; this translation is taken from the York Manual (London: Henry Bradshaw Society, 1875).

that is to saye, of this man and of this woman,
that they be from this tyme forth
but one body and two soules
in the faythe and lawe of God and holy Chyrche,
for to deserve everlastynge lyfe,
what soever that they have done here before.

I therefore admonish you
that if any of you have anything to say
why these young people
should not be joined lawfully together,
let him now speak.

*. . . And if anyone wishes to allege an impediment and there seems reason to investigate it, the marriage (*sponsalia*) should be postponed until the truth is known. But if no impediment is alleged, the priest should enquire after the woman's dowry, namely the sponsal arrhas. The arrhas are the rings or coins or other goods given to the bride by the groom. . . .*[60]

3.
Then the priest shall say to the man in the hearing of all, using the mother tongue:[61]

N., wylt thou haue this woman to thy wyfe
and loue her and wirschipe her and keep her,
in sykenes and in helthe,
and in all other degrees
be to her as a husband should be to his wyfe,
and all other forsake for her,
and holde the only to her to thy lyues ende.

The man shall respond in this way:

I wyll.

Again the priest addresses the bride as follows:

N., wylt thou haue this man to thy husbande,
and to be buxum[62] to hym,
luf hym, obey to hym, and wirschipe hym,
serue hym and kepe hym in syknes and in helthe,
and in all other degrees
be unto hym as a wyfe should be to her husbande,

---

[60] Extensive canonical regulations follow relating to the reading of the banns and to the penalties incurred by priests who assist at clandestine marriages.

[61] English text from York Manual.

[62] Obedient, compliant.

and all other to forsake for hym,
and holde the only to hym to thy lyues ende.

The woman shall respond in this way:

I wyll.

4.
Then the woman is given by her father or by a friend. If she is a maiden, her hand is bare; if a widow, she keeps it gloved. The man takes her hand, to hold in faith to God and to her, as he has vowed before the priest, and he holds her by the right hand in his right hand. And then the man pledges his troth to the woman with words de presenti, *saying after the priest:*

I, N., take the, N.,
to my weddyd wyfe,
to haue and to holde
(from this day forward),
for better for wurs,
for rycher for porer,
in syckenes and in helthe
tyll deth us departe
(yf holy Chyrche will it ordeyn),
and therto I plyght the my trouth.

He withdraws his hand.

Then the woman says after the priest:

I, N., take the, N.,
to my weddyd husbande,
to haue and to holde
(from this day forward),
for better for wurs,
for rycher for porer,
in syckenes and in helthe,
to be bonoure and buxum,[63]
in bed and at borde,
tyll deth us depart
(yf holy Chyrche will it ordeyn)
and thereto I plyght the my trouth.

She withdraws her hand.

5.
Then the groom puts gold or silver and a ring on a dish or book. And

---

[63] To be agreeable and compliant.

then the priest asks whether the ring was previously blessed or not; if
the answer is that it was not, then he blesses the ring as follows:

The Lord be with you.
And also with you.

Let us pray:
Eternal God,[64]
creator and sustainer of the human race,
giver of spiritual grace
and bestower of eternal salvation,
send your blessing upon this ring +;
may she who wears it
be armed with the strength of heavenly protection
and may it profit her unto eternal salvation.
Through.
Amen.

Let us pray:
Bless, O Lord, this ring,[65]
which we bless in your holy name.
May she who wears it be kept in your peace
and remain in your will
and live and increase and grow old in your love
and be multiplied unto length of days.
Through.

Then the ring is sprinkled with holy water. . . .

6a

If the ring had been blessed previously, the priest picks up the ring as
soon as the groom has placed it on the book and gives it back to the
groom. The groom takes it in the three main fingers of his right hand,
holding the bride's right hand with his left. Following the priest, he
says:

6b

With this rynge I the wed
and this gold and silver I the geve;
and with my body I the worshipe,
and with all my worldely cathel I the endowe.

6c

Then the groom puts the ring on the finger of the bride, saying:

---

[64] See Robert, 12b.
[65] See Robert, 12a.

In the name of the Father,

at the first finger,

and of the Son,

at the second,

and of the Holy Spirit,

at the third, and

Amen

at the fourth, and there he leaves it; for in that finger there is a vein which runs to the heart; and the clink of coins signifies interior love which is always to be fresh between them.

6d
Then, as they bow their heads, the priest pronounces a blessing over them:

May you be blessed by the Lord
who made the world out of nothing.
Amen.

6e
Then the following psalm is said:[66]

Send, O Lord, your power;
confirm, O God, what you have wrought among us.
From your holy temple which is in Jerusalem;
there kings offer you gifts.
Put down the beasts of the reeds;
may the assembly of bulls
among the cows of the peoples
keep afar off those
who have been tested by money.
Glory be.
As it was.

6f
Kyrie eleison.
Christe eleison.
Kyrie eleison.
Our Father . . .
And lead us not into temptation.
But deliver us from evil.

[66] Ps 67:29-31. See Robert, 12a.

Let us bless the Father, the Son, and the Holy Spirit.
Let us praise and exalt him for ever.
Let us praise the Lord the angels praise.
To whom cherubim and seraphim cry,
"Holy, holy, holy."
Lord, hear my prayer.
And let my cry come unto you.
The Lord be with you.
And also with you.

6g

Let us pray:
May the God of Abraham,[67]
the God of Isaac,
and the God of Jacob
be with you
and join you together
and fill you with his blessing.
Who lives and reigns with God the Father
in the unity of the Holy Spirit
one God for ever and ever.
Amen.

6h

Another prayer.

Let us pray:
May God the Father + bless you;[68]
may Jesus Christ keep you;
may the Holy Spirit illuminate you;
may the Lord show his face to you
and be merciful to you;
may he turn his countenance towards you
and give you peace;
may he fill you with every spiritual blessing
for the forgiveness of your sins,
that you may have eternal life
and live unto ages of ages.
Amen.

[67] See Tobit 7:15; Robert, 12e.

[68] A common version of the Aaronic blessing adapted for marriage. See Egbert, 1a.

II

1.

Here they enter into the church, going as far as the altar steps. The priest, accompanied by his ministers, says the following psalm as he enters,

Blessed are those who fear the Lord . . .
. . . and on Israel peace. [Ps 127]
Glory be. As it was.

without music, followed by

Kyrie eleison.
Christe eleison.
Kyrie eleison.

2.

Then, with the bride and groom prostrate before the altar steps, the priest invites the congregation to pray for them, saying:

2a
Our Father.
Lead us not into temptation.
But deliver us from evil.
Save your servant and your handmaid,
who put their trust in you, my God.
Lord, send them help from your holy place.
And defend them out of Sion.
Be a tower of strength to them, O Lord.
In the face of the enemy.
Lord, hear my prayer.
And let my cry come to you.
The Lord be with you.
And also with you.

2b
Let us pray:
May the Lord bless you from Sion,
that you may see the good things of Jerusalem
all the days of your life;
may you see your children's children
and peace upon Israel.[69]
Through Christ.

[69] Ps 127:5-6.

2c
Let us pray:
God of Abraham . . .[70]

2d
Let us pray:
Look down, O Lord . . .[71]

2e
Let us pray:
Look down with mercy, Lord,
upon your servant and your maidservant.
May they receive the blessing of heaven +
in your name;
may they be kept hale
to see the children of their sons and daughters
to the third and fourth generation;
may they ever persevere in your will
and in the future come to share
in the heavenly kingdom.
Through.

2f
Let us pray:
May the almighty, everlasting God . . .[72]

2g
Then he blesses them, saying:

Let us pray:
May almighty God bless you +
with every heavenly blessing;
may he make you both worthy in his sight;
may he lavish the riches of his glory upon you;
may he instruct you with the word of truth,
that you may be pleasing to him
both in body and in mind.
Amen.

3.
*After the prayers, which are said over the couple as they lie prostrate
at the altar steps, the couple is led into the presbyterium, viz., be-*

---

[70] Egbert, 5a.
[71] Egbert, 5b.
[72] Robert, 9.

tween the choir and the altar on the south side of the church. The woman stands to the right of the man, between him and the altar.

III

THE SERVICE BEGINS[73]

1.

Blessed be the Holy Trinity and Undivided Unity:
let us praise him,
for he has shown us his mercy.
In Paschaltide the antiphon ends with
Alleluia alleluia.
Psalm: We bless the Father and the Son
with the Holy Spirit. *No more is said.*

Kyrie *is said with its verses. At this Mass, all is done as on doubles of the first class, as follows:*

Gloria in excelsis.

2.

The following two collects are said under one Oremus *and one* Per Dominum.

2a

Almighty and everlasting God
you have granted your servants
by profession of the true faith
to acknowledge the glory of the eternal trinity;
and in the power of your divine majesty
to worship the unity;
we pray that
by remaining firm in that faith
we might be protected against all adversity.

2b

Hear us . . . .[74]

3a

To the Corinthians: Brethren, do you not know that your bodies are members of Christ? . . . Glorify and bear God in your body. [I Cor 6:15-20]

---

[73] *Incipiatur officium.* The Mass is that of Trinity Sunday. The divine unity and self-giving of the three Persons are presumably what inspired this common medieval practice.

[74] Greg, 1.

3b

Graduale: Blessed are you, Lord, who gaze into the depths and who are seated above the cherubim.

Verse: Bless the God of heaven, who has dealt with us according to his mercy.

The gradual is not repeated at Nuptial Masses.

Alleluia.

Verse: Blessed are you, Lord, God of our ancestors, and worthy of praise for ever.[75]

3c

According to Matthew: At that time, the scribes and pharisees came to Jesus . . . What therefore God has joined together let no one put asunder. [Matt 19:3-6]

3d
Credo

4. OFFERTORY

4a

Blessed be God the Father
and his only-begotten Son
and the Holy Spirit,
for he has shown us his mercy. *P.T.* Alleluia!

4b

The odor of blessed incense is never offered to bride and groom in the church. Thus, after the gifts on the altar have been incensed, fresh incense must be put in if the thurible is taken to the clergy and laity.

OVER THE GIFTS

4c

Holy Trinity, Lord, our God,
sanctify the offering of this oblation
by the invocation of your holy name
so that, with the help of the Holy Spirit,
we who offer might ourselves become
an everlasting gift to you.

---

[75] The text gives a series of alternative Alleluia verses for use in paschaltide, plus a sequence (hymn) celebrating the divine names. Both belong to the Mass of the Trinity rather than to the celebration of marriage.

4d
Be present, O Lord, to our prayers.[76]
Accept with pleasure and kindness
the gift we offer for your servants,
whom you have deigned
to bring to the state of maturity
and to the day of marriage.
Through Christ.

5a PREFACE [OF THE TRINITY]

5b
After the Sanctus, *the couple prostrate themselves at the foot of the altar steps, and the veil is spread over them. It is held by four clerics dressed in surplices, one at each corner. Unless one or both of them have been married before and received the blessing. In that case, the veil is not held over them and the blessing is not given.*

6a
Then, following the Per omnia saecula saeculorum, *after the* Our Father *and before the* Pax Domini *is said, the priest breaks the host as usual and lays the three pieces on the paten. Then he turns to the couple, kneeling under the veil, and pronounces the following prayers over them, in the reading tone.*

6b
The Lord be with you.
And also with you.

Let us pray:
Be present . . . .[77]

6c
O God, you made all things . . . .[78]

6d
The section, O God, you have consecrated the bond of marriage *down to* God, through you a woman is joined to her husband, *is omitted in second marriages. A man or woman marrying for a second time should not be blessed again by a priest; since they were blessed before, the blessing should not be repeated; for the flesh which is blessed draws unto itself the flesh which is not blessed.*

---

[76] Cf. Gel, 3.
[77] Gel, 3.
[78] Greg, 6.

It should be noted that the Capitulum extra *on second marriages prohibits the giving of the blessing in second marriages. This is what Ambrose says:* First marriages are instituted by the Lord; second marriages are merely permitted. First marriages are celebrated with every blessing; second marriages without any blessing. *But since there are many blessings in the celebration of marriage, viz., at the entrance to the choir, under the veil, after Mass, and later over the marriage bed, I wonder which blessing should be repeated at a second marriage and which not.*

The answer is that in the prayer O God, you have made all things, *there are three clauses which begin in the same way, with O, God. The middle one is entirely to be omitted in second marriages, viz.,* O God, you have consecrated the bond of marriage . . ., *for this blessing focuses on the unity of Christ and his Church, which is represented in first marriages, but not in second. . . .[79]*

Here it might be asked why second marriages are not blessed. To this I say that while second marriage, considered in itself, is a complete sacrament, nevertheless, when compared with first marriage, it is somewhat defective sacramentally, for it does not bear the fulness of meaning since it is not one to one, as is the marriage of Christ and the Church. Because of this defect, the nuptial blessing is not given. This holds whenever it is a second marriage for both the man and the woman, or even just for the woman. But if a virgin married a man previously married, the marriage would nevertheless be blessed. For in this case the signification is to some extent safeguarded, even in reference to first marriage. For a bishop, though married to one Church, has nevertheless many persons to whom he is espoused in that one Church. But the soul can have no other spouse than Christ, for that would be to fornicate with demons and would not be a spiritual marriage. For this reason, when a woman marries for the second time, the marriage is not blessed on account of the defect in the sacrament.

6e

After these things, the priest turns back to the altar and says the Pax Domini *and* Agnus Dei *in the usual way. Then, the veil being removed, the bride and groom arise from their prayer. The groom receives the* pax *from the priest and takes it to his bride, kissing her. But neither of them kiss anyone else, but a cleric, receiving the* pax *from the priest, takes it to the others, as is the custom.*

---

[79] A large section of this discussion on second marriages is omitted here, including a decree of John XXII which is cited at length.

COMMUNION

7.
We bless the God of heaven
and confess him before all living things,
for he has shown his mercy towards us.
P.T. Alleluia, alleluia!

POSTCOMMUNION

8a
May the reception of this sacrament, Lord,
profit us in health of body and soul,
and the confession of the eternal holy Trinity
and the same undivided Unity.

8b
We beseech you . . . .[80]

IV

1.
*After Mass, bread and wine, or other drink in a cup, are blessed, and
they drink in the name of the Lord, as the priest says:*

The Lord be with you.
And also with you.

Let us pray:
Lord, bless this bread
and this drink
and this cup,
as you blessed the five loaves in the wilderness
and the six water pots at Cana of Galilee,
so that those who drink thereof
may be healthy, sober and free from sin,
O Redeemer of the world,
who live and reign with God the Father
in the unity of the Holy Spirit.

2.
*The night following, when the bride and groom have gone to bed, the
priest should come and bless the marriage chamber, saying:*

The Lord be with you.
And also with you.

[80] Greg, 11.

2a

Let us pray:

Bless, O Lord, this marriage chamber . . . .[81]

ANOTHER BLESSING OF THE MARRIAGE BED

The Lord be with you.
And also with you.

2b

Let us pray:

O God, who neither sleep nor slumber,
bless this bed chamber;
you who watch over Israel,
watch over your servants
as they sleep in this bed,
protecting them from all demonic dreams;
watch over them while they are awake,
that they might meditate on your law;
watch over them while they are asleep
that even sleeping they may know your presence;
here and everywhere
may they enjoy the help of your protection.
Through.

Then this blessing is said over them in bed:

2c

The Lord be with you.
And also with you.

    Let us pray:

i   May God bless + your bodies and your souls,
    and confer his blessing upon you
    as he did on Abraham, Isaac and Jacob.
    Amen.

    Let us pray:

ii   May the hand of the Lord be upon you
    and may he send his holy angel
    to guard you all the days of your life.
    Amen.

[81] Bury St Edmunds, IV.3.

Let us pray:
iii **May Father, Son and Holy Spirit + bless you,**
three in number,
one in name.
Amen.

2d
After all this, the priest sprinkles them with holy water. Then he leaves and dismisses them in peace.

21. MISSALE ROMANUM (1570)

In December 1563, the Council of Trent, already in process for nearly twenty years, decided that it could not itself undertake the task of reforming the liturgical books of the Western churches in communion with Rome, so it handed the task over to the pope. Five years later, the revised Roman Breviary appeared and, in 1570, the Missal. However, the Missal only contained the texts used in the celebration of the Mass. For the revised marriage rite, Catholics had to wait until the new Ritual was published in 1614.

Thus the contracting of marriage was separated from its solemnization: the order for the former being found in the Ritual, while the Mass and nuptial blessing were contained in the Missal. The two dimensions of the rite were frequently separated in practice, since marriages contracted in the "closed seasons" and marriages in which one partner was not a Catholic or where the woman was marrying for the second time could not be "solemnized" and were celebrated without Mass or without the blessing.

Nonetheless, the Council of Trent did more for marriage than order a revision of the rites. A major preoccupation of the Council was with the social mischief created by clandestine marriages, i.e. marriages entered into simply through the couple's exchange of consent, without public ceremony. Such was the concern of the Council that it took the unprecedented step of declaring such marriages simply void and invalid, despite the long history of the axiom that "consent makes marriage." One of the consequences of this was that Catholic marriages, to be considered valid, had to be celebrated now in the presence of a priest and in accordance with ecclesiastical law. Consequently, while we can never be quite sure whether ordinary people were wedded ceremoniously with the rites we have seen so far, it is certain that from the sixteenth century, all marriages took place in church, with or without the nuptial Mass.

The text of the Wedding Mass is characteristic of the Tridentine Missal in that it is not at all innovative. It approximates to many local missals of the fifteenth and sixteenth centuries, but is relatively simple and sober. The Gregorian Mass formularies stand alone, no longer accompanied by the various non-Roman texts that had continued to cluster around them throughout the Middle Ages, though the old Spanish prayer, "May the God of

Abraham,"[1] is retained for a final blessing of the couple at the end of Mass. Fortunately, instead of the Mass of the Trinity which was so common in the Middle Ages, the Roman Missal opted to reclaim the proper texts for the Mass for Bride and Groom from the twelfth century Roman Pontifical.

TEXT

Missale Romanum ex decreto sacrosancti concilii tridentini restitutum . . . Turin, 1952.

BIBLIOGRAPHY

Stevenson, 1982:169–172.

INTROIT

1.
May the God of Israel join you together,[2]
and may he be with you
who was merciful to two only children;
and now, O Lord,
make them bless you more and more.

Blessed are they who fear the Lord;
who walk in his ways.
V. Glory be to the Father.

May the God of Israel . . .

COLLECT

2.
Hear us . . .[3]

EPISTLE

3.
Ephesians 5:22-33

---

[1] See Tob 7:15; Robert, 12e; Vich, 1425.
[2] Cf. Vich, 1408.
[3] Greg, 1.

GRADUAL

4a

Your wife shall be like a fruitful vine
on the walls of your house. [Ps 127]
V. Your children like olive plants
around your table.
Alleluia, alleluia!
May the Lord send you help from his holy place,
and defend you out of Sion. [Ps 19:3]
Alleluia!

TRACT, AFTER SEPTUAGESIMA

4b

Thus shall be blessed every man
who fears the Lord. [Ps 127:4-6]
V. May the Lord bless you out of Sion;
and may you see the good things of Jerusalem
all the days of your life.
V. And may you see your children's children.
On Israel peace.

4c

P.T. Alleluia, alleluia!
May the Lord send you help from his holy place,
and defend you out of Sion. [Ps 19:3]
Alleluia!
May the Lord bless you from Sion,
he who made heaven and earth. [Ps 133:3]
Alleluia!

GOSPEL

5.
Matthew 19:3-6

OFFERTORY

6.
In you, O Lord, have I hoped.
I said, You are my God,
my times are in your hands. [Ps 30:15-16]
(P.T. Alleluia.)

OVER THE GIFTS

7.
Receive, we beseech you . . .[4]

8.
Following the Pater noster, *and before he says the* Libera nos
quaesumus, *the priest stands on the Epistle side of the altar and
faces the bride and groom, who kneel before the altar, and he says the
following blessings over them:*

Be present . . .[5]

9.
O God, you have made all things . . .[6]

10.
Then the priest returns to the middle of the altar and says the Libera
nos *and the rest as usual. After he has received the Blood, he shall
give Communion to the couple; and the Mass continues.*

COMMUNION

11.
Behold, thus shall be blessed
every man who fears the Lord;
and you shall see your children's children.
Peace upon Israel.

POSTCOMMUNION

12.
We beseech you . . .[7]

13.
After saying Benedicamus Domino *or, if appropriate for the Mass of
the day,* Ite missa est, *the priest turns to the bride and groom before
blessing the people and says:*

May the God of Abraham,
the God of Isaac
and the God of Jacob
be with you
and may he fulfill his blessing in you,[8]

---

[4] Greg, 2.
[5] Gel, 3.
[6] Greg, 6-10.
[7] Greg, 11.
[8] Robert, 12e.

that you may see your children's children
even to the third and fourth generation;
and afterwards may you enjoy
eternal life without end;
with the help of our Lord Jesus Christ,
who lives.

14.

Then let the priest warn them seriously that they are to remain faith-
ful to one another and to observe continence in times of prayer and,
especially, of fasting, and on solemnities; that the man is to love his
wife and the woman her husband; and that they should remain in the
fear of God. Thereafter he sprinkles them with holy water and, having
said the Placeat tibi, sancta Trinitas, *he gives the blessing.*

Then he reads the Gospel of John, In principio erat verbum, *as is*
customary.

22. RITUALE ROMANUM (1614)

The Council of Trent seems to have had two goals where marriage was concerned: to ensure its public celebration out of respect for the social character of marriage, and to secure its reverent celebration out of respect for its sacramental character. The result was a series of prescriptions concerning the publication of banns, marriage before the church in the presence of the parish priest, the ascertaining of the couple's consent to the marriage, and the exchange of vows in the presence of the priest. In addition, the priest was to seal the marriage with a formula such as "I join you together in matrimony . . ." (from Rouen, fourteenth-fifteenth cent.) or some local equivalent. Records of all marriages were to be kept in parish churches. Moreover, the couple were exhorted not to live together before marriage, but to confess their sins and to receive the Eucharist three days before the wedding, or at least three days before they consummated their marriage.[9]

However, the Council of Trent, in a note reproduced in the Roman Ritual itself, stated that "if any provinces have herein any praiseworthy customs and ceremonies besides the aforesaid, the holy Synod earnestly (*vehementer*) desires that they be by all means retained."[10] Given this option, and given the extreme spareness of the service provided in the Ritual, what we have here is less a nuptial liturgy than a formula for ensuring that all the conditions for a clearly valid marriage are met, and one must doubt that it was ever intended to be used as it stood. Indeed, the use of the Ritual itself, unlike the other liturgical books, was not originally mandatory, but was merely to serve as a model for reform of local rites. Where it was eventually adopted in place of customary forms of marriage, there was considerable impoverishment, but the *Rituale Romanum* did not begin to supplant local rituals on any scale until the second half of the nineteenth century. Even then many local communities, such as Roman Catholics in England, continued to follow their own traditional rites of marriage into which the Roman requirements were simply incorporated.

TEXT

Rituale Romanum Pauli V pontificis maximi iussu editum . . . Rome, 1847.

[9] Trent, session 24, ch. 1.
[10] *Ibid.*

BIBLIOGRAPHY

Stevenson, 1982:169–172; 1987:99–102.

Pierce J. "A Note on the *Ego vos conjungo*," *Ephemerides liturgicae* 99 (1985) 290–299.

Duval, A. "La formule *Ego vos conjungo* au Concile de Trente," *La Maison-Dieu* 99 (1969) 144–153.

Fischer, B. "Das Rituale Romanum (1614–1964): Die Schicksal eines liturgischen Buches," *Trierer Theol. Zeitschrift* 73 (1964) 5, 257–271.

RITE FOR THE CELEBRATION OF THE SACRAMENT OF MATRIMONY

1.

After publishing the banns on three feast days, as aforesaid, and if no lawful impediment stands in the way, the parish priest who is to celebrate the marriage, being vested in surplice and white stole and attended by at least one cleric likewise vested in a surplice and carrying the book and the vessel of holy water with its sprinkler, shall, in the presence of two or three witnesses, in the church, ask the man and the woman separately, preferably in the presence of their parents or relatives, the question about their consent to the marriage, using the vernacular tongue and the following form:

N., will you take N.,
here present,
to be your lawful wife,
according to the rite of holy mother Church?

The bridegroom answers:

I will.

Then the priest asks the bride:

N., will you take N.,
here present,
to be your lawful husband,
according to the rite of holy mother Church?

The bride answers:

I will.

The consent of one does not suffice; it must be of both. And it must be expressed in some sensible sign, either by the parties themselves or through an intermediary.

2.

Having understood the mutual consent of the parties, the priest orders them to join their right hands, saying:

I join you in matrimony,
in the name of the Father +
and of the Son
and of the Holy Spirit.

Or other words may be used according to the received rite of each province. Afterwards, he sprinkles them with holy water.

3.

Then he blesses the ring.

BLESSING OF THE RING

V. Our help is in the name of the Lord.
R. Who made heaven and earth.
V. Lord, hear my prayer.
R. And let my cry come to you.
V. The Lord be with you.
R. And also with you.

Let us pray:
  Bless +, O Lord,
  this ring which we bless + in your name,[11]
  so that she who shall wear it,
  remaining totally faithful to her husband,
  may remain in peace and in your will,
  and live always in mutual charity.
  Through Christ, etc.

Then the priest sprinkles the ring with holy water in the form of a cross.

4.

Receiving the ring from the priest's hand, the bridegroom places it on the ring finger of his bride's left hand, while the priest says:

In the name of the Father +,
and of the Son, and of the Holy Spirit.
Amen.

5.

Then he adds:

V. Confirm, O God, what you have wrought among us.

[11] See Robert, 12a.

R. From your holy temple, which is in Jerusalem.
    Kyrie eleison.
    Christe eleison.
    Kyrie eleison.
    Our Father. *silently*
V. And lead us not into temptation.
R. But deliver us from evil.
V. Save your servants.
R. Who put their trust in you, my God.
V. Lord, send them help from your holy place.
R. And defend them out of Sion.
V. Be a tower of strength to them, O Lord.
R. In the face of the enemy.
V. Lord, hear my prayer.
R. And let my cry come to you.
V. The Lord be with you.
R. And also with you.

Let us pray:
Look down, we beseech you, O Lord,[12]
upon these your servants,
and graciously assist this ordinance of yours,
which you have provided
for the propagation of the human race;
that those who are joined together
by your authority
may be preserved by your help.
Through Christ our Lord.
Amen.

6.
When all this is done, and if the marriage is to be blessed, the parish priest celebrates the Mass for Bride and Groom, as found in the Roman Missal, observing everything prescribed there.

7.
Moreover, if, besides the above, some provinces are accustomed to using other laudable customs and ceremonies in the celebration of the sacrament of matrimony, the holy Council of Trent desires that they should be retained.

8.
When everything has been completed, the parish priest enters in the register of marriages, in his own hand, the names of the couple, of the

[12] See Ver, 5.

witnesses and the other things required; and that he, or some other priest delegated either by him or by the ordinary, has celebrated the marriage.

23. RITUAL OF COUTANCES

A visitor to Châlons-sur-Marne in the winter of 1609–1610 noted in his journal that, "I see in this town that the marriage customs are different from those of our own region for, one must understand, the Council of Trent has not yet been promulgated by the bishops in many areas of France, as a result of which it is not followed on all points." Such diversity continued to be characteristic of liturgical life in France in the seventeenth and eighteenth centuries, but, as the disciplinary decrees of Trent came to be incorporated into local rituals in diocesan reforms, the result was the kind of ritual of which that of the diocese of Coutances is a fine example.

This rite for betrothal and marriage reflects many of the characteristics of eighteenth century Catholic life in France. It is marked by a new concern about legal niceties, characteristic of the Catholic Counter-Reformation, as well as a profound seriousness about the dignity and sanctity of the Christian vocation. These are overlaid on what is still fundamentally a medieval rite, with its separate rite of betrothal (falling into desuetude in eighteenth century France), its marriage rite with the blessing of rings and coins and the exchange of vows, its nuptial mass and blessing (with the rite of legitimation following the final blessing!), and its provision still for the blessing of the nuptial chamber. The appended rite for freeing the couple from the curse of infertility witnesses to the shadow side of rural Christianity in this period, its preoccupation with witchcraft, a preoccupation which the Church, judging by the restrictive guidelines, was attempting to keep under control.

Nonetheless, it is the moral seriousness of these rites, rather than their consciousness of the demonic or their canonical rigor or their theological depth, which is their hallmark. The model exhortations, reproduced here in full, nicely capture the spirit of the age and the reforming emphasis upon the sanctity of the married state and upon the seriousness of the Christian call to holiness.

TEXT

Rituale Constatiense. Paris: Typis J.-B. Coignard, 1744.

BIBLIOGRAPHY

Brooks-Leonard, J. K. "Another Look at Gallican Reform: A Comparison of Marriage Rites in Coutances." *Ephemerides liturgicae* 98 (1984), 458–485.

Paris, C. B. *Marriage in XVIIth Century Catholicism.* Tournai: Desclée [Montreal: Bellarmin], 1975.

Stevenson, 1982:173–175.

I

ORDER FOR THE CELEBRATION OF BETROTHAL[13]

1.

Those who are to be betrothed by a promise of future marriage come to the parish church and there take their place before the parish priest or vicar or other priest delegated by the parish priest in the nave or other public place in the church. There the pastor, vicar, or other priest, wearing surplice and white stole and accompanied by a cleric or other server carrying holy water and an aspergille, calls those present to order, if necessary, and then prays with all the others for a while in silence. Then he rises up and turns to those to be betrothed, the man facing him on the left, the woman on the right. He questions them without using any titles when he mentions their names, no matter what their exalted status.

First he says to each of them:

P.   What is your name?

Then, having established their names, he asks with head covered:

P.   N. and N.,
        do you swear and promise to God
        to tell the truth concerning the matters
        about which I am going to question you?

Each of them responds:
        Yes, Monsieur, I swear and promise.

P.   Do you profess the Catholic,
        apostolic and Roman faith and religion,
        and is it your intention to live and die in it,
        so help you God?
R.   Yes, Monsieur.

---

[13] *Ordo Celebrandi Sponsalia.*

(P. Are you from this parish and, if so, since when? This question can be omitted when the parish priest knows them to be his parishioners.)

P. Are you sure there is no lawful impediment which would render you incapable of promising yourselves to each other in marriage?

R. Yes, Monsieur.

P. Are you sure you are not bound by any vow of religion, chastity or continence, or any vow not to marry?

R. Yes, Monsieur.

P. Are you sure you are not already married or related in those degrees of affinity or consanguinity within which marriage is forbidden?

R. Yes, Monsieur.

The parish priest should not ask the following questions unless, in his prudent judgement, they need to be posed to those to be betrothed.

P: Are you sure there is no spiritual bond between you, i.e., that neither of you baptized the other, nor stood as godparent for the other or stood as godparent for the other's child?

R. Yes, Monsieur.

P. Are your fathers and mothers, or your guardians, or other persons in whose custody you belong, in agreement and do they consent to your betrothal?

R. Yes, Monsieur.

P. Do you come here entirely of your own free will, not compelled by threat, violence or authority?

R. Yes, Monsieur.

2.

If the priest discovers any impediment to marriage, he may not proceed further. If not, he continues; and in order to avoid any profanation of marriage, which the Apostle calls a great sacrament, in the name of the Lord Bishop he commands both the couple and the witnesses to speak up immediately if they know of any impediment or have even the least suspicion of such, under pain of excommunication. He must indicate particularly that those who contract marriage while knowing there to be an impediment are ipso facto *excommunicated and must remain excommunicate as long as they continue in the unlawful union.*

3.

*After giving this warning, and if no impediment is brought to his at-
tention, he may give a brief sermon to those to be betrothed concerning
the institution of marriage, its dignity, holiness, and the goods of marriage, and about the obligations arising from betrothal. He should also
enjoin upon them that they live piously and chastely throughout the
whole period of their betrothal, as befits the children of saints; nor
should they live together under the same roof until they are lawfully
joined in wedlock. Finally, they should beseech God's mercy that their
future marriage might be a happy one.*

*Bearing in mind their condition and state of life, he may address
them in these or similar words:*

EXHORTATION

3a

The rite of betrothal has been established in the Church to prepare the faithful for the blessings which Jesus Christ has attached to the sacrament of matrimony. Would it be proper,
then, to rush haphazardly into a state of life which can never
be a happy one without the call and grace of our Lord? Christian marriage is not something indifferent or profane, that God
and the Church should take no interest in it. Earthly advan-
tages can be left to children by those who brought them into
the world, but God alone can give one a prudent wife and ar-
range for a virtuous spouse. And they will be happy in their
marriage if God presides over it, if God blesses it, if God
sanctifies it.

You, N. and N., can promise yourselves such happiness if
you are as wise as the couple mentioned in the Gospel and also
invite Jesus Christ to your wedding and ask him himself to
marry you. Earn this privilege by your fervent prayers, by
generous almsgiving, by frequenting the sacraments. Meditate
before God upon the duties of the state of life you are choos-
ing, and remind yourselves that the children of saints must
marry in other wise than those who know not the Lord. That is
to say, you must be united in your Christian outlook and intend to live a pure and edifying life in marriage, so that you
never misuse a sacrament intended for the sanctification of
souls and so that you fulfill your obligations worthily and never
have to ward off the dangers of marriage which, like its obligations, have infinite consequences for the salvation of your souls
once they are seen, not from the perspective of the ways of the

world, but in the light of the correct ideas which Christianity proposes to us.

OR

3b

The ceremony we are about to celebrate is not a sacrament. The Church has instituted it as a preparation for holy matrimony; a preparation both holy and respectable, and which confers the blessing of heaven on the promises you are about to make to each other. These promises cannot be broken, except for just and lawful reasons. These promises will bind you before the eyes of God as well as in human eyes, yet they do not permit you to live together without further ado. On the contrary, just as you must not receive the sacrament of matrimony unless you are in a state of grace, so these promises will remind you to live with even greater circumspection and blamelessness until the time of marriage. And then you will merit, by your holy dispositions, all the temporal and spiritual blessings you need for the state of life you are entering. Take care, then, in the little time that remains before your wedding, to avoid anything which might be contrary to chastity or Christian modesty, for fear of calling down upon yourselves the maledictions of the Lord. Moreover, to avoid the occasions when Satan might overcome you, I forbid you, in the name of the Church, to stay together in the same house. The fruit of your obedience and your holy preparations will be both prosperity for your marriage and eternal happiness in the life to come.

4.

When the exhortation is finished, the priest addresses the man first, without using any honorific title:

P. N., do you promise God before holy Church
that you will take
N. (*name and surname of the woman*), here present,
to be your wife and lawful spouse,
when she will require you
and if holy Mother Church
does not place any impediment in the way?
R. Yes, Monsieur, I promise.

Then the priest says to the woman:

P. N., do you promise God before holy Church
that you will take

N. *(name and surname of the man)*, here present,
to be your husband and lawful spouse,
when he will require you
and if holy Mother Church
does not place any impediment in the way?

R.   Yes, Monsieur, I promise.

5.

After each has given and received the troth, the parish priest tells them to join right hands and, with head uncovered, making the Sign of the Cross at the point indicated, he says:

P.   I betroth you
in the name of the Father
and of the Son +
and of the Holy Spirit.

R.   Amen.

6.

Then he sprinkles them with holy water and, after a short period of prayer, all depart in silence. Betrothals are not to be recorded in the register or records, but they should be mentioned in the Marriage Deed.

II

ORDER FOR THE CELEBRATION OF THE SACRAMENT OF MATRIMONY

1.

At the appointed time (in the morning and not after noon, nor before 4 a.m. in the summer or 6 a.m. in the winter, except by dispensation) the parish priest puts on a surplice and a white stole (or, if the nuptial Mass immediately follows, amice, alb, cincture and white stole, but not the maniple). He is accompanied by a cleric in a surplice, or at least a server, who holds the Ritual and the holy water and aspergille, along with a small dish in which is placed a single ring of gold or silver (without decoration, precious stones, or inscription) and a coin or coins symbolizing the settlement agreed for the bride.

2.

Then the bride and groom, who have previously made their confession and received communion and who are, if possible, fasting, are led solemnly and modestly into the church by the parish priest and his assistants, accompanied by their parents, friends and invited guests of

*both sexes. They proceed to the main entrance to the choir, if there is
a crucifix there, or to the main altar, or to some other altar.*

3.
*The parish priest, in the presence of four witnesses and parents and
friends asks the husband-to-be for the ring and coin(s) which he places
in the above-mentioned dish which the cleric or server holds in front of
the priest. The parish priest stands facing the couple, the man to his
left, the woman to his right, and greets them and the company with a
moderate bow. Then he checks visually, or verbally, if necessary, to be
sure that, if one or both of the parties are minors, the parents or
guardians are present. Then, making the sign of the Cross, he begins:*

P.   In the name of the Father . . .

4.
Then the ring and coin(s) are held before him to be blessed.

BLESSING OF THE RING

4a

P.   Our help is in the name of the Lord.
R.   Who made heaven and earth.
P.   The Lord be with you.
R.   And also with you.
P.   Let us pray:

      Bless, O Lord, this ring[14]
      which we bless in your name,
      that she who wears it,
      being wholly faithful to her husband,
      may abide in your peace and your will
      and live always in mutual love.
      Through Christ our Lord.
R.   Amen.

BLESSING OF A COIN OR COINS

4b

P.   O Lord, sanctify these coins,
      offered as a symbol of the settlement
      which has been agreed.

[14] See Robert, 12a and *Rituale Romanum*, 3.

As the bride has been well settled,
so instruct her also in the ways of heaven.
Through Christ our Lord.

R.   Amen.

4c
*Then the parish priest sprinkles the ring and the coin(s) with holy
water in the sign of the Cross. Baring his head, the priest continues:*

5a

P.   Christian people,
we hereby declare and certify
that the publication of the promise of marriage
between N. and N.,
which we call "banns,"
has been previously carried out
on three different Sundays (or holy days)
in this church (and in the church of N.),
and that no one has raised any objection.
Since the parties are now ready for the next step,
we publish these banns of marriage for the last time.
On behalf of his Lordship the Bishop,
we command you all, under pain of excommunication,
to speak now if you know of any reason
why this marriage may not lawfully be celebrated;
and we likewise forbid you,
under pain of excommunication,
to raise any objection that is baseless or malicious.

5b
*Any diocesan dispensation from impediments, from the banns, or dis-
pensation relating to the time or place of the marriage should be ex-
pressly announced, lest ignorance thereof should give rise to doubt or
scandal.*

5c
*If no one raises any objection, and if the parents, guardians, or other
appropriate persons give their consent—which the parish priest may
prudently require to be expressed anew if one or both of the parties are
minors—the priest uncovers his head and declares as follows:*

P.   There being no impediment,
we beseech the goodness and majesty of God
that he will vouchsafe to ratify and affirm
the holy proposition
which he has inspired in these spouses-to-be,

and that all might be accomplished
to the glory of his name.

5d

Then, covering his head, he says:

P.   In the name of almighty God,
         and with the authority of his holy Church,
         we hereby excommunicate all those,
         men and women,
         who may now be engaged in using
         magic, superstition or witchcraft
         to impede the use of the marriage
         which this couple is about to contract.

5e

*Here the parish priest may say a few words to the bride and groom
concerning the sacrament of matrimony: its institution and dignity,
the holy use thereof, and the blessings of marriage. He may use this
or a similar exhortation in the vernacular, depending on how he
judges the situation of those present.*

EXHORTATION

P.

Marriage is a holy estate. God established this alliance in the
time of innocence and ratified it after the fall. It is a covenant
sanctified in the Old Testament by faithful servants of the Lord
and it was raised to the dignity of a sacrament in the new Law
by our Lord Jesus Christ. St. Paul, too, called it a sacrament, a
great sacrament, its greatness deriving from the mystery it
represents (for it is a symbol of the union of Christ with his
Church), from the blessing which God bestows upon it, and
from the duties it imposes.

But, just as faith represents marriage to us as a holy alliance,
so it also teaches us the necessity of entering upon it and living
it out in holiness, according to the Lord and not according to
the dictates and customs of a corrupt world. Faith teaches us
that the estate of marriage is to be respected and honored by
purity of manners and truly Christian behavior. Whereas immorality dishonored this estate among the pagans and divorce
degraded it among the Jews, Jesus Christ has restored it to its
original condition in restoring the unity and indissolubility of
the marriage bond. What he has established in all its purity is a
holy society, ordained for the increase of the children of faith
and for the creation, within the womb of the Church, of heirs

for his kingdom. This is a covenant whose dignity and happiness can never adequately be described, according to Tertullian's mind. For it is holy Church herself who establishes the bond, the offering of the august sacrifice which confirms it, the blessing of the priest which seals it, the angels who serve as witnesses to it, and the heavenly Father who ratifies it. We are the children of saints, as young Tobias told his wife, and we should not live in marriage as do the nations who do not know the Lord. We might address these selfsame words to ourselves today and with greater justification. You are the children of saints; you are yourselves saints at least by vocation, for you are Christians and the children of Christians. You cannot live in marriage, then, as those who know not the Lord, nor observe the Law. On the contrary, you must hallow your union with living faith, burning charity and a mutual desire and zeal for progress in the path of virtue. The Christians who are joined in marriage are two people who join together to work for their sanctification, to run their race together to the finish, to share their sufferings, to support and sustain each other in the difficulties they will have to face, in the hope of the same end: for the end of your race is in heaven. Learn from this instruction, Christian spouses, with what spirit of recollection and religiosity you should receive this sacrament and with what single-mindedness and zeal you should strive throughout your life to obtain from God the preservation and increase of the graces he has attached to the marriage of his faithful servants.

6.
Having completed the exhortation, the priest asks for their right hands. He then addresses the groom as follows, without using any titles or honorifics. And he should make sure that the man answers in a clear, audible voice.

P.   N., do you declare, state, and swear
       before God and in the face of his holy Church,
       that you now take N., here present,
       to be your wife and lawful spouse?
R.   I do.
P.   Do you promise to be faithful to her in all things
       as a man should be faithful to his wife,
       according to the command of God?
R.   I do.

Then he addresses the bride, without title or honorifics, ensuring that she replies in a clear voice.

P.   N., do you also declare, state, and swear
        before God and in the face of his holy Church,
        that you now take N., here present,
        to be your husband and lawful spouse?
R.   I do.
P.   Do you promise to be faithful to him
        in all things
        as a wife should be faithful to her husband,
        according to the command of God?
R.   I do.

7.
Next, the priest gives the coin(s) to the bridegroom, who places them in the bride's right hand. He repeats the following words after the priest:

        N., I give you the settlement
        which has been agreed
        between your parents and mine,
        of which these coins are the sign and symbol.[15]

8.
Next, the priest gives the bridegroom the ring which he places on the ring finger of the bride's left hand (i.e. the finger next to the little finger), saying:

        I give you this ring
        as a sign of the marriage we are contracting.

9.
When he has said these words, the priest makes the sign of the Cross over the bride's hand, saying:

P.   In the name of the Father,
        and of the Son,
        + and of the Holy Spirit.
R.   Amen.

10.
Stretching out his hand, he says:

P.   The Lord be with you.
R.   And also with you.
P.   Let us pray:
        May the God of Abraham,[16]

[15] Alternate forms are provided for the cases in which either one or both parties are independent.
[16] Robert, 12e.

the God of Isaac
and the God of Jacob
· bless you and fullfil his blessing in you.
And I join you in matrimony.[17]
In the name of the Father +
and of the Son +
and of the Holy + Spirit.

R.   Amen.

11.

He then sprinkles them with holy water, saying:

P.   What God has joined
let no one put asunder.

Let us pray:
Look down upon these your servants, O Lord,[18]
that they may remain in your will
and grow old
and be multiplied unto length of days.
Through Christ our Lord.

R.   Amen.

12.

*This done, the parish priest tells the husband to take the bride's right
hand and lead her to the altar where Mass is to be celebrated, unless
they have already attended Mass earlier. The Mass for Bride and
Groom provided in the Missal is said, unless the feast is a double or
higher, or the day falls within a major octave. In such cases, the Mass
of the day is said, with a second collect from the Nuptial Mass. But
even on a feast day the nuptial blessing (if it is conferred at all) is
given in its usual place.*

BLESSING OF THE COUPLE

13.

*(This blessing is omitted when the bride is a widow or a woman who
has already conceived children out of wedlock.)*

After the Libera nos, *the priest replaces the particles of the host
upon the paten, before saying the* Pax domini. *The bride and groom,
kneeling before the altar, are covered with a white veil. The priest,
moving to one side of the middle of the altar, turns round and
stretches his right hand over them. He says the following prayer in a
low voice, without* Dominus vobiscum, *the server holding the book.*

---

[17] Rituale Romanum, 2.
[18] Egbert, 2b.

13a

P.   Let us pray:
          Listen graciously . . .[19]
          Through our Lord Jesus Christ your Son,
          who lives and reigns with you
          in the unity of the Holy Spirit.

Then he continues in a loud voice:

P.   For ever and ever.
R.   Amen.

13b

P.   The Lord be with you.
R.   And also with you.
P.   Lift up your hearts.
R.   We lift them up to the Lord.
P.   Let us give thanks to the Lord our God.
R.   It is right and fitting.
P.   It is truly right and fitting,
          just and for our salvation,
          that we should give you thanks
          always and everywhere, Lord,
          Holy Father, almighty and eternal God.
          You made all things out of nothing by your power.[20]
          When you had laid the foundations of the universe
          you created made man in the image of God,
          and made woman as man's inseparable helper,
          bringing the woman's body into being
          out of the man's flesh;
          teaching us thereby
          that what it had pleased you to create
          out of an original unity
          must never be put asunder.
          O God, you have consecrated the bond of marriage
          with such an excellent mystery
          as to prefigure in the covenant of marriage
          the sacrament of Christ and his Church.
          O God,
          through you a woman is joined to her husband
          and society is chiefly ordered by that blessing
          which was neither lost by original sin
          nor washed away in the flood.

[19] Ver, 5.
[20] Greg, 6-7.

O God,
in whose hands alone rests power over the human heart
and who know and direct all things by your providence,
what you have joined no one may sunder,
what you have blessed no one may curse.
We beseech you,
so join these two people in singleness of mind,
so infuse their hearts with love,
that, as you alone are one,
true and all-powerful,
so may they be one in you.

13c

(If there is more than one bride, the following is put in the plural.)

Look graciously upon your maidservant[21]
who is to be joined in marriage,
and who now seeks the help of your protection.
May her yoke be one of love and peace.
May she marry in Christ,
faithful and chaste.
May she remain an imitator of holy women:
amiable to her husband, like Rachel;
wise, like Rebecca;
long-lived and faithful, like Sarah.
May the author of lies
never subvert a single one of her acts;
may she remain steadfast in fidelity
and in keeping the commandments;
loyal to one marriage bed,
may she flee all unlawful relations;
let her shore up her weakness
with the strength of discipline.
May she be sober and modest,
her honor above reproach,
learned in heavenly wisdom.
May she be fruitful with children,
a person of integrity and above suspicion;
and may she come at last
to the repose of the blessed
and to the heavenly kingdom.
May they both see their children's children
to the third and fourth generation,

---

[21] Greg, 8-10.

and come to a desired old age.
Through the same Jesus Christ.

13d
The priest sprinkles them with holy water and the veil is removed.

14.
Turning back to the altar, the priest picks up the smallest particle of the host and makes the sign of the Cross with it over the chalice in the usual way, saying Pax domini, *etc. After the prayer,* Domine Jesu Christe qui dixisti, *etc., the server hands the pax-board to the priest who kisses it, saying:*

Peace be with you, brother,
and with the holy Church of God.

Then the server carries the pax-board to the bride and groom for them to kiss, saying:

Peace be with you.

15.
After the server has responded to the Ite missa est, *the priest turns to the bride and groom, and with hands joined, says:*

P.   The God of Abraham,
the God of Isaac,
the God of Jacob
be with you,
and fulfill his blessing in you,
that you may see your children's children
unto the third and fourth generation.
And thereafter
may you enjoy eternal life,
with the help of our Lord Jesus Christ,
who lives and reigns with the Father
and the Holy Spirit,
one God for ever and ever.
R.   Amen.

16.
If the bride has had a child by the man she is marrying, the child is legitimated by placing the veil over the man, the woman and the child(ren). The priest turns to them and says the following with hands joined:

P.   Let us pray:
O God,
you always open the fountain of your mercy

to sinners who have recourse to you.
Look graciously upon
the repentant hearts of this couple.
Remit the debt of punishment
which they have contracted by their sin
and passed on to their offspring.
Let the birth
which has been regenerated by baptism
to the hope of an eternal
and heavenly inheritance
be made eligible also
by this our ministry
to inherit earthly and temporal goods
as well, and be publicly declared legitimate.
Through Jesus Christ our Lord.

However, should the parish priest judge that this public legitimation might give rise to scandal, the rite can be conducted privately apart from the Mass. But, however it is done, the act of legitimation should be recorded in the register. After the prayer Placeat tibi sancta Trinitas, *the final blessing is given as usual.*

III

BLESSING OF THE NUPTIAL CHAMBER

1.

Since the blessing of the marriage chamber is established for the overcoming of all obscene and indecent spirits and the fire of intemperate passion, the parish priest should ensure that it is conducted with all piety and modesty. It should take place in the morning, before the banquet, and never in the evening hours. Only the friends of the couple and two or three decorous persons should be present. If there is any risk of scandal, the parish priest should exercise his judgement and not perform the blessing.

2.

The bride and groom kneel beside the nuptial bed. The priest, wearing a surplice and white stole, sprinkles the couple and the chamber with holy water, saying:

P.   Sprinkle me with hyssop, O Lord,
        and I shall be clean;
        wash me and I shall be whiter than snow.

Let us pray:
Visit, we beseech you, O Lord, this dwelling[22]
and drive far from it all the snares of the enemy.
Let your holy angels dwell herein
who may keep these newlyweds in peace;
and may your blessing be always upon them.
Through Christ our Lord.

R.   Amen.

3.

Then he recites Psalm 127, alternating verses with the server, together with the versicles that follow:

P.   Blessed are those who fear the Lord,
        and walk in his ways.
R.   Of the labors of your hands you shall eat;
        you are blessed
        and it shall go well with you.
P.   Your wife like a fruitful vine,
        beside your house.
R.   Your children like shoots of the olive,
        around your table.
P.   Thus shall the man be blessed,
        who fears the Lord.
R.   May the Lord bless you from Sion;
        may you see a prosperous Jerusalem
        all the days of your life.
P.   May you see your children's children.
        Peace upon Israel.
R.   Glory be to the Father.
P.   As it was in the beginning.
        Lord have mercy.
R.   Christ have mercy.
P.   Lord have mercy.
        Our Father.
        And lead us not into temptation.
R.   But deliver us from evil.
P.   Save your servant and your maidservant.
R.   Who put their trust in you, my God.
P.   Send them help, O Lord,
        from your holy place.
R.   And defend them out of Sion.

---

[22] Concluding prayer from Compline in the Roman Breviary, lightly adapted.

P.   Be a tower of strength to them, O Lord.

R.   In the face of the enemy.

P.   Lord, hear my prayer.

R.   And let my cry come unto you.

P.   The Lord be with you.

R.   And also with you.

P.   Let us pray:
        Lord, bless this couple
        and this marriage chamber,
        that they may be established in your peace,[23]
        remain in your will,
        live in your love
        and grow old
        and be multiplied unto length of days.
        Through Christ our Lord.

R.   Amen.

4.

Then, raising his right hand, the priest blesses the couple, saying:

P.   May the Lord bless you in body and soul
        and give you his blessing,
        as he blessed Abraham, Isaac, and Jacob.
        May the Lord's holy hand be upon you
        and may he send his angel to guard you
        all the days of your life.

R.   Amen.

P.   May the Father bless you,
        and the Son
        and the Holy Spirit.

R.   Amen.

5.

*The priest then sprinkles the husband, the wife, the marriage chamber
and those in attendance in the room. If it seems to him appropriate, he
may explain the purpose for which the blessing of the marriage chamber was instituted.*

[23] Egbert, 2a.

IV

OF THOSE WISHING TO IMPEDE
THE USE OF MARRIAGE

MONITUM

Since it can happen, God permitting, that married couples are impeded in the use of their marriage by witchcraft, the parish priest should know how to advise, warn, counsel and observe; and he should also know what countermeasures are available from the Church and how to proceed in such cases with discretion and prudence.

Wherefore:

1.
Since those who have a lively faith in God and who, entering upon marriage or using it, do so with a right intention and a pure conscience have less to fear from witchcraft, the faithful who are thinking of so committing themselves are to be warned to sin no more by lack of faith, or by lack of a pure intention or failure to live chastely, since God's most just judgement permits these faults and other sins to be punished in this way.

2.
Since the Church has always condemned such superstitions and depraved practices as inventions of the devil, the parish priest must neither have recourse to any superstitious practice himself, nor permit the married couple to do so.

3.
Because the inability to consummate marriage is very often a punishment for lust, whereby God vindicates the sanctity of holy matrimony, the spouses are to be reconciled by the Sacrament of Penance and the priest should exhort them to follow the example of Tobit and Sarah, spending some days of their life in total chastity and preparing themselves by fasting, prayer, almsgiving and other pious works. If this does not lift the spell, then they should make a vow to God to do some pious work of supererogation; or they should have a Mass said for themselves; or they should religiously take holy water with them when they enter the bedroom, intending to use marriage purely and chastely and with the sole purpose of conceiving a child. Where the existence of the problem has been established by doctors and where natural remedies have been tried, the priest, after receiving authorization from the Bishop, may recite the following prayers over the couple. This should be done in the church, but privately, not in public, and with only other such persons present as the couple may invite.

SERVICE FOR UNDOING WITCHCRAFT[24]

*After the couple has heard the Mass of the Holy Spirit (or other Mass
if they piously desire), the priest or another priest delegated by him,
removing his chasuble, maniple, and stole, puts on a purple stole over
his alb . . . and, in some place aside, blesses the couple who have
been bewitched as follows:*

P.   Our help is in the name of the Lord.

R.   Who made heaven and earth.

P.   Save your servant and your maidservant.

R.   Who place their hope in you, my God.

P.   Send them help from your holy place.

R.   And defend them out of Sion.

P.   Let the enemy not succeed against them.

R.   And the son of iniquity not attack them to harm them.

P.   Be a tower of strength to them, O Lord.

R.   In the face of the enemy.

P.   O Lord, hear my prayer.

R.   And let my cry come unto you.

P.   The Lord be with you.

R.   And also with you.

P.   Let us pray:

         Hear us . . .[25]

R.   Amen.

P.   The Lord be with you.

R.   And also with you.

P.   A reading from the holy Gospel according to John.

R.   Glory to you, O Lord.

Gospel: John 2:1-11, the marriage feast at Cana.

R.   Thanks be to God.

P.   Let us pray:
         Lord Jesus Christ,
         who became man for us,
         you raised marriage,
         which had been instituted as a natural function
         in the earthly paradise,
         even to the dignity of a sacrament,
         deigning to honor it by your presence.

---

[24] *Ordo ad solvendum maleficium.*
[25] *Ver,* 1.

Through the merits
of the Blessed Virgin Mary your Mother,
and of all the saints,
vouchsafe to bless +
your servant and your maidservant,
and to free them from every spell, evil eye
or work of witchcraft wrought by Satan,
in the name of the Father +
and of the Son +
and of the Holy + Spirit.

R.   Amen.

The priest then recites Psalms 3, 90, and 127, alternating verses with the servers.

P.   Lord have mercy.
R.   Christ have mercy.
P.   Lord have mercy.
        Our Father *silently until*
P.   And lead us not into temptation.
R.   But deliver us from evil.
P.   Lord, hear my prayer.
R.   And let my cry come unto you.
P.   The Lord be with you.
R.   And also with you.

P.   Let us pray:
        Almighty and everlasting God,
        who marvelously fructified
        the womb of the Blessed Virgin Mary
        that it might conceive your Son,
        true God and true man,
        by the Holy Spirit;
        we beseech your mercy
        that you would bless + these your servants
        and make them fruitful
        by removing every impediment
        and spell of the devil.
        Through the same Christ our Lord.

R.   Amen.

        He sprinkles them with holy water.

24. MARTIN LUTHER:
THE ORDER OF MARRIAGE
FOR COMMON PASTORS (1529)

The importance of Martin Luther for Protestant and thus for
modern conceptions of marriage can hardly be overestimated.
In *The Babylonian Captivity of the Church* (1520), Luther had
denied the sacramentality of marriage and begun his attack on
the legalistic and ritual superstructure which had grown up
around it, especially the whole system of canonical impediments and the machinery for dispensing them. In his 1522 trea-
tise on *The Estate of Marriage*, he defends the necessity of
marriage, dismantles the "eighteen distinct reasons for prevent-
ing or dissolving a marriage," establishes what he considers
three biblically-based grounds for divorce and, most im-
portantly, develops what must be one of the first real spirituali-
ties of marriage: "how to live a Christian and godly life in that
estate."

For Luther, marriage is divinely instituted and was blessed by
God at the beginning of the world, yet it remains a secular reality, not a sacrament instituted by Christ. From this Luther drew
the fateful conclusion that the regulation of marriage was a
proper matter for the civil authority rather than the Church,
thereby opening the door to purely civil marriage. Nonetheless,
since it is part of God's order in this world, the Church should
be prepared to bless marriages when asked to do so, in order
"to honor this divine estate and gloriously bless and embellish
it and pray for it," and "to teach the young people to take this
estate seriously, to honor it as a divine creation and command
and not to act so disgracefully at weddings, making fools of
themselves with laughing, jeering and other nonsense, as has
been common till now, just as though it was a joke or child's
play to enter into the married estate or to have a wedding."

To this end he proposed a simplified wedding rite in 1529. It
is in three parts: the publication of the banns, the exchange of
consent and rings at the entry to the church, and then the short
service—a reading, sermon, and prayer—at the altar. He makes
no provision for a betrothal rite, which would in any case have
been celebrated separately. The traditional German marriage
rites he was replacing were frequently much less complex than
the other later medieval rites represented in this collection, so
his reform is not as radical as it might seem. Nevertheless,
Luther's positive, if somewhat lugubrious, view of marriage is

well represented by the rite, which speaks of it as God's "creation, ordinance, and blessing."

TEXT

Luther's Works. Vol. 33. Edited by Ulrich S. Leupold. Philadelphia: Fortress, 1965, 110–115.

BIBLIOGRAPHY

Luther, Martin. *The Babylonian Captivity of the Church*, in *Luther's Works.* Vol. 36, 92ff; *The Estate of Marriage*, in idem, Vol. 44, 5–14.

Spinks, B. D. "Luther's Other Major Liturgical Reforms: 3. The *Traubuchlein*," *Liturgical Review* 10 (1980) 33–38.

Stevenson, 1982:126–128; 1987:87–89.

. . . Whoever desires prayer and blessing from the pastor or bishop indicates thereby—even if he does not express it in so many words—into what peril and need he now enters and how greatly he stands in need of the blessing of God and common prayer for the estate which he enters. For every day we see marriages broken by the devil through adultery, unfaithfulness, discord and all manner of ill.

Therefore we will deal in the following way with the bridegroom and bride (if they desire and ask for it).

1.
First, publishing the banns from the pulpit with such words as these:

Hans N. and Greta N.
purpose to enter into the holy estate of matrimony
according to God's ordinance.
They desire that common Christian prayer
be made on their behalf
so that they may begin it in God's name
and prosper therein.

And should anyone have anything to say against it,
let him speak in time or afterward hold his peace.
God grant them his blessing.
Amen.

2.
Marrying them at the entrance to the church with words such as these:

Hans,
dost thou desire Greta to thy wedded wife?

He shall say:
Yes.

Greta,
dost thou desire Hans to thy wedded husband?

She shall say:
Yes.

3.
Then let them give each other the wedding rings and join their right hands together, and say to them:

4.
What God hath joined together,
let no man put asunder.

Then shall he say:

Since Hans N. and Greta N.
desire each other in marriage
and acknowledge the same here publicly
before God and the world,
in testimony of which they have given each other
their hands and wedding rings,
I pronounce them joined in marriage,
in the name of the Father,
and of the Son,
and of the Holy Ghost.
Amen.

5.
Before the altar he shall read God's word over the bridegroom and bride, Genesis, the second chapter.

6.
Thereupon, he shall turn to both of them and speak to them thus:

Since both of you have entered the married estate in God's name, hear first of all God's commandment concerning this estate. Thus speaketh St. Paul: Husbands, love your wives, even as Christ also loved the Church and gave himself for it; that he might sanctify and cleanse it with the washing of water by the word, that he might present it to himself a glorious Church, not having spot, or wrinkle or any such thing; but that it should be holy and without blemish. So ought men to love their wives as their own bodies. He that loveth his wife loveth himself. For no man ever yet hated his own flesh; but nourisheth and cherisheth it, even as the Lord the Church.

Wives, submit yourselves unto your husbands, as unto the Lord. For the husband is head of the wife, even as Christ is the head of the Church; and he is the savior of the body. Therefore, as the Church is subject unto Christ, so let wives be to their own husbands in everything. Second, hear also the cross which God has placed upon this estate.

God spake thus to the woman: I will greatly multiply thy sorrow and thy conception; in sorrow thou shalt bring forth children; and thy desire shall be to thy husband, and he shall rule over thee. And God spake to the man: Because thou hast hearkened unto the voice of thy wife, and hast eaten of the tree of which I commanded thee, saying, Though shalt not eat of it: cursed is the ground for thy sake; in sorrow shalt thou eat of it all the days of thy life; thorns and thistles shall it bring forth to thee; and thou shalt eat the herb of the field; in the sweat of thy face shalt thou eat bread, till thou return to the ground; for out of it wast thou taken; for dust thou art, and unto dust shalt thou return. Third, this is your comfort, that you may know and believe that your estate is pleasing to God and blessed by him. For it is written: God created man in his own image, in the image of God created he him; male and female created he them. And God blessed them, and God said unto them, Be fruitful, and multiply, and replenish the earth and subdue it; and have dominion over the fish of the sea, and over the fowl of the air and over every living thing that moveth upon the earth. And God saw everything that he had made, and, behold, it was very good. Therefore, Solomon also says: Whoso findeth a wife findeth a good thing, and obtaineth favor of the Lord.

7.

And he shall spread forth his hands over them and pray:

O God, who hast created man and woman
and hast ordained them for the married state,
hast blessed them also with fruits of the womb,
and hast typified therein
the sacramental union of thy dear Son,
the Lord Jesus Christ,
and the Church, his bride:
we beseech thy boundless goodness and mercy
that thou wouldst not permit this thy creation,

ordinance and blessing to be disturbed or destroyed,
but graciously preserve the same,
through Jesus Christ our Lord.
Amen.

25. THE BOOK OF COMMON PRAYER (1559)

The *Book of Common Prayer* went through a series of revisions after its first appearance in 1548, notably in 1552, 1559, and 1662, but the marriage rite remained remarkably intact and has exercised a powerful cultural influence in the English-speaking world. Its formula for the marriage vows, directly taken from the Sarum Rite (q.v.), has been adopted in the postconciliar reform of the Roman Marriage Rite.

The text presented here is that of the Elizabethan settlement of 1559, but it is identical with Cranmer's own rite as it appeared in the Second Prayer Book of 1552 and is substantially the same as that of the 1662 Book. One exception is that in the 1662 Book the rubric requiring the couple to receive Communion at their wedding was revised to read: "It is convenient that the newly married persons should receive the holy Communion at the time of their marriage, or at the first opportunity after their marriage."

Relying heavily on the *Sarum Manual*, this Anglican rite focuses on the consent of the partners (no longer at the door of the church, but at the front of the nave, before the choir) and on the prayers for the couple (at the altar). Remarkably it retains not only the practice of celebrating the Eucharist at weddings, but even such practices as the joining of hands and the exchange of rings. (The giving of coins, which survived among the recusant English Catholics, disappeared in the Church of England with this 1552 revision, though it lingered informally in some areas.) The nuptial blessing, pronounced over the couple kneeling at the altar table before the Communion Service begins, is adapted to pray for both the man and the woman. A catechesis, to be read if there is no sermon, follows the Gospel, but it is little more than a catena of Pauline texts on the duties of husband and wife.

TEXT

The Prayer Book of Queen Elizabeth, 1558. Edinburgh, 1909, 122–128.

BIBLIOGRAPHY

Brightman, F. E. *The English Rite*. London: Rivingtons, 1915, vol. 1, cxxii–cxxv; vol. 2, 800–817.

Cuming, G. J. *A History of Anglican Liturgy*. Second edition. London: Macmillan, 1982, 21ff.

Wickham Legg, J. "Notes on the Marriage Service in the Book of Common Prayer," in his *Ecclesiological Essays*. London: De la More Press, 1905, 181–226.

Stevenson, 1982:134–152.

THE FOURME OF SOLEMPNIZACION OF MATRIMONYE

First, the banes must be asked thre seuerall Sondaies or holy daies, in the tyme of seruice, the people beyng present, after the accustomed maner.

And yf the persons that would be maryed dwell in diuerse Paryshes, the banes must be asked in both Parishes and the Curate of the one Paryshe shall not solempnize matrimonye betwyxt them, wythout a certifycate of the banes beyng thryse asked, from the Curate of the other Parysh.

I

At the daie appoincted for solempnizacyon of Matrimonye, the persones to be maryed shal come into the body of the Churche, wyth theyr frendes and neighbours. And there the Pryest shall thus saye.

1.
Dearely beloued frendes,[26]
we are gathered together here in the sight of God,
and in the face of his congregacion,
to ioyne together this man and this woman
in holy matrimony,
which is an honorable state,
instytuted of God in Paradise,
in the time of manes innocencie,
signifiyng vnto vs the mistical vnion
that is betwixt Christ and his Churche:
which holy state Christe adourned and beautified
with his presence and firste myracle
that he wrought in Cana of Galile,
and is commended of sainct Paul
to be honourable emong all men,
and therfore is not to be enterprised,

---

[26] Cf. Sarum I.2.

nor taken in hande
vnaduisedly, lightly or wantonly,
to satisfye mennes carnall lustes and appetytes,
lyke brute beastes that haue no vnderstandyng;
but reuerently, discretely, aduisedly,
soberly, and in the feare of God,
duely consideryng the causes
for the which matrimony was ordeined.
One was the procreation of children,
to be brought vp in the feare
and nurtoure of the Lorde,
and praise of God.
Secondly,
it was ordeined for a remedy agaynste sinne
and to auoide fornication,
that suche persones
as haue not the gifte of continencie might mary,
and kepe themselues vndefiled membres of Christes body.
Thirdly,
for the mutual societie, helpe, and comfort,
that the one ought to haue of the other,
bothe in prosperity and aduersitye,
into the whiche holy state
these two persones present,
come nowe to be ioyned.
Therefore
if any man can shewe any iust cause,
why thei may not lawfully be iouned together
let hym now speake,
or els hereafter for euer holde his peace.

2.
And also speakynge to the persons that shalbe maryed, he shall saie.

I require and charge you
(as you wil aunswere at the dreadful day of iudgement,
when the secretes of all hartes shalbe disclosed)
that if either of you doe knowe any impedyment,
why ye may not be lawfully ioyned together
in Matrimony,
that ye confesse it.
For be ye well assured,
that so many as be coupled together,
otherwyse than Goddes worde doeth allowe,

are not ioyned together by God,
neither is their Matrimonye lawfull.

At whyche day of Maryage, if any man do allege and declare any im-
pediment, why they may not be coupled together in matrymony by
Gods law, or the lawes of thys realme, and wyll be bound, and suffi-
cient sureties with him, to the parties, or els put in a cautyon to the
ful value of suche charges, as the persons to be maryed do susteine, to
proue hys allegation: then the solempnization must be deferred vnto
suche tyme as the truthe be tried. If no impedyment be alledged, then
shall the curate saye vnto the man,

3.
N., wilt thou haue thys woman to thy wedded wyfe,[27]
to lyue together after Goddes ordynaunce
in the holye estate of Matrimony?
Wylt thou loue her, comforte her,
honour, and kepe her,
in sickenes, and in healthe?
And forsakyng al other,
kepe the onely to her,
so long as you both shall liue?

The man shall aunswere,
I will.

Then shall the Priest saye to the woman,

N., wilt thou haue this man to thy wedded housband,
to lyue together after Goddes ordynaunce
in the holy estate of matrimony?
Wilt thou obey hym and serue him,
loue, honour, and kepe him,
in sycknes, and in health?
And forsakynge al other,
kepe the onely to him
so long as ye bothe shal liue?

The woman shall aunswere,
I will.

Then shall the Minister saie,

4.
Who geueth this woman to be maried vnto this man?[28]

---

[27] Sarum, I.3.
[28] Sarum, I.4 (York).

And the Minister, receiuyng the woman at her father or frendes handes, shall cause the man to take the woman by the right hand, and so either to geue their trouth to other, the man first saying.

5.

I, N., take the, N.,[29]
to my wedded wyfe,
to haue and to hold from thys day forward,
for better, for worse,
for richer, for porer,
in sickenes, and in healthe,
to loue and to cheryshe,
tyll death vs departe;
according to Gods holy ordinaunce,
and therto I plight the my trouth.

Then shall they louse their handes, and the woman takyng againe the man by the right hande, shall saie.

I, N., take the, N.,
to my wedded husbande,
to haue and to holde,
from this day forward,
for better, for worse,
for richer, for porer,
in sickenes, and in health,
to loue, cherish, and to obey,
till death vs departe;
accordynge to Godes holy ordinaunce,
and therto I geue the my trouth.

6.

Then shall they again louse theyr handes, and the man shal geue vnto the woman a ring, laying the same vpon the booke, with the accustomed dutie to the Priest and Clerke. And the Priest taking the ryng, shal delyuer it vnto the man, to put it vpon the fourth finger of the womans left hand. And the man taught by the Priest, shal say.

With this ring I the wed:[30]
with my body I the worship:
and with all my worldly goodes, I the endow.

[29] Sarum, I.4.
[30] Sarum, I.6b.

In the name of the Father,
and of the Sonne,
and of the holy Ghost.
Amen.

Then the man leauyng the ryng vpon the fourth finger of the womans left hande, the Minister shall saye.

O eternall God,[31]
creatoure and preseruer of all mankynd,
giuer of all spirytuall grace,
the aucthour of euerlastyng life:
send thy blessyng vpon these thy seruauntes,
thys man and this woman,
whom we blesse in thy name,
that as Isaac and Rebecca
lyued faithfully together:
So these persons may surely performe
and kepe the vow and couenaunt betwixte them made,
whereof this ring geuen, and receiued,
is a token and pledge,
and may euer remain
in perfect loue and peace together,
and liue according vnto thy lawes,
through Jesus Christ our Lorde.
Amen.

7.
Then shal the Priest ioyne their right handes together and say.

Those whome God hath ioyned together,[32]
let no man put a sonder.

8.
Then shall the Minister speak unto the people.

For asmuche as N. and N.
haue consented together in holy wedlocke,[33]
and haue witnessed the same before God,
and thys company,
and therto haue giuen and pledged,
their trouth eyther to other,
and haue declared the same
by geuyyng and receiuyng of a ryng,

[31] Sarum, I.5.
[32] See Luther, 4.
[33] See Luther, 4.

and by ioynyng of handes
I pronounce that thei be man and wife together.
In the name of the father,
of the sonne
and of the holy Ghost.
Amen.

9.
And the Minister shal adde this blessyng.

God the Father,[34]
God the Sonne,
God the holy Ghost,
blesse, preserue, and kepe you,
the Lorde mercifully wyth his fauour loke vpon you,
and so fil you with al spiritual benediction, and grace,
that you may so lyue together in thys life,
that in the world to come,
you may haue life euerlastyng.
Amen.

II

1.
Then the Ministers or Clerckes goyng to the Lordes table, shall saie,
or syng this Psalme folowyng Beati omnes. *[Ps 127]*

Blessed are all they that feare the Lorde, and walke in his waies.
For thou shalt eate the labour of thy handes, O wel is the, and
   happy shalt thou be.
Thy wife shalbe as the fruitfull vine vpon the walles of thy
   house.
Thy children like the Oliue braunches rounde about thy table.
Lo thus shall the man be blessed: that feareth the lorde.
The Lorde from out of Sion shal blesse the: that thou shalt see
   Hierusalem in prosperitie, al thy life long:
Yea, that thou shalt see thy childres children, and peace vpon
   Israel.
Glory be to the Father. &c.
As it was. &c.

Or elles this Psalme folowyng Deus misereatur. *[Ps 67]*

God be mercifull vnto vs and blesse vs:
and shewe vs the lyght of his countenaunce,
and be merciful vnto vs.

[34] See Sarum I.6h.

That thy waie maie be knowen vpon the earth: thy sauyng
  healthe among al nacions.
Let the people prayse the (O God) yea, let all the people praise
  the.
O let the nacions reioyce and be glad, for thou shalt iudge the
  folke ryghteously, and gouerne the nacions vpon the earth.
Let the people praise the (O God), lette all the people
  praise the.
Then shall the earthe bryng furthe her encrease, and God, euen
  our God, shal geue vs his blessyng.
God shall blesse vs, and al the endes of the worlde shall feare
  him.
Glory be to the Father. &c.
As it was in the beginning. &c.

2.

*The Psalm ended, and the man and the woman knelyng afore the
Lordes table: The Priest standyng at the Table, and turnyng hys face
towarde them, shal saie,*

2a

Lorde haue mercie vpon vs.[35]
Aunswere. Christe haue mercie vpon vs.
Minister. Lorde haue mercie vpon vs.

Our Father which art. &c.
And leade vs not into temptation.
Aunswere. But deliver vs from euil. Amen.
Minister. O Lorde, saue thy seruaunt, and thy handmaide.
Aunswere. Whyche put their trust in the.
Minister. O Lorde, sende them helpe from thy holy place.
Aunswere. And euermore defende them.
Minister. Be vnto them a towre of strength.
Aunswere. From the face of their enemie.
Minister. O Lorde, heare our praier.
Aunswere. And let our crie come vnto the.

The Minister.
2b
O God of Abraham,[36]
God of Isaac,
God of Jacob,
blesse these thy seruauntes,
and sowe the sede of eternal life in their mindes,

---

[35] Sarum, II.1-2.
[36] Sarum, II.2c.

that whatsoeuer in thy holy worde
they shal profitably learne,
they may in dede fulfil the same.

Loke, O Lorde[37]
mercifully vpon theim from heauen,
and blesse them.
And as thou diddest send thy blessing
vpon Abraham and Sara to their greate comforte:
so vouchesaufe to sende thy blessing
vpon these thy seruauntes,
that they,
obeiyng thy will,
and alway beyng in saufetie vnder thy protection,
may abide in thy loue vnto their liues ende,
throughe Jesu Christe our Lorde.
Amen.

2c
This prayer next folowyng shal be omitted where the woman is past childe birth.

O mercifull Lorde, and heauenly Father,[38]
by whose gracious gifte mankynde is encreased,
we beseche the
assiste with thy blessyng these two persones,
that they may bothe be fruitefull
in procreation of children,
also liue together
so long in godly loue and honestie,
that they may see their childers children,
vnto the thirde and fourthe generacion
vnto thy praise and honour:
through Jesus Christe our Lorde.
Amen.

2d
O God
whiche by thy mightie power[39]
hast made all thinges of naught,
which also after other thinges set in ordre,
diddest appoinct that out of man
(created after thyne owne ymage and similitude)

[37] Sarum, II.2d.
[38] Sarum, cf. II.2e.
[39] Sarum, I.6c.

woman should take her beginning,
and knitting them together,
diddest teache
that it shoulde neuer be lawfull to put a sonder
those whome thou by matrimonie haddest made one:
O God
which haste consecrated the state of matrimonie
to suche an excellent misterie,
that in it is signified and represented
the spiritual mariage and vnitie
betwixte Christe and his Churche:
Loke mercifully vpon these thy seruauntes,
that both this man may loue his wife,
accordyng to thy worde
(as Christe did loue his spouse the Churche,
who gaue himselfe for it,
louyng and cherishing it,
euen as his owne fleshe).
And also that this woman may be
louyng and amiable to her housband as Rachel,
wise as Rebecca,
faithfull and obedient as Sara,
and in all quietnes, sobrietie, and peace,
be a folower of holy and Godly matrones,
O Lorde blesse them bothe,
and graunt them
to enherite thy euerlastyng kyngdome:
throughe Jesus Christe our Lorde.
Amen.

Then shall the Priest saye,
Almightie God,
which,
at the beginnyng did create our firste parentes[40]
Adam and Eue,
and did sanctifie and ioyne them together in mariage,
powre vpon you the richesse of his grace,
sanctifie, and blesse you,
that ye may please hym both in body and soule,
and liue together in holy loue,
vnto your liues ende.
Amen.

[40] Sarum Missal.

III

Then shal begyn the Communion, and after the Gospel shalbe saied a Sermon, wherin ordinarily (so oft as there is any mariage) thoffice of a man and wife shalbe declared, accordyng to holy Scripture, or if there be no sermon, the Minister shal reade this that foloweth.

Al ye which be maried, or whiche entend to take the holy estate of Matrimonie vpon you: heare what holy scripture doth say, as touching the dutie of housbandes towarde their wiues, and wiues toward their housbandes.

Saincte Paul (in his Epistle to the Ephesians, the v Chapiter) doeth geue this commaundement to all maried men.

Ye housbandes loue your wiues, euen as Christ loued the Churche, and hath geuen hymselfe for it, to sanctifie it, purgyng it in the fountaine of water, throughe the worde, that he might make it vnto hym selfe a glorious congregacion, not hauyng spot or wrincle, or any suche thyng, but that it shoulde be holy and blameles. So men are bounde to loue their owne wyues, as their owne bodies. He that loueth his owne wife loueth hym selfe. For neuer did any man hate his owne fleshe, but nourisheth and cherisheth it, euen as the Lorde doeth the congregacion, for we are membres of his body: of his flesh and of hys bones.

For this cause shall a man leaue father and mother, and shalbe ioined vnto his wife, and thei two shalbe one flesh. This mistery is great, but I speake of Christe and of the congregacion. Neuerthelesse, let euery one of you so loue his owne wyfe, euen as hym selfe.

Likewise the same sainct Paule (wrytyng to the Collossians) speaketh thus to all men that be maried. Ye men, loue your wyues, and be not bitter vnto them. Heare also what saincte Peter Thapostle of Christe, whiche was him selfe a maried man (saith vnto al men) that are maried. Ye housbandes, dwel with your wyues according to knowledge. Geuynge honour vnto the wyfe as vnto the weaker vessell, and as heires together of the grace of lyfe, so that your praiers be not hyndred.

Hetherto ye haue hearde the dutie of the housbande toward the wyfe. Now likewise ye wyues heare and learne your dutie towarde your housbandes, euen as it is plainely sette furth in holy scripture.

Saincte Paule (in the forenamed Epistle to the Ephesians) teacheth you thus: Ye women, submit youre selfes vnto youre owne housbandes as vnto the Lorde: for the housbande is the

wyues headde, euen as Christe is the headde of the Churche.
And he is also the sauioure of the whole bodye. Therefore as
the Churche or congregacion, is subiecte vnto Christe. So likewyse lette the wyues also be in subiection vnto their owne
housbandes in al things. And againe he sayeth: Let the wife re-
uerence her housbande. And (in his Epistle to the Collossians)
Sayncte Paule geueth you thys shorte lesson. Ye wyues, sub-
mitte youre selues vnto youre owne housbandes, as it is
conuenient in the Lorde. Saincte Peter also doeth instructe you
verye godly thus, saiynge. Let wyues be subiecte to their owne
housbandes, so that if anye obey not the woorde, they may be
wonne withoute the woorde by the conuersacion of the wyues,
whyle they beholde your chaste conuersacion coupled with
feare, whose apparell let it not be outward, with broided haire
and trymmyng aboute with golde, eyther in puttinge on of gor-
geous apparell, but let the hidde manne, whiche is in the harte,
be without all corruption, so that the spirite be milde and
quiete, whiche is a precious thynge in the sighte of God. For
after thys maner (in the olde tyme) did the holy women whiche
trusted in God apparell them selues, beynge subiect to their
owne housbandes: as Sara obeyed Abraham, callynge hym
Lorde, whose daughters ye are made, doynge well, and be-
yinge not dismayde with any feare.

*The newe maried persones (the same day of their mariage) must
receyue the holy Communion.*

26. THE REFORMED TRADITION: JOHN KNOX

John Knox, born in Edinburgh in 1505, was converted to the Reform by the preaching of George Wishart, who had been a disciple of Calvin at Geneva. Under Cranmer's protection, Knox became a chaplain to the young Edward VI, but fled to Geneva when Edward died and was succeeded by his Catholic sister, Mary Tudor. Returning to Scotland under Elizabeth I, he became the chief architect of the Scottish Reformation and assured its more radical Calvinist character.

The marriage rite given here is the classic Scots Presbyterian rite originally worked out by John Knox for the use of English-speaking exiles in Geneva and was published in 1556 in *The Form of Prayers and Ministration of the Sacraments*. As the title indicates, Knox followed very closely on the provisions made by John Calvin himself in his *Form of Prayers and Manner of Ministering the Sacraments according to the Use of the Ancient Church* (1542), while Calvin, in turn, based himself on the earlier radical revision of Guillaume Farel (1533).

After a triple publication of the banns of marriage, the rite takes place at public worship before the sermon and, characteristic of the Reformed tradition, is very long on didacticism and very short on ritual and symbol. The declaration of freedom is retained, but this, like the marriage vows themselves, is in the passive form. Calvin had done away with the wedding rings, but Knox goes further and scraps all prayer for the couple except for the brief blessing at the end and the singing of Psalm 127. However, he also echoes the *Book of Common Prayer* in the opening of the address to the people.

TEXT

The Liturgy of John Knox Received by the Church of Scotland in 1564. Glasgow: University Press, 1886, 147–152.

BIBLIOGRAPHY

Spinks, B. D., "The Liturgical Origins and Theology of Calvin's Genevan Marriage Rite," *Ecclesia Orans* 3 (1986), 195–210.

Stevenson, 1982:152–155.

von Allmen, J. J., "Benediction nuptiale et mariage d'après quelques liturgies de l' Eglise Reformée," in *Mélanges liturgiques offerts au R. P. Bernard Botte*. Louvain: Abbaye de Mont César, 1972, 1–18.

THE FORME OF MARRIAGE

1.

*After the banes or contracte hathe byn publisshed thre severall dayes
in the Congregation, (to the intent that if any person have intereste or
title to either of the parties, they may have sufficient tyme to make
theyr challenge), the parties assemble at the begynning of the sermon,
and the Minister, at tyme convenient, sayeth as followeth:*

THE EXHORTATION

2.

Dearlie beloved Bretherne,[1]
we are here gathered together in the sight of God,
and in the face of his Congregation,
to knytt and joyne these parties together
in the honorable estate of Matrimony,
which was instituted
and auctorised by God hym selff in Paradise,
man beyng then in the state of innocencie.
For what tyme God made heaven and earth,
and all that is in theym,
and had created and fasshoned man also
after his owne similitude and likenes,
unto whome he gave rule and lordship
over all the beastes of the earth,
fisshes of the sea,
and fowles of the ayre;
he sayd,
It is not good that man lyve alone;
let us make hym an helper like unto hym selff.
And God brought a faste sleape uppon hym
and toke one of his ribbes
and shaped Eva therof;
doying us therby to understand,
that man and wife are one body,
one flesshe and one blood.
Signifyinge also unto us the mysticall union
that is betwixt Christe and his Churche;
for the which cawse
man leaveth his father and mother
and taketh hym to his wife,
to kepe company with her;

---

[1] Cf. *Book of Common Prayer*, I.1.

the which also he ought to love,
even as owr Saviour loveth his Churche,
that is to say,
his electe and faithfull congregation,
for the which he gave his liffe.

And semblably also,
it is the wives dewtie to studie
to please and obey her howsband,
servyng hym in all thynges that be godlie and honeste;
for she is in subjection,
and under the governance of her howsband,
so long as they contynew bothe alyve.
And this holie mariage,
beyng a thynge most honorable,
is of suche vertew and force,
that therby the howsband hathe
no more right or power over his own bodie,
but the wyfe;
and likewyse the wyfe hathe
no power over her own bodie,
but the howsband.
Forasmoche as God hathe so knytte theym together
in this mutuall societie
to the procreation of children,
that they should bryng theym up
in the feare of the Lorde,
and to the increase of Christes kyngdome.

Wherefore,
they thatt be thus couppled together by God,
can not be severed or put a parte,
oneles it be for a season,
with th'assent of bothe parties,
to th'end
to gyve theym selves the more ferventlie
to fastyng and prayer;
gyvyng diligent hede, in the meane time,
that their longe beyng aparte be not a snare
to bryng them into the daunger of Satan
through incontinencie.
And therefore to avoyde fornication,
every man aughte to have his own wyffe,
and every woman her owne howsband:
so that so many as can not lyve chaste,

are bownde by the commandment of God to mary,
that therby the holye temple of God,
which is our bodies,
may be kept pure and undefiled.
For synce owre bodies are now become
the very members of Jesus Christe,
howe horrible and detestable a thyng is it
to make theym the members of an harlot!
Every one oght therfore
to kepe his vessel in all pureness and holines;
for whosoever polluteth and defileth the temple of God,
hym will God destroye.

3.

*Here shall the Minister speake to the parties that shalbe mariede, in
this wise:*

I require and charge you,[2]
as you will answer at the daye of judgement,
when the secretes of all hartes shalbe disclosed,
that if either of you do knowe any impediment
whie ye may not be lawfully joyned together in matrimony,
that ye confesse it;
for be ye well assured,
that so many as be coupled
otherwise than Godes Woorde dothe allowe,
are not joyned together by God;
neyther is theyr matrimony lawfull.

If no impediment be knowen, then the Minister sayeth:

I take you to wittenes that be here present,
besechyng you all to have good remembraunce hereof;
and moreover,
if there be any of you which knoweth
that either of these parties
be contracted to any other,
or knoweth any other lawfull impediment,
let theym nowe make declaration therof.

4.

If no cawse be alleged, the Minister procedith, sayinge (to the man):

Forasmuche as no man speaketh agaynste this thynge,

---

[2] *Book of Common Prayer, I.2.*

4a

you, N.,
shall proteste here
before God and his holy congregation,
that you have takyn
and are now contented to have
N., here present,
for your lawfull wyfe and spowse;
promisyng to kepe her,
to love and intreate her
in all thynges accordynge
to the dewtie of a faythful howsband,
forsakyng all other durynge her lyfe;
and briefelie,
to lyve in a holy conversation with her,
kepynge faythe and trewthe in all poyntes,
according as the Woorde of God and his holie Gospell
dothe commaunde.

The answere:
Even so I take her before God,
and in presence of this his congregation.

4b

The Minister to the spowse also sayethe:

You, N.,
shal proteste here before the face of God,
in the presence of this holy congregation,
that ye have takyn,
and are now contented to have
N., here present,
for your lawful howsband;
promisynge to hym subjection and obedience,
forsakyng all other duryng hys lyfe;
and fynallie,
to lyve in a holy conversation with hym,
kepinge faithe and truethe in all poyntes,
as Godes Worde doth prescribe.

The answere:
Even so I take hym before God,
and in the presence of this his congregation.

5.

The Minister then sayeth (to the married couple):

Give diligent care to the (words of the) Gospell,
that ye may understande how our Lorde
wolde have this holy contracte kept and observed;
and howe sure and faste a knott it is,
which may in no wyse be lowsed,
accordyng as we be taughte
in the 19 chapter of S. Mattewes Gospell:
   "The Pharisies came unto Christe to tempte hym and to
grope hys mynde, sayinge, Is it lawfull for a man to put away
his wife for every lighte cawse? He answered, sayinge, Have ye
not read, that He which created man at the begynnynge, made
theym male and female? sayeng, For this thyng shall man leave
father and mother, and cleave unto his wife, and they twayne
shalbe one flesshe; so that they are no more two, but are one
flesshe. Let no man therfore put asonder that which God hathe
cowpled together."

If ye beleve assuredlie these woordes
which owr Lorde and Saviour did speake,
(according as ye have hard them now rehearsed
owte of the holy Gospell),
then may you be certayne,
that God hathe evyn so knytt you together
in this holy state of wedlocke.
Wherefore applie your selves
to lyve a chaste and holie lyfe together,
in godlie love, in Christian peace and good example;
ever holdinge faste the band of charitie
withowte any breache,
kepinge faithe and trueth th'one to the other,
even as Godes Woorde dothe appoynte.

6.

*Then the Minister commendeth theym to God in this or suche like
sorte:*

The Lorde sanctifie and blesse you;
the Lorde powre the riches of hys grace uppon you,
that ye may please hym,
and lyve together in holy love
to youre lyves ende.
So be it.

7.

Then is songe the 128 Psalme [=127],

"Blessed are they that feare the Lorde," etc.,

or some other appertaynyng to the same purpose.

27. THE DIRECTORY FOR THE PUBLICK WORSHIP OF GOD

Agreed upon by the Assembly of Divines at Westminster . . . 1645.

In 1645, a number of English and Scottish divines, impatient with the compromises of the *Book of Common Prayer*, met to draw up guidelines for what they considered a more biblically-based form of worship. The guidelines for marriage, incorporated into the Westminster Directory, have served ever since as the basis of the various Free Church traditions.

The text begins with the by-now familiar Reformation assertion that marriage is a part of this world's order, established by God at creation, but not a sacrament. Nonetheless, because it is a way of life which the baptized may adopt, it should be entered upon and lived in the right spirit. The possibility of formal betrothal is recognized, if only as constituting an impediment to marriage to a third party, but the Church seems not to be involved in its celebration. Church involvement begins with the customary three-fold publication of the marriage banns. (Consent of parents or guardians is required in the case of the marriage of minors: Calvin required such consent for girls under eighteen and boys under twenty.) The wedding itself is not to take place on a Sunday, contrary to Calvin's prescription. The service opens with spontaneous prayer by the minister (2), followed by a discourse on marriage (3) which is to be based on the Scriptures. Then follows a final effort to assure the couple's freedom to marry. The marriage vows that follow are even shorter than those of John Knox, but the joining of hands is restored. Finally, the minister pronounces the couple man and wife and offers a short prayer on their behalf (5). The registration of marriage, required in English law since Elizabeth I, appears for the first time in these texts.

This abbreviated rite did not last long, for in 1653 the so-called "Barebones Parliament" enacted that "all persons intending to marry shall come before some justice of the peace within the county, city, or town corporate" where they live and where the banns have been published. After presenting proof of the publication of banns and, as may be appropriate, proof of parental consent, the couple exchanged vows. "After this, the justice may and shall declare the said man and woman to be from henceforth husband and wife . . . and no other marriage whatsoever, within the commonwealth of England, after the 29th of September, 1653, shall be held or accounted a marriage according to the law of England." Though the latter provision was repealed by Cromwell's restored Parliament of 1656 and the *Book of Common Prayer* was reimposed after the Restoration of 1660, the tendency towards a strictly civil marriage was now irreversible.

TEXT

Breward, I., ed. *The Westminster Directory*. Bramcote: Grove Publications, 1980, 24–26.

BIBLIOGRAPHY

Stevenson, 1982:155–157.

THE SOLEMNIZATION OF MARRIAGE

1a
Although Marriage be no Sacrament, nor peculiar to the Church of God, but common to Mankind, and of publick Interest in every Common-wealth; yet, because such as marry are to marry in the Lord, and have special Need of Instruction, Direction, and Exhortation, from the Word of God, at their Entring into such a new Condition; and of the Blessing of God upon them therein; we judge it expedient, that Marriage be solemnized by a lawful Minister of the Word, that he may accordingly counsel them, and pray for a Blessing upon them.

1b
Marriage is to be betwixt one Man and one Woman only; and they, such as are not within the Degrees of Consanguinity or Affinity prohibited by the Word of God; and the Parties are to be of Years of Discretion, fit to make their own Choice, or, upon good Grounds to give their mutual Consent.

1c
Before the solemnizing of Marriage between any Persons, their Purpose of Marriage shall be published by the Minister, three several Sabbath-days, in the Congregation at the Place or Places of their most usual and constant Abode respectively. And of this Publication, the Minister who is to join them in Marriage, shall have sufficient Testimony, before he proceed to solemnize the Marriage.

1d
Before that Publication of such their Purpose (if the Parties be under Age) the Consent of the Parents, or others under whose Power they

are (in case the Parents are dead) is to be made known to the Church-Officers of that Congregation, to be recorded.

1e
The like is to be observed in the Proceedings of all others, although of Age, whose Parents are living, for their first Marriage. And in After marriages of either of those Parties, they shall be exhorted not to contract Marriage without first acquainting their Parents with it (if with Conveniency it may be done), endeavouring to obtain their Consent. Parents ought not to force their Children to marry without their free Consent, nor deny their own Consent without just Cause.

1f
After the Purpose or Contract of Marriage hath been thus published, the Marriage is not to be long deferred. Therefor the Minister, having had convenient Warning, and nothing been objected to hinder it, is publickly to solemnize it in the Place appointed by Authority for publick Worship, before a competent Number of credible Witnesses, at some convenient Hour of the Day, at any Time of the Year, except on a Day of publick Humiliation. And we advise that it be not on the Lord's Day.

2.
And, because all Relations are sanctified by the Word and Prayer, the Minister is to pray for a blessing upon them, to this Effect:

Acknowledging our Sins,
whereby we have made ourselves
less than the least of all the Mercies of God,
and provoked him to imbitter all our Comforts;
earnestly, in the Name of Christ, to intreat the Lord
(whose Presence and Favour
is the Happiness of every Condition,
and sweetens every Relation)
to be their Portion,
and to own and accept them in Christ,
who are now to be joined
in the honourable Estate of Marriage,
the Covenant of their God:
And that,
as he hath brought them together by his Providence,
he would sanctify them by his Spirit,
giving them a new Frame of Heart,
fit for their new Estate;
enriching them with all Graces,

whereby they may perform the Duties,
enjoy the Comforts,
undergo the Cares,
and resist the Temptations
which accompany that Condition,
as becometh Christians.

3.

The Prayer being ended, it is convenient that the Minister do briefly declare unto them, out of the Scripture, The Institution, Use, and Ends of Marriage, with the Conjugal Duties, which in all Faithfulness, they are to perform each to other; exhorting them to study the holy Word of God, that they may learn to live by Faith, and to be content in the Midst of all Marriage Cares and Troubles, sanctifying God's Name, in a thankful, sober, and holy Use of all conjugal Comforts; praying much with, and for one another; watching over, and provoking each other to love and good Works; and to live together as the Heirs of the Grace of Life.

4.

After solemn charging of the Persons to be married, before the great God, who searcheth all Hearts, and to whom they must give a strict Account at the last Day, that if either of them know any Cause, by Precontract or otherwise, why they may not lawfully proceed to Marriage, that they now discover it: The Minister (if no Impediment be acknowledged) shall cause first the Man to take the Woman by the right Hand, saying these Words,

I, N., do take thee N.,
to be my married Wife,
and do, in the Presence of God,
and before this Congregation,
promise and covenant
to be a loving and faithful Husband unto thee,
until God shall separate us by Death.

Then the Woman shall take the Man by his right Hand, and say these Words,

I, N., do take thee N.,
to be my married Husband,
and I do, in the Presence of God,
and before this Congregation,
promise and covenant
to be a loving, faithful, and obedient Wife unto thee,
until God shall separate us by Death.

5.

Then, without any further Ceremony, the Minister shall, in the Face of the Congregation, pronounce them to be Husband and Wife, according to God's Ordinance; and so conclude the Action with Prayer to this Effect; That the Lord would be pleased to accompany his own Ordinance with his Blessing, beseeching him to enrich the Persons now married, as with other Pledges of his Love, so particularly with the Comforts and Fruits of Marriage, to the Praise of his abundant Mercy, in and through Christ Jesus.

6.

A Register is to be carefully kept, wherein the Names of the Parties so married, with the Time of their Marriage, are forthwith to be fairly recorded in a Book, provided for that Purpose, for the Perusal of all whom it may concern.

28. AN ECUMENICAL MARRIAGE RITE (1985)

Since the 1960s, most Western Churches have undertaken a revision of their marriage rites and have established a definite pattern of convergence in the way they celebrate the rites. Instead of selecting from among all these new rites, it seems better to choose, as representative of this new ecumenical convergence, the rite drawn up by the Consultation on Common Texts (CCT). The CCT is a forum for consultation on the renewal of worship which embraces many of the mainline churches of North America and Canada. The value of this text is not only that it provides for the ritualization of interchurch marriages, but that it is rather representative of the way the mainline churches envisage the celebration of marriage at this point in history.

The Ecumenical Marriage Rite is clearly heir to the long Western evolution of the marriage liturgy, especially as it was shaped in the English-speaking world after the Reformation. This gives it a rather conservative or traditional character. As in all postconciliar liturgies, there is a clear preference for public celebration in the presence of friends and acquaintances. In accordance with the longstanding Western legal and theological axiom that "consent makes the marriage," the couple are clearly seen to be marrying each other, rather than "being married" by the minister. Reflecting socio-cultural developments in the modern world, marriage is presented very much as a partnership between equals. Open to the possibility that ministers from both communities of faith may actively participate in the service, the rubrics remain rather generic: "A minister says . . ."

Compared with most of the historic marriage rites of the Christian tradition, this one is relatively short on symbols but represents a fairly solid consensus concerning the significance of marriage for believing Christians. In providing exclusively for the "church part" of the process of marrying—unlike earlier rites which accompanied the couple from betrothal to bedding— the rite also reflects the sharp modern dichotomy between liturgy and life or, better, between religious rituals and secular rituals; in this instance, between the part of the celebration that takes place in church and the rest of the customary practices associated with getting married.

TEXT

A Consultation on Common Texts. *A Christian Celebration of Marriage: An Ecumenical Liturgy.* Copyright 1985.

BIBLIOGRAPHY

Henderson, J. F. "A Christian Celebration of Marriage: An Ecumenical Liturgy," in Farnedi, 1986, 375–385.

Stevenson, 1987:179-181.

Tegels, A. "An Ecumenical Rite of Marriage." *Worship* 59 (1985) 5, 446–449.

ORDER OF SERVICE[3]

GATHERING

Greeting
(Questions to the Congregation and the Couple)
Public Declaration of Intention
Affirmation by Families and Congregation
Prayer of the Day

WORD OF GOD

THE MARRIAGE

Marriage Vows
Exchange of Rings
Announcement of the Marriage

PRAYERS

Prayers of Intercession
Prayer of Blessing
Lord's Prayer

CONCLUSION

Kiss of Peace
Dismissal

Music is suggested as a preference or as an option in the following places: at the gathering; the psalm following the first reading; follow-

---

[3] Portions in brackets are optional.

*ing the sermon; following the announcement of the marriage; at the
dismissal.*

I

GATHERING

1.

*The people gather, forming a community of friends of the couple, in
order to offer thanks to God, to serve as witnesses, and to assure the
couple of their continuing support and love.*

*It is important that hospitality be shown to welcome all those who
are not part of the local congregation.*

2.

The congregation stands.

*The ministers enter and go to the entrance of the church to welcome
the wedding party. After they have greeted the bride and groom, the
entire party enters the church and goes to a place in front of the assembly. The procession may take this order: cross and torches, assisting ministers, host and guest presiding ministers, attendants, parents
and bride and bridegroom. It is appropriate that a hymn or psalm be
sung during the entrance, or music performed by instrumentalists or a
choir.*

*(If a simpler entrance is desired, the ministers come before the as-
sembly. The bride and bridegroom and their attendants enter the
church together and stand before the ministers and the assembly.)*

GREETING

3.

A minister says:

The grace of our Lord Jesus Christ,
the love of God
and the communion of the Holy Spirit
be with you all.

All: And also with you.

4.

Dear friends:
We have come together in the presence of God
to witness the marriage of N. and N.,
to surround them with our prayers,
and to share in their joy.

The Scriptures teach us
that the bond and covenant of marriage
is a gift of God,
a holy mystery
in which man and woman become one flesh,
an image of the union of Christ and his Church.

As this man and woman give themselves
to each other today,
we remember that at Cana in Galilee
our Lord Jesus Christ made the wedding feast
a sign of God's kingdom of love.

Let us enter into this celebration confident
that, through the Holy Spirit,
Christ is present with us also:
we pray that this couple may fulfill God's purpose
for the whole of their lives.

If required by law or local custom:

5.
QUESTIONS TO THE CONGREGATION
AND THE COUPLE

5a
A minister says to the congregation:

These two persons have come here
to become one in this holy union.
But if any of you can show just cause
why they may not be lawfully married,
declare it now
or hereafter remain silent.

5b
A minister says to the couple:

N. and N.,
have you come here freely
and without reservation
to join together lawfully in marriage?

The bride and bridegroom separately respond:

I have.

6.
PUBLIC DECLARATION OF INTENTION

6a
A minister says to the bride:

N., will you have N.[4]
to be your husband,
to live together in holy marriage?
Will you love him, comfort him,
honor and keep him,
in sickness and in health,
and, forsaking all others,
be faithful to him as long as you both shall live?

The bride responds:

I will.

6b
A minister says to the bridegroom:

N., will you have N.
to be your wife,
to live together in holy marriage?
Will you love her, comfort her,
honor and keep her,
in sickness and in health,
and, forsaking all others,
be faithful to her as long as you both shall live?

The bridegroom responds:

I will.

AFFIRMATION BY FAMILIES AND CONGREGATION

6c
A minister says to the families:

Do you, the families of N. and N.,
give your love and blessing to this new family?
R: We do.

6d
Members of the families may share expressions of encouragement and love with the couple.

---

[4] *Book of Common Prayer,* I.3.

7.

A minister says to the congregation:

Will all of you,
by God's grace,
do everything in your power
to uphold and care for these two persons
in their life together?
R: We will.

8.

PRAYER OF THE DAY

A minister says:

Let us pray.

Gracious God,
you sent your Son Jesus Christ into the world
to reveal your love to all people.
Enrich these your servants with every good gift,
that their life together may show forth your love;
and grant that at the last
we may all celebrate with Christ
the marriage feast that has no ending.
In the name of Jesus Christ our Lord.
R: Amen.

The congregation is seated.

II

THE WORD OF GOD

*Suggested Bible readings are given below.[5] Three (or two) readings
may be chosen, one of which is always from the Gospels.*

1.

Before the first reading, the reader may say:

A reading from (the name of the book of the Bible).

First reading.

At the conclusion of the first reading, the reader may say:

The Word of the Lord.

And the congregation may respond:

Thanks be to God.

[5] Cf. Appendix I.

2.

A psalm or hymn is sung as a response to the first reading.

Psalm.

3.

Before the second reading, the reader may say:

A reading from (the name of the book of the Bible).

Second reading.

At the conclusion of the second reading, the reader may say:

The Word of the Lord.

And the congregation may respond:

Thanks be to God.

4.

An acclamation (Alleluia) or hymn may be sung as a preparation for the Gospel.

All may stand for the Gospel.

Before the Gospel, the minister who reads it may say:

The Holy Gospel of our Lord Jesus Christ
according to (the name of the Gospel).

And the congregation may respond:

Glory to you, O Lord.

Gospel.

At the conclusion of the Gospel, the minister may say:

The Gospel of the Lord.

And the congregation may respond:

Praise to you, Lord Jesus Christ.

The congregation is seated.

5.

A sermon or homily is then preached.

6.

A hymn may be sung.

III

THE MARRIAGE

MARRIAGE VOWS

1.
The congregation is seated.

The bride and bridegroom stand in view of the congregation and face each other.

A minister says:

Join your hands and declare your vows.

2.
The bride and bridegroom join their hands and speak so that all can hear. The minister discreetly helps the couple proclaim their vows.

The bridegroom says:

In the presence of God and this community[6]
I, N., take you, N.,
to be my wife;
to have and to hold from this day forward,
in joy and in sorrow,
in plenty and in want,
in sickness and in health,
to love and to cherish,
as long as we both shall live.
This is my solemn vow.

The bride says:

In the presence of God and this community
I, N., take you, N.,
to be my husband;
to have and to hold from this day forward,
in joy and in sorrow,
in plenty and in want,
in sickness and in health,
to love and to cherish,
as long as we both shall live.
This is my solemn vow.

3.
EXCHANGE OF RINGS

---

[6] See *Book of Common Prayer*, I.5.

3a

It is preferable that two rings be exchanged. The rings are placed on a suitable plate, or on the service book of the minister,[7] or are held by an assisting minister.

A minister says:

3b

Bless, O Lord,
(the giving of) these rings:[8]
may they who wear them
live in love and fidelity,
and continue in your service
all the days of their lives,
through Christ our Lord.
R: Amen.

(If only one ring is exchanged:

Bless, O Lord,
(the giving of) this ring;
may he who gives it
and she who wears it
live in love and fidelity,
and continue in your service
all the days of their lives,
through Jesus Christ our Lord.
R: Amen.)

3c

The bridegroom places the ring on the ring finger of the bride, and speaks so that all can hear:

N., I give you this ring,
as a sign of the covenant we have made today.
(In the name of the Father and of the Son
and of the Holy Spirit.)

The bride places the ring on the ring finger of her bridegroom, and speaks so that all can hear:

N., I give you this ring,
as a sign of the covenant we have made today.
(In the name of the Father
and of the Son
and of the Holy Spirit.)

[7] See *Book of Common Prayer,* 6.
[8] See Sarum, I.5.

(If only one ring is exchanged, the appropriate omission is made.)

3d

If it is customary, other suitable tokens may be exchanged or used at this time.

4.

ANNOUNCEMENT OF THE MARRIAGE

A minister says:

Now that N. and N.
have given themselves to each other
by solemn vows,
with the joining of hands,
and the giving of ring(s),
I announce to you that they are husband and wife.

Those whom God has joined together,
let no one put asunder.

R: Blessed be the Lord our God now and forever. Amen.

5.

A hymn may be sung.

IV

PRAYERS

PRAYERS OF INTERCESSION

The congregation stands.

1.

A minister says:

Friends of Christ,
in the midst of our joy
let us pray also for this broken world.

For all people in their daily life and work;
for our families, friends and neighbors,
and for all whose lives touch ours.
R: We pray to you, our God.

For this holy fellowship of faith
in which we seek your grace;
for the world, the nation and this community,
in which we work for justice, freedom and peace.
R: We pray to you, our God.

For the just and proper use of your creation;
for the victims of hunger,
injustice and oppression.
R: We pray to you, our God.

For all who are in danger, sorrow
or any kind of trouble;
for those who minister to the sick,
the friendless and the needy.
R: We pray to you, our God.

For those who have suffered
the loss of child or parent,
husband or wife;
for those to whom love is a stranger.
R: We pray to you, our God.

Most gracious God,
you have made us in your image
and given us over to one another's care.
Hear the prayers of your people,
that unity may overcome division,
hope vanquish despair,
and joy conquer sorrow.
Through Jesus Christ our Lord.
R: Amen.

2.
PRAYER OF BLESSING

The couple may kneel.

A minister says:

Blessed are you, Lord God, Heavenly Father.
In your great love you created us male and female
and made the union of husband and wife
an image of the union between you and your people.
You sent Jesus Christ to come among us,
making your love visible in him,
to bring new life to the world.

Send your Holy Spirit to pour out
the abundance of your blessing on N. and N.,
who have this day given themselves
to each other in marriage.

Bless them in their work
and in their companionship;

in their sleeping and their waking;
in their joys and in their sorrows;
in their life and in their death.

(Give them the gift and heritage of children
in accordance with your will,
and make their home a haven of peace.)
Let their love for each other
be a seal upon their hearts,
a mantle about their shoulders,
a crown upon their foreheads.

Bless them
so that all may see in their lives together
in the community of your people
a vision of your kingdom on earth.
And finally, in the fullness of time,
welcome them into the glory of your presence.
Through your Son Jesus Christ
with the Holy Spirit in your holy Church
all honor and glory is yours, Almighty Father,
now and for ever.
R: Amen.

3.
LORD'S PRAYER

A minister says:

And now,
with the confidence of the children of God,
let us pray:

All: Our Father in heaven . . . now and forever.
Amen.

4.
The couple rises.

V

CONCLUSION

1.
KISS OF PEACE

The husband and wife may greet each other with a kiss.

Greetings may be exchanged throughout the congregation.

2.
DISMISSAL

A minister says:

The Lord bless you and keep you.
The Lord make his face shine on you
and be gracious to you.
The Lord look upon you with favor
and give you peace.
R: Amen.

3.
A minister says:

Go in peace
to love and serve the Lord.
R: Thanks be to God.

4.
The wedding party then leaves the church. A hymn, psalm or choral music may be sung, or instrumental music may be played.

MARRIAGE RITES AS DOCUMENTS OF FAITH: NOTES FOR A THEOLOGY OF MARRIAGE

Whether or not the marriage of Christians be considered a sacrament in the strict sense of the term, however that be defined, it is rarely understood as a simply secular undertaking. Because it is lived by two baptized people and constitutes their common life, it cannot but be the form in which their Christian vocation and their engagement in the mystery of salvation is lived out. But for many, especially for those who belong to the Catholic and Orthodox Churches, marriage between two baptized people is considered a visible sign of the unfolding of the hidden mystery of God in this world and thus significant not only for the couple themselves, but for the wider community to which they belong. Precisely because marriage is understood as an integral part of the whole economy of grace, itself conceived in sacramental-incarnational terms, this understanding of marriage has to be integrated into any adequate and coherent theology. And this presents particular problems, for while sacramentality, by definition, means the intersecting of two worlds of reality—the divine and the human, the invisible and the visible—the relation of these two orders in marriage is not particularly easy to identify. Marriage has always existed and continues to exist without being a sacrament: not every marriage is sacramental. A marriage between two non-believers is not regarded by the Church as sacramental, nor is a marriage between a baptized and an unbaptized person. The status of marriages contracted by baptized persons who lack faith continues to be disputed, though in law they are treated as sacramental marriages. A further problem relates to what it is precisely that constitutes the sacrament, a problem that continues to vex the Catholic Church in particular.[1] This is not the place to rehearse the canonical issue, but a sketch of the development of Christian thinking about marriage will help situate the texts of this collection and underline their significance.

[1] See Theodore Mackin, S.J. *What Is Marriage?* (New York: Paulist, 1982).

I

CHRISTIAN MARRIAGE IN HISTORY

Marriage in the Early Christian Centuries

It is important to realize from the outset that marriage was originally considered a "Christian marriage," or a marriage contracted and lived "in the Lord" (I Cor 7:39), because it was a marriage between two baptized believers in Christ. In other words, the sacramentality of marriage as a *state*, depended not on a wedding rite but on the baptismal identity of the couple. Their life together was a form of the Christian life, a form which, in the mutual love and reciprocal service for which marriage afforded occasion, was capable of iconicizing the mutual relationship between Christ and the Church (Eph 5:21-33).

In the early centuries, the way Christians contracted marriage differed little, if at all, from the way non-Christians got married, viz., through the customary domestic rites of betrothal, the handing-over of the bride, and the celebration of cohabitation, as these were done in different societies. It did not exclude marriage by cohabitation alone, where this was a socially acceptable way of marrying as, for example, among the lower classes. Nor did it fear to recognize marriages which the state would not recognize, as when the Roman Church recognized as marriage the permanent relationship between a free woman and a slave. The arranging, celebrating and consummating of these marriages were matters, usually, for the families concerned, though it appears that, in the East, the local bishop did on occasion take an active role in finding suitable spouses for orphaned or abandoned children. Marriage was a domestic matter in all societies, being arranged by the two families and celebrated in the two households. Christians seem to have taken this entirely for granted although, as was only to be expected, their faith prompted them, on the one hand to suppress or adapt the religious (i.e. "pagan") dimensions of the inherited customs, and on the other to invite the bishop or priest, as leader of the faith community, to pronounce a blessing on the couple as they began their life together.

For many centuries, the presence of the clergy and the giving of the nuptial blessing seems to have been something rather like the blessing of a house today: a privilege sought by the devout rather than an obligation incumbent upon all. In fact, it only began to be urged upon couples who were marrying if the bridegroom was a member of the clergy. From the late fourth century, clerics who married were expected to seek the blessing of the bishop upon their marriage and to dispense with the traditional raucous and often rather ribald custom of the *domum-ductio* (procession to the groom's house). The fact that the traditional Roman Rite, as found in the Verona, Gelasian and Gregorian sacramentaries, consisted of a Nuptial Mass and blessing, without any exchange of vows, reflects this non-involvement of the Church in the actual arrangement and conduct of the betrothal and wedding (texts 4, 5, and 6). In the East, however, in the fourth to seventh centuries, matters took a different direction, and the clergy become closely involved in both the rites of betrothal (which, in the solemn form involving the *arrhas*, were considered binding and virtually irrevocable) and in the rites associated with the beginning of married life. This seems to have happened in part because the need for the Church to regulate marriages seems to have asserted itself rather earlier in the East than in the West, and in part because of a rather vivid sense of the identity of the Church itself as the Bride of Christ. Whatever the reasons, we find, beginning in Armenia in the late fourth century and spreading to the rest of the Eastern empire in the centuries following, that the priest or bishop is coming to assume a central role in the conduct of the marriage ceremonies. Central to these ceremonies from ancient times were the rites of the joining of the couple's hands, the handing over of the bride to her husband, and the crowning of the couple with garlands. These came to constitute the central elements of what quickly emerged as a specifically Christian wedding liturgy, and the last of them came to lend its name (*stephanoma*: "crowning") to the whole liturgy (see texts 7 and 8). Sometimes this rite took place on the same day as the secular or domestic aspects of the celebration, sometimes the day before. Even so, it was not until the late ninth century that Constantinople ruled that this marriage liturgy, conducted by the clergy, would henceforth become the *only* way of marrying recognized by the Church as valid.

If the Eastern Church had a strong sense of the community of believers as constituting the Bride of Christ, that awareness in the West became somewhat obscured by the writings of Tertullian (died c. 220) and Cyprian (martyred 258) in North Africa. Responding perhaps to the fact that women considerably outnumbered men in North Africa, they both encouraged young women to dedicate themselves to a life of virginity by applying to the individual woman who so dedicated herself the title that had previously and properly belonged to the whole community: bride of Christ. In the late fourth century, we find Ambrose of Milan talking about a public ceremony in which women were dedicated to God, a ceremony called "the veiling of virgins." The veil in question was the orange-colored *flammeum*, customarily worn by the Roman bride on her wedding day: if the virgin was to be the bride of Christ, she should be publicly espoused to Christ and given the veil.

Although this whole history of the development of the "veiling of virgins" and its connection with the developing Christian marriage rite at Rome remains obscure, it is certain that there was some connection. In the *Verona Sacramentary*, the marriage rite is called "the nuptial veiling"; in the *Gregorian* it is "the veiling of brides." In pre-Christian Roman tradition, however, the veiling of the bride was not part of the ceremonies: when she appeared for her wedding, she was already dressed and veiled. There is reason, however, to think that, in the late fourth and early fifth centuries, the newly developed rite for the consecration of a virgin (the so-called *velatio virginum*) began to influence Christian marriage rites at Rome and lead to the introduction of a ceremony of "nuptial veiling" of the bride, comparable to the public veiling of the woman in the rite for the consecration of virgins. In both instances, the underlying motif would be that of the dedication of the young woman as "bride of Christ," in the one case through a life of virginity, in the other through married life. Nevertheless, there are several difficulties with this hypothesis: it is hard to see how the priest or bishop could actually give the veil (did the bride appear in public bare-headed?); there are no extant rubrics or descriptions to indicate how it was done; later medieval sources, like the *Liber Ordinum*, refer to a veiling of *both* husband and wife; there is no mention in the prayers of any veil or act of veiling. In support of the hypothesis, on the other hand, is the whole tenor of the nuptial blessing and of most of the Mass prayers in the sacramentaries, which pray almost exclusively for the bride, and constitute a sort of consecration of the woman to married life. Certainly the very close parallel between the nuptial blessings and the prayers for the consecration of virgins in these Roman documents from late antiquity is unmistakable and has often been commented on.[2]

[2] See P. d'Izany, "Mariage et consécration virginale au 4e siècle," *La vie spirituelle: 'Supplément,* 24 (1953), 92–118. J. P. de Jong, "Brautsegen und Jungfrauweihe: Eine Rekonstruktion des altrömischen Trauungsritus als Basis für

Whatever the truth of the matter concerning the origins and inspiration of the Roman nuptial blessing, the fact is that the role of the clergy, and thus the liturgical celebration of marriage, did not usually include, in the West, their involvement in the arrangement of the dowry and the contract of betrothal, nor in the handing over of the bride to her husband's family, nor in the joining of hands, nor in the customs associated with the bringing of the bride to her new home. The only exception might have been the marriage of orphans who were under episcopal protection or, as we see with Paulinus of Nola's marriage ode (text 3), the marriage of clergy. But the mindset revealed in the ode also shows that the clergy wanted to keep a clear distance between the marriage liturgy and whatever else popular custom might require.

Here we catch a glimpse of another, more problematic dimension of the parallel established in Christian antiquity, especially in the West, between the life of marriage and the life of virginity. The preference for virginity had already been unequivocally expressed by St Paul in I Corinthians 7: "he who marries his betrothed does well; and he who refrains from marriage will do better." But, whereas Paul, in expressing a personal preference for virginity, particularly in view of the imminent end of the world ("the appointed time has grown very short"), also took pains to insist that marriage was not sinful, there was always a strong dualistic strain of Christianity which thought otherwise. In this gnostic tradition, later taken up by the Manichees, all matter is evil and all involvement with the life of the flesh, as in marriage, sinful. Now, while the leaders of the Church defended the legitimacy and even the sanctity of marriage, they could not quite get over a deep-rooted cultural suspicion of sexuality, so tied up did it seem with the world that was passing away, with mortality and corruption, with passions that threatened to cloud the rational mind and thereby possibly to shipwreck the soul on its journey to salvation. It thus came to be the common opinion of teachers and theologians in the West that while marriage was a legitimate way of life for Christian people, sexual pleasure was always sinful and sexual intercourse could only excuse such pleasure (reducing it to a minor sin) when it was undertaken exclusively for the purpose of conceiving a child. For this reason, perhaps, the amount written on

theologische Besinnung," *Zeitschrift fur Theologie und Kirche*, 84 (1962), 300–302. R. Metz, *La consécration des vièrges dans l'Eglise romaine*. Paris: Presses universitaires de France, 1954.

marriage in the patristic period is miniscule compared with the amount written in praise of virginity.

Marriage in the Middle Ages

The Middle Ages begin when the Roman Empire is replaced in the West by a new civilization bringing together the old Roman peoples in Italy, Spain and Gaul with the new peoples who had migrated West in waves from Eastern Europe, the steppes of central Asia and ultimately from Mongolia. The Vandals, the Goths, the Franks and others burst through the defenses of the Roman Empire along the Rhine and Danube, and came to settle in what is now Western Europe, bringing with them their own languages, their own laws, and their own customs. In what concerned marriage these Germanic peoples shared one thing in common that differentiated them from their new Roman neighbors: for them marriage rested not upon consent of the couple, but upon cohabitation. The bride was treated pretty much as a family asset, which might be lost to another family by elopement or capture perhaps, but was preferably transferred in orderly fashion and to the satisfaction of both families by purchase agreement. This agreement involved drawing up a contract between the heads of the respective families which stipulated the dowry the girl might bring to the marriage and the compensation to be given the girl's family for the loss of her. This agreement constituted a betrothal, and penalties were reckoned if one of the families reneged on the agreement and failed to go through with the marriage. Some time after this betrothal, at a time and place stipulated in the agreement, the girl would be handed over to the authority of her husband's family and the couple would then be married. The Gallican and Celtic traditions of the blessing of the marriage chamber, with or without the blessing of the food and drink and of the ring, reflects this Germanic tradition and the domestic setting in which it was celebrated (texts 9 and 10).

A tension thus arose between Roman practice based on consent and Germanic practice based on the bride price and cohabitation, between negative patristic views of sexuality and Germanic understandings of marriage which defined it almost exclusively in terms of sexual relations. From this tension arose juridical conflicts which were not resolved for several centuries, while from the unsettled social conditions of the so-called "Dark Ages" sprang the problems of widespread infidelity, divorce, abuse of women, disinheritance of lawful heirs, and so on, that so taxed serious-minded churchmen of the time. The compromise eventually arrived at, beginning with Hincmar of Rheims in the ninth century, was to define an indissoluble marriage as one that was both *ratum* and *consummatum*, i.e. freely and lawfully entered into and then consummated by sexual intercourse. This canonical combination of both the Roman and the Germanic definitions of marriage was the reason, it has been suggested, why marriages in the later Middle Ages were commonly celebrated at dusk![3] The combination is seen in our texts, however, in the Anglo-Norman synthesis represented by the *Benedictional of Archbishop Robert* (11), and especially by *Bury St Edmunds* (18) and *Barbeau* (19), which lead through *Sarum* (20) to the modern rites.

Nonetheless, while such a solution may have satisfied the lawyers, it did little to resolve the conflict of mentalities. From the eleventh century, the Church began to assert its juridical authority over marriage in a series of reforming synods. From these synods emerged legislation affecting the public nature of marriage and intended to curb the worst abuses of clandestine marriages. But these synods, in attempting to reform marriage, also contributed to the denigration of marriage by imposing celibacy upon the higher clergy. Thus the reform movement perpetuated the negative attitudes towards sexuality found in Jerome and Augustine, suggesting that it was incompatible with service at the altar. Of course, most of the writers and reformers of the early Middle Ages were monks, who naturally tended to view women as a temptation and sexuality as the plaything of the devil. These attitudes seep over into preaching and into the exhortations that married people should abstain from sex during Lent, on the vigils of major feasts, on Sundays, and before approaching the Eucharist.[4] Such teaching derived from Paul's exhortation to couples not to refuse each other "except perhaps for a season, to devote yourselves to prayer," but suc-

---

[3] James A. Brundage. *Law, Sex and Christian Society in Medieval Europe*. (Chicago: University of Chicago Press, 1987) 136.

[4] Conversely, the newly-married could be barred from attending church. So Gregory I to Augustine of Canterbury: "It has always been the custom of the Romans from olden times that [a married man] should seek purification and reverently abstain awhile from entering the church after intercourse with his wife. In holding this view, we do not mean that the couple are at fault. It is just that marital intercourse cannot take place without the desire of the flesh and so they should stay away from entering the sacred place because such desire can never be aroused without sin." (PL 72:89) See Gel, 6. "Infra actionem for the thirtieth day after marriage, or for the anniversary."

ceeded in turning it into a prohibition of intercourse under pain of sin. The Book of Tobit which, in its interpolated form, also played a crucial role as the model which had inspired the fourth century *Statuta ecclesiae antiqua* to advocate continence on the first night of marriage "out of respect for the blessing," was now invoked to propose more extended periods of continence.

There is very little evidence, however, that such teaching was ever taken very seriously by most lay people, who went on living and loving and lusting pretty much as people had always done. Certainly, historical research on the sex lives of medieval Christians suggests that fornication, adultery, prostitution and concubinage all had their acknowledged place in medieval life and, apart from occasional outbursts of reform in response to zealous itinerant preachers, tended to be taken pretty much in stride by the local clergy.[5] But then the local pastors tended to be closer to their flocks than reformist preachers and episcopal synods. When clerical marriage was outlawed, it was not infrequently replaced by clerical concubinage, especially in more remote areas. Those few couples who took the Church's teaching on married sexuality seriously and made a mutual vow of continence were often considered candidates for canonization.

Christian Marriage: Tradition or Traditions?

Although the rites of marriage documented in this book were increasingly shaped by the emerging canon law relating to marriage, they remain (until the sixteenth century) essentially anonymous creations, the work, presumably, of local pastors who were asked to "say something" at the marriage of members of their flocks. It is essential, then, to recognize that there are at least three traditions of Christian marriage in the West.

First, there is the doctrinal, moral and canonical tradition developed and preserved in the teaching of the Fathers, and in the theological and canonical works of bishops and theologians. It is this which is the usual source for a Catholic "theology of marriage," but it is only one such source and cannot be safely used in isolation.

---

[5] See Jean-Louis Flandrin, "Sex in married life in the early Middle Ages: the Church's teaching and behavioural reality," in Philippe Ariès and Andre Bejin, *Western Sexuality. Practice and Precept in Past and Present Times.* (Oxford: Basil Blackwell, 1985) 114–129. Also, Jacques Rossiaud, "Prostitution, sex and society in French towns in the fifteenth century," *ibid.*, 76–94.

There is, second, the way Christian people through the centuries actually contracted their marriages and lived their married lives. For the most part, it must be said, history has not associated marrying with falling in love, but with doing one's duty as a son or daughter in a matter affecting the well-being of the family. Among the lower classes, it is quite likely that, at least up until the sixteenth-century Protestant and Catholic reforms, people frequently married without benefit of clergy. The canonical reforms of the eleventh century and the rites developed in response to them were primarily aimed at men of property and power, for the protection of their women and children. It did not prevent clandestine marriage or marriage by cohabitation, it merely delegitimized it; but that would not have had much effect on those who had neither name nor property worth speaking of to pass on to prospective heirs. Thus, while the lay tradition of marriage must be distinguished from the far better documented clerical tradition of marriage, within that lay tradition we need to distinguish marriage with the blessing of the Church from what one might call simply "marriage by cohabitation." Unfortunately, it is not possible at the present time to say with any confidence what percentage of the population of any given country at any given time used the rites presented in this collection.

Third, there is the romantic tradition which, historically, probably bore as little relation to most people's lived experience of marriage as did the theological tradition. It is represented by the much-discussed phenomenon of "courtly love" in the high Middle Ages, as reflected both in works of the creative imagination, such as the legend of Tristan and Isolde and the lays of the troubadours, and in the writings of mystical theologians.[6] Both in its medieval form and in its reviviscence in nineteenth century romanticism, and again in the twentieth-century idealization of "falling in love," it represents a drive to transcend the mundaneness of the institution of marriage in a *grand amour* for an idealized object, whether it be Christ, or the Virgin, *la belle dame sans merci* or some "dream woman." Paradoxically, under this heading have to be grouped two forms of other-worldliness: that which attempts to transcend the flesh in asceticism, and

---

[6] Denis de Rougemont, *Love in the Western World*, 1940, 1956. Martin d'Arcy, *The Mind and Heart of Love*, 1947, 1956. C. S. Lewis, *The Allegory of Love*. Georges Duby, *The Knight, the Lady and the Priest. The Making of Modern Marriage in Medieval France*, 1983. Jean Leclercq, *Monks on Marriage. A Twelfth-Century View*, 1982.

that which plunges into unbridled eroticism. Both are "other worldly" from the perspective of marriage; both are romantic in their flight from the realities of mundane living and in their quest for an immediacy of experience of an ideal lover. What they have in common is their unwillingness to hold together the two dimensions of the *sacramentum*: the visible and the invisible, the tangible and the intangible, the sacred and the secular, the ecstatic and the mundane, the life of the Spirit and the life of the flesh. A theology of marriage will have to define itself, in part at least, in opposition to the romantic tradition, and not just as "better to marry than to burn," especially today when popular culture exalts immediacy of experience and romantic love to the detriment of marriage as an institution. In so doing, it will need to develop a positive understanding of asceticism and its role in transforming a Christian marriage into a credible sacrament of divine love in human form.

Finally, there are the documents of the marriage liturgy. They have rarely served as anything more than a useful source of quotations in treatises on the theology of marriage, or as evidence of the development of canonical legislation on marriage. But the importance of these marriage documents lies elsewhere. As was suggested above, most of the documents in this book were not the work of theologians or canonists, but of anonymous and long-dead pastors whose apt invocations in the context of marriage survived to accompany and interpret and partially to transform the old, inherited ways of doing things. The Fathers and the moralists may have had negative views of sexuality and marriage; the assembled families may have had very specific economic goals or social ambitions in mind in marrying off their children. In their presence, and before this young, barely pubescent couple, what was a man of faith to say? Liturgy is always a moment of decision, when the theorizing has to end and the ideal has to yield to the practical: something has to be said and something has to be done. These documents witness to what nameless believers have found to say about marriage in the concrete, about the life and relationship that is opening up before this couple, and about the *sacramentum*. The *sacramentum* of matrimony—using the term in a broader sense than Augustine—is what holds the order of faith and the order of experience together. It is not an ideal, but a given reality. At a wedding it may be more or less clearly evoked, more or less overlaid by the social or even the erotic; but it is never moralizing. It is what it is. In the liturgy of mar-

riage it draws the couple and the attendance—more or less wit-
tingly, more or less willingly—into its ambit. Over against all
forms of dualism, these texts bear witness to the struggle of
Christians to hold the two dimensions of the Christian life
together in all their wholeness. Holism is the heart of Catholicism. These documents of the marriage liturgy show, more than
the writings of the theologians, and more than those who
romanticize the erotic, a balanced and forward-looking vision of
how the mystery of marriage can be understood and lived.

II

MOTIFS FOR A THEOLOGY OF MARRIAGE

A complete analysis of the theologies implicit in these documents of the marriage liturgy is beyond the scope of this essay.
Instead it will suffice to draw attention to certain themes or motifs that recur in different ways in the different traditions, allow-
ing the reader to explore the presence and form of these motifs
in the texts themselves.

1. *Anamnesis*

While a sense of anticipation is perhaps the chief hallmark of
modern weddings—anticipation of a life of love, of success, of
children, etc.—these traditional rites are strongly marked by
memory, or *anamnesis*. The meaning of this moment and of this
transaction is assessed not so much in reference to the hopes of
the couple, as to the memories of the community. Marriage in
general, and now this marriage in particular, is contextualized
in the economy of divine salvation, seen as a long, continuous
history of God's presence and assistance as generation after
generation of believers have tried to live in marriage a life of
faith.

   This anamnesis has the effect of relating the present couple to
the ancestors: to Adam and Eve, Abraham and Sarah, Isaac and
Rebeccah, Jacob and Rachel, Tobit and Sarah, Joachim and
Anna, Zachary and Elizabeth, and the anonymous couple at
Cana. Thus each new couple takes its place in the succession of
generations, hopeful of doing its duty by God's grace, and of
being blessed with children and an old age in which they see
the succession continued in their children's children, before
they pass to their reward. Even more than that, the whole succession of generations is somehow summed up in this bridal

pair: in a certain sense, they *become* Adam and Eve, Abraham and Sarah, and the rest. They become more than themselves, assuming a role which transcends their individual lives and loves and faith: they become Everyman and Everywoman, the archetypal Man and Woman, king and queen,[7] icons of the holy nation (text 2) wedded to its God.

In Christian usage, the image of the couple representing Israel yields, of course, to the image of the couple as living icons of Christ and the Church, based on Ephesians 5.[8] The importance of this for a theology of Christian marriage has already been discussed, but it is in the Byzantine and Coptic liturgies that this making of the couple into icons of Christ and his Church reaches full bloom. Properly understood, this could provide a starting point for a theology of the household as a domestic church constituted by marriage.

The divine sanction on marriage in general and on this marriage in particular is constantly recalled. Marriage is the first, original blessing conferred by God on humankind, a blessing that has survived the fall and the vicissitudes of history (and one might add, though the texts do not, a negative theological press in Christian history). In marrying before God, the couple take up what is their divine vocation, a way of life ordained by God and sanctified by its submission to God's plan for his creation. And the presence of Christ at the marriage feast of Cana, while simply the context for the first "epiphany" of Christ's glory in John's Gospel, has been seen in the ritual tradition as indicating the assumption of marriage into Christ's work of redemption. There, still, the Lord may manifest his glory in those who invite his presence in their lives.

In short, the role of remembering or anamnesis is to situate this marriage in a larger context of God's creative and redemptive work, to identify these two people with the couples who flit across the history of that work as recorded in the Scriptures, and to turn them into icons of the redeeming Christ and redeemed humanity. The couple do not merely minister the sacrament to each other: they become sacrament in assuming,

---

[7] So the Coptic liturgy:
    Crown them with glory and honor.
    The Father blesses,
    the Son crowns,
    the Holy Spirit sanctifies and makes perfect . . .

[8] Curiously, the image of the wedding feast of the Church and the Lamb in Revelations (Rev 19 and 21, *passim*) seems to have found no echo in our texts.

fully, consciously and actively, the sacramental role or vocation that the liturgy celebrates.

2. *Invocation*

Although the Jewish wedding liturgy maintains a mood of unqualified joy, content simply to bless God for the blessings of marriage, in all Christian traditions such a high vision of the married life evokes a corresponding call for divine assistance in living out this vocation. Out of anamnesis flows intercession, as the memory of God's economy prompts the request for help on behalf of those who are to be participant in it.

This pattern is common enough, but in the solemn blessings of the Roman Rite—the blessing of the font, the prayer of ordination, the Eucharistic prayer—the first and chief blessing that is invoked is the descent of the Holy Spirit upon the action of the Church, to ensure that the sacramental sign be capable of effecting what it signifies. The nuptial blessing is the equivalent prayer of the marriage rite and becomes the central element in the nuptial liturgies of the West. Yet, for all its similarities to the other solemn prayers, it passes directly from *anamnesis* to intercession without an *epiclesis* invoking the Spirit. (The same is true in the rite for the consecration of virgins.) Can it be that the importance attached to the exchange of consent as constituting marriage, (or to the intent to live a life of virginity, independent of any public ceremony of consecration), was such that the nuptial blessing was simply that: a blessing on a marriage that was already in place? If so, it is remarkable that later, when the marriage rite came to include the exchange of vows at the door of the church, no prayer for divine assistance was insinuated at that point.

The rest of the blessings prayed for inevitably reflect the social and cultural conditions of each liturgy and deserve closer comparison than can be undertaken here.

a. The *Roman* texts (4-6) tend to speak rather generically about God's lending assistance to the institutions he has ordained, but then become much more specific in the nuptial blessing. Here we have the mold, as it were, for the features of the ideal wife in late antiquity. She is to be, first and foremost, a lady: faithful, serious, modest, "a person of integrity and innocence," wise, and above suspicion. In her marriage "she devoutly serves the living God"; marriage is not so much for "lawful pleasures" as it is for fidelity both to God and to her

husband. A contemporary theological note creeps in with the
assertion, first found in an anonymous late-fourth century
Roman writer, that woman is (morally) weaker than man, because her likeness to God is one step removed: God made man
in his own image, but he made woman like man![9] Hence the
prayer for grace to protect her against her own weakness, and
to enable her to live a life of religious discipline. These prayers
doubtless survived in the marriage rite less because they bore
any direct relation to normal human experience (which would
suggest, if anything, that it has usually been men rather than
women who need such discipline), than because they matched
the negative picture of woman fostered early by ascetics, culti-
vated by monks, and promoted by the clergy. While the anam-
netic sections of the Roman prayers have some positive things
to say about the divine institution of marriage and its procreative purpose in God's plan, their brevity, their focus on the
woman, and their endorsement of the cultural stereotype of the
wife-as-matron make them rather poor sources for a theology of
marriage.

b. The Gallican tradition is that of the non-Roman West, though
it came to be compromised early on by Roman influence and
was eventually suppressed in favor of Roman Rites. Nonetheless, the conquest was not complete, for Gallican prayers and
rites have continued to appear in Western marriage rites to the
present day. They are represented in our collection by *Bobbio* (9)
and *Egbert* (10), with their characteristic blessing of the couple
in the nuptial chamber. In *Bobbio* the prayer is chiefly for those
graces that make marriage companionable: peace of mind, oneness of heart, charity. In *Egbert* there is more of a sense of what
might be called the religious dimension of marriage: "holiness,
chastity, meekness, fulfillment of the law and obedience to
God." But it is not purely moralizing, like the Roman prayers.
The *sacramentum* is not overlooked: "may [the Holy Trinity]
preserve your body, save your soul, shine in your heart, guide
your senses, and lead you to everlasting life." But just as *Bobbio*
asks for the graces of friendship, so *Egbert* is not ashamed to
ask for long life. Both ask for the blessing of children, but
neither seems defensive about sex or worried about the possibility of infidelity, though hints of this appear in the later Gallican
documents, from Canterbury and Northern Italy (12 and 13).

---

[9] Ambrosiaster, *In Epistolam I ad Corinthios*, 11:3-25 (PL 17:252-254).

c. In the Visigothic or old Spanish tradition, the most characteristic prayer is perhaps that for "united hearts" and "virtuous
children." They are not afraid to ask for the material security
which makes a happy marriage possible as well as for appropriate spiritual gifts, but there is an edge of anxiety, creeping in
from time to time, that the goods of this world, including the
joys of the marriage bed, might be a cause of their spiritual undoing. All in all, though, these Spanish prayers pray for the
couple that they may enjoy all blessings of body, heart and
mind.

d. The Eastern texts pray repeatedly for blessings that are
poured out, pressed down and running over, but like the
Visigothic texts they pray for material as well as spiritual, temporal as well as eternal goods. In the Byzantine liturgy, we see
this overflowing to the benefit of others:

Fill their houses with wheat, grain and oil
and with every good thing,
so that they may give in turn to those in need.

The Coptic liturgy is similar, except that here the joy of the day
and its promises are edged with the recognition of danger. Like
the Byzantine liturgy, it asks God to strengthen the promises
the couple have made to each other and to keep them united,
but it adds "Save them from the wiles of the evil one, and
from all diabolical temptation" and characterizes the anointing
as "protection against evil spirits."

e. The later medieval rites are largely a synthesis of the earlier
Western traditions, both Roman and non-Roman. *Sarum* (20),
for example, adds little to those earlier traditions in terms of
blessings prayed for. With the medieval Western rites, as with
the Eastern rites, one gets the impression that a general,
elaborate and repeated request for God's blessing outweighs
much attention to specifics, though the ancient Roman blessing
continues to present its profile of the ideal bride of late antiquity and the Gallican prayers qualify the austerity of the
Roman texts with their mutuality and homeliness.

f. The modern rites, those of the Reformation era and later, are
different again. The *Roman Missal* (21) is content to reproduce
the Mass prayers of the Gregorian sacramentary, but to set
them in the context of chants based on Tobit and thus redolent
of the whole medieval tradition. The final blessing of the couple
is an ancient Gallican prayer asking for children, long life in

this world and eternal life in the world to come. The *Roman Ritual* (22), as we noted in the introduction to the text, is less a liturgy than a canonical formula. It has only two brief prayers: one, for the blessing of the ring, asks that the woman remain faithful to her husband and to God's law; the other, at the end, asks God to keep together those whom he has joined together.

Curiously, the rites of the Churches of the Reformation—apart from Cranmer's *Book of Common Prayer* (25) which retains much of the Sarum rite—tend to be long on exhortation and short on prayer. Luther (24), for example, has only one prayer, asking that

thou wouldst not permit this
thy creation, ordinance and blessing,
to be disturbed or destroyed . . .

John Knox (26) has merely a blessing at the end, in which the minister prays that God will enable the couple to please him and to live together in holy love to their lives' end.

The *Ritual of Coutances* (23) on the other hand is remarkable not only for the sober and exalted view of marriage it proposes but also for the prayers for protection against, or deliverance from, the evil eye, which was thought to be responsible for infertility and impotence in marriage.

3. Marriage as a Way to Salvation

Thus, in sundry and divers ways, these documents testify to an acknowledgement of the light and the dark of marriage, and such a double dimension deserves to be retained even if the way in which it is expressed is thought to be archaic. It deserves to be retained as underlining a conviction running all through the prayers: namely, that marriage, for all its splendor as established by God and blessed by God, is a venture that can go astray. It is this realization that prompts prayer in the first place, of course, but it also points to a recognition that in marriage Christians have to work out their salvation in a life of faithful obedience to God. Marriage creates its own exigencies, as Luther indicates in speaking of the cross as well as the joy that God has given to married people. Prayers for peace, for singleness of heart, for obedience and mutual love make sense because marriage is potentially a cauldron of conflict, a battleground of conflicting needs and demands. Prayers for chastity and fidelity recognize the temptation to seek a way out, to avoid the discomfort, to seek to assuage one's hurts and one's unsatisfied desires elsewhere.

That is why marriage is spoken of as a bond, a law, an institution: what Martin d'Arcy called, in a felicitous phrase, "a quiet ordered love."[10] That order is not something the couple create for themselves, but something established by God and blessed by Christ and sanctified by generations of faithful couples for them to enter into. The crowning of the couple in the Byzantine rite captures this well. These are not the crowns of arrogance, or of make-believe princes and princesses, but the crown of martyrs, suggesting that married couples, too, faithful unto death, witness to Christ and make up what is to be made up in his sufferings. In other words, marriage is a pathway to salvation, a crucible for the transformation of faithful souls, a way to eternal life.

One thing all the texts pray for, but which we deliberately omitted from our brief survey of the nuptial *epiclesis*, is that the couple now being married may come at last to life everlasting. None of the rites pray that the couple may be happily married: they all pray that the couple may be found worthy to enter into eternal life. *Bury St Edmunds* (18), for example, prays God to bless the couple so that

. . . cleansed of all sin
the love of your love may grow in their hearts
which will please you on the dread judgement day . . .

On removing the crowns from the bridal pair, the priest prays in the Byzantine rite:

Receive their crowns into thy kingdom
preserving them spotless, blameless and without reproach
unto ages of ages.

In this way, a certain eschatological note enters into the marriage liturgy and qualifies the joy of the occasion by subordinating it to the final goal and purpose of human life: eternal life with God in the kingdom of heaven. Though the couple may still be young, the rites look beyond the hoped for years to come to the frontier of death. In the words of the old Gallican prayer retained at the end of the Nuptial Mass in the Roman Missal:

[10] D'Arcy, *op. cit.*, 48.

May you see your children's children
even to the third and fourth generation
and afterwards may you enjoy
eternal life without end.

Conclusion

Between the preoccupations of the families and the negativity of
theologians, pastors, it seems, still found positive vision of marriage to present to believers on the occasion of their betrothal
and their wedding. It is unclear to what extent their practice
can serve as a model for renewing Christian marriage today,
but the vision preserved in their prayers and blessings can continue to inspire.

It has been argued, for example, that a return to the practice
of marrying in stages might be helpful in today's de-Christianized
world, because it would help raise the consciousness of Christians about the splendor and seriousness of marrying "in
Christ." Whether separate rites of betrothal or blessings for the
beginning of married life could usefully surround and protract
the celebration of the wedding is uncertain. It may well help
the faithful, but it may do little for those whose faith is little
more than notional. Among such people the most common
pastoral problem today seems to be not only that they have no
inkling of what a sacramental marriage might mean, but that
they are often already living together or intend to do so with or
without the blessing of the Church, which then appears as a
more or less dispensable ceremony for helping them celebrate
their relationship. In the Catholic Church, at least, the most
pressing problem to be decided is whether marriage between
two baptized but only nominal Christians is always and *ipso
facto* an indissoluble and sacramental marriage. Unless it is
decided that two baptized but practically unchurched Christians
can be validly but non-sacramentally married, there seems little
hope of being able to differentiate between those who are ready
to celebrate a sacramental marriage and those who are not.

Once the possibility of full conscious and active participation
in a sacramental marriage is established, then the kind of vision
offered by these rites comes into play. They offer, we have tried
to suggest, elements for a theology of marriage in which the va-
lidity of the experience of married people is fully accepted and
provides a context of faith in which to interpret such experience. In doing so, they provide a timely reminder of the objec-
tivity of the married state, work to counter an excessive psy-

chologization of the married relationship, restore a sense of marriage as a vocation to be followed in faith and fidelity, and thus propose a view of marriage as a salvific reality, a participation in the dying and rising of Christ.

One final thought. The axiom upon which the whole Roman theology of marriage, and the whole jurisprudence of marriage in the West, has come to be built is that marriage is made by consent. This has led to the view that it is the couple themselves who are the ministers of the sacrament to each other. It is to be noted, however, that this is a legal axiom and relates primarily to the *sine qua non* of freedom as a condition for entering the married state.

The Eastern tradition makes the presiding priest the minister of the sacrament, because he represents Christ joining the couple together, just as when he is baptizing it is not he who baptizes, but Christ the Lord. This takes the experience of the liturgy of marriage as its starting point, instead of the legislation governing marriage as a contract. And here it must be said, too, that in the West the dramatic iconography of the rite is the same: Christ presides over the wedding in the person of his priest. Liturgically, the priest is more than just the official witness to the marriage. According to the Liturgy Constitution, no. 7, Christ is present in the person of the priest-presider and he is "present by his power in the sacrament, so that when a man baptizes it is really Christ himself who baptizes." Of course, in marriage Christ is also represented by the couple as icon of Christ and the Church, but they are constituted as such an icon by the liturgy, celebrated "in the sight of God and this congregation," over which the priest presides in the name of Christ the Head. This is not to suggest that the Western conception of the sacramentality of marriage is wrong, but only that, for a catechesis based on the actual rite of marriage, it needs to be complemented by the Eastern view.

But perhaps the one thing that these marriage rites call us most urgently to consider is the loss and gain involved in the gradual removal of Christian marriage celebrations out of the domestic sphere into the church. The result was not a sacralization of marriage, for marriage "in Christ" was always sacred, but a split between the "church marriage" and the "secular celebration," which led to a secularization of the domestic and its alienation from the realm of the sacred, now identified with the church. It was part of the same development which led to the imposition of clerical celibacy and is intelligible in a so-called Christian world. When all the world is Christian, the sacred-profane dichotomy will run through the Church, instead of between the Church and the as yet unredeemed world. But in a post-Christian world, the divide has to be redrawn and the unity of the holy Church, composed of all baptized believers, can be re-asserted over against the purely secular life of the world, which Christians are to redeem. The renewal of Christian marriage, then, would seem to be inseparable, finally, from the renewal of baptismal consciousness and from the profound consequences that will flow therefrom not only for the life of the family, but for the structures of the Church itself. Thus we shall have come full circle, back to the baptismal foundations of "marriage in Christ" with which the Church's theology of marriage began.

APPENDIX I
LECTIONARY READINGS

1. EASTERN RITES: BYZANTINE

1. Hebrews 12:28–13:8   Codex Sinaiticus, 10th cent.
2. Ephesians 5:20-33   Printed euchologia, 15-16th cents.
3. John 2:1-11   Codex Sinaiticus, 10th cent.

2. WESTERN RITES: SPANISH

1. Jeremiah 29:5-7   Liber Comicus, 11th cent.
2. I Corinthians 7:1-14   ibid.
3. John 2:1-11 or Mt 19:3-6   ibid.

3. WESTERN RITES: ROMANO-GALLICAN

1. I Corinthians 6:15-20[11]   Comes of Wurzburg, 7th cent.
2. I Corinthians 7:32-35   ibid.
3. Isaiah 61:10ff.   Pontifical of Poitiers, 9th cent.
4. Ephesians 5:22-33   Missal of Troyes, 12th cent.
5. John 2:1-11   Lindisfarne, c. 700.
6. Matthew 19:1-6   Most common Gospel in M.A.
7. Mark 10:1-9   Parallel to Matt 19:1-6
8. Matthew 22:2-14   Found in four lectionaries

4. MODERN RITES: CONSULTATION ON COMMON TEXTS (1987)[12]

1. Genesis 1:26-28, 31a [Genesis 1:26-28]
2. Genesis 2:18-24 [Genesis 2:4-9, 15-24]
3. Song of Songs 2:8-10, 14, 16a; 8:6-7a [Song of Songs 2:10-13 or 2:8-13; 8:6-7]
4. Jeremiah 31:31-32a, 33-34a [Jeremiah 31:31-34]
5. Isaiah 54:5-8
6. Hosea 2:16-23
7. Tobit 7:9c-10, 11c-17
8. Tobit 8:4-9 [Tobit 8:5-9]

---

[11] Most commonly used text in medieval rites.

[12] Consultation on Common Texts. *A Christian Celebration of Marriage. An Ecumenical Liturgy.* (Philadelphia: Fortress, 1985) 23–25. Where more than one text reference is given, this reflects the usages of different churches.

9. Ecclesiasticus [Sirach] 26:1-4, 16-21
10. Psalm 23
11. Psalm 33 [Ps 33:12, 18, 20-21, 22]
12. Psalm 34 [Ps 34:2-9]
13. Psalm 37:3-7
14. Psalm 67
15. Psalm 100
16. Psalm 103 [Ps 103:1-2, 8, 13, 17-18a]
17. Psalm 112 [Ps 112:1-9]
18. Psalm 121
19. Psalm 127
20. Psalm 128 [Ps 128:1-5]
21. Psalm 136
22. Psalm 145 [Ps 145:8-10, 15, 17-18]
23. Psalm 148 [Ps 148:1-4, 9-14]
24. Psalm 115
25. Romans 8:31b-35, 37-39 [Romans 8:31b-39]
26. Romans 12:1-2, 9-18 [Romans 12:1-2, 9-13]
27. I Corinthians 6:13c-15a, 17-19 [I Cor 6:15-20]
28. I Corinthians 12:31-13:8a [I Cor 13:1-13]
29. Ephesians 3:14-21
30. Ephesians 5:2a, 21-33
31. Colossians 3:12-17
32. I Peter 3:1-9
33. I John 3:18-24
34. I John 4:7-12 [I John 4:7-16]
35. Revelation 19:1, 5-9a
36. Matthew 5:1-12 [Matt 5:1-10]
37. Matthew 5:13-16
38. Matthew 7:21, 24-29
39. Matthew 19:3-6
40. Matthew 22:35-40
41. Mark 10:6-9 [Mark 10:6-9, 13-16]
42. John 2:1-11
43. John 15:9-12 [John 15:9-17]

APPENDIX II
SAMPLE MARRIAGE DEEDS

1. *A list of the arrhas which Rodrigo Diego pledged to his wife, the daughter of the Duke of Asturia, on their wedding day. In the year 1047.*[13]

In the name of the holy and undivided Trinity, viz., Father, Son and Holy Spirit, who created all things, visible and invisible, existing as one and worthy of wonder, the inseparable Trinity: whose kingdom and dominion remain for ever. Amen. May it be known by as many as possible, but proclaimed by as few.

I, therefore, Rodrigo Diego, have taken to wife Scemena, daughter of the Duke Diego of the land of Asturia. When I come to my wedding day, I have promised to confer upon the aforesaid Scemena all the villas mentioned above [sic!] and to make a firm written bequest, through the notaries of Sir Pedro Assuriz and Sir Garcia Ordoniz, of all that is in the territory of . . . [Here follows a long list of hamlets and villages]. And I grant unto you the estates mentioned above, for those which have been made over to me by my cousins Alvaro Fanniz and Alvaro Alvariz: and with them I grant you all the lands, vineyards, trees, with pastures, swamps, ponds, apple trees, with all their hedges and the products of their mills.

These arrhas are made in favour of you, my wife Scemena, in the square of Legion. And it was agreed between me, Rodrigo Diaz, and you, my wife Scemena, that we should write a writ of inheritance. I give unto you all the lands that are not included in these arrhas and which you will learn of from me as to their location, both those in our possession and those which we might add to them henceforth. — But if I, Rodrigo Diaz, should pass on before you, my wife Scemena Diaz, and you indeed outlive me, and assume the headship and refuse to take another husband, you will have all the above-mentioned lands as your inheritance, both the arrhas and all the rest besides: the estates and the livestock, both horses and mules, armor and

---

[13] This marriage was between Rodrigo Diaz del Vivar, better known as "El Cid," who was to become a national hero of Spain, and Jimena of Oviedo, a cousin of the king, Alphonso VI of Castile. The text is published by M. Ferotin in Appendix VIII of his *Liber ordinum en usage dans l'église wisigothique et mozarabe d'Espagne du V au XI siècle* (Paris, 1904) 545–547.

weapons, and all the furnishings of our house. And without your express will and consent, none of these things shall pass to your sons, or to any man born of woman, without your will; but after your death it shall all pass to your children, born of me.

Thus, if I, Scemena, should happen to take a second husband, I will thereby forfeit all the inheritance recorded in these writings and others, and all my arrhas, to the children born of us two. Moreover, I, Scemena Diaz, likewise make over to you, Rodrigo Diaz, the arrhas and all the furnishings and all my inheritance, as we have often said beforehand: that is, estates, gold, heirlooms, silver, horses and mules, armor and weapons, and the furnishings of our house in their entirety. But if I, Scemena Diaz, die before you Rodrigo Diaz, my husband, all my inheritance shall fall, as I have said, to you, and shall be confirmed as your possession, and you shall have the right to give and grant it as you wish. And after your death, Rodrigo Diaz, your sons and mine shall inherit it all, who are born of you and me.

All this I have promised and confirmed with an oath, I, Rodrigo Diaz, to my wife, Scemena, for the loveliness of her beauty and in covenant of virginal marriage.

And we, the aforesaid Sir Pedro Assuriz and Sir Garsea Ordoniz, were witnesses and shall be witnesses. This, I, the oft-aforementioned Rodrigo Diaz, make over to you in plain writing all the inheritances mentioned above and promise you firmly, concerning the inheritance still to come; so that you, like me, will have them and hold them and do with them what your will desires.

If anyone, from this day forth, whether from my own family, such as sons and nephews, or those not my heirs, should wish to disregard this writ or deed, or to challenge it: whosoever shall so act shall pay to you or your agent twice the amount that was in contention, or triple it, plus two talents in gold for the king. And all these shall be yours in perpetuity for all ages.

Signatures follow.

2. *Clermont, 1490.* In the name of Christ. Amen. I, N.N., take N.N. to wife, giving her in marriage 10 sous of Tours; Charles de Bourbon being bishop of Clermont, Louis [XII] being our King of France. Given . . . .

3. *Lyon, 1568.* In the name of the Holy Trinity, Father, Son and Holy Spirit. Amen. I, Charles Noyrat, merchant, citizen of Lyon, take as my wife and loyal spouse, Louise, daughter of the noble Guillaume Roville, citizen of Lyon. And I commend to you my almsgiving as God has commanded and St Paul has written and the law of Rome has confirmed. What God has joined in marriage, let no one put asunder. Given at Lyon, at St Nysier, the 18th day of May, 1568.

4. *Vienne, 1578.* In the name of the Lord. Amen.
At the creation of the world, God created woman from one of the ribs of Adam; and he blessed them saying: "Increase and multiply and fill the earth." And he said through the lips of the same Adam: "The man shall leave his father and mother and cleave to his wife, and they will be two in one being." And the Apostle has written, "Husbands, love your wives as Christ has loved the Church." From these and other sacred texts, it is clear that marriage is instituted of God. That is why I, N., desiring to live honestly in the married state, give and deliver myself to N., daughter of N., my betrothed, as her lawful spouse, with the agreement of God and the Church. (And reciprocally) I, N., give and deliver myself as spouse to my betrothed, and I accept him as my lawful spouse, with the agreement of God and the Church. Given, etc. This is so. *(Signature).* The cure of the church of . . . .

5. *A contemporary Jewish marriage contract (Ketubah).*
This is to certify that on the ____ day of the week, the ____ day of the month _____ in the year 57____, corresponding to the ____ day of _____ 19____, the holy Covenant of Marriage was entered into, in _____, between the Bridegroom _____ and his Bride
_____.

The said Bridegroom made the following declaration to his Bride: "Be thou my wife according to the law of Moses and Israel. I faithfully promise that I will be a true husband unto thee. I will honor and cherish thee; I will work for thee; I will protect and support thee, and I will provide all that is necessary for thy due sustenance, even as it becomes a Jewish husband to do. I also take upon myself all such further obligations for thy maintenance as are prescribed by our religious statute."
And the said Bride has plighted her troth unto him, in affec-

tion and sincerity, and has thus taken upon herself the fulfillment of all the duties incumbent upon a Jewish wife.

This Covenant of Marriage was duly executed and witnessed
this day according to the usage of Israel.

[*Signatures of rabbi and witnesses.*]